In the second edition of *Reproductive Trauma, Psychot*
Experiencing Infertility and Pregnancy Loss, Jaffe expe
the clinical practice of clients coping with infertility and
and experienced clinicians alike can use this easy-to-read yet in-depth book to
enhance their practice working with diverse clients, particularly clients in the
LGBTQ+ community, whose reproductive traumas are too often overlooked. This
edition includes the most recent transformations in the field of genetics and
cryopreservation, and truly prepares clinicians to help clients process and grow
from their reproductive trauma in the ever-changing and always evolving complex
world of fertility.
—*Rayna D. Markin, Associate Professor in Counseling,* Villanova University,
Villanova, PA; Licensed Psychologist; Author of *Psychotherapy for Pregnancy Loss:
Applying Relationship Science to Clinical Practice*

This compassionate guide offers a wealth of helpful information for anyone
struggling with infertility or pregnancy loss, as well as for clinicians treating
patients navigating these issues. Dr. Jaffe distills the latest cutting-edge research
in a clear direct style, offers many helpful clinical examples, and includes several
chapters about the clinician's perspective and the patient-therapist dynamic. I
highly recommend this book to everyone struggling to make sense of infertility or
pregnancy loss, as well as to their friends, families, and therapists.
—*Shira Keri, MD,* psychiatrist in private practice, La Jolla, CA

This book provides a powerful and unparalleled exploration of the depths of
loss that accompany the journey to parenthood. Dr. Jaffe provides foundational
knowledge for any health care provider supporting individuals who have
experienced reproductive trauma.
—*Kendra Schaa, ScM,* Johns Hopkins Bloomberg School of Public Health,
Baltimore, MD; Certified Genetic Counselor; Founder of Allay Life

Dr. Jaffe has written a must-read book for all professionals—psychologists,
counselors, social workers, physicians, and nurses who work with fertility patients.
It provides a comprehensive understanding of the psychological and emotional
challenges faced by those experiencing infertility, as well as clear well-researched
approaches to help these patients move forward. Dr. Jaffe's depth of knowledge
about fertility and her compassionate presentation make this an informative,
readable, and important book. Bravo!
—*Lauren Magalnick Berman, PhD,* Emory University, Atlanta, GA; Fertility Psychology
Center of Atlanta, GA

2nd
Edition

Reproductive
TRAUMA

2nd Edition

Reproductive TRAUMA

Psychotherapy With Clients Experiencing
Infertility and Pregnancy Loss

Janet
JAFFE

 AMERICAN PSYCHOLOGICAL ASSOCIATION

Published by
American Psychological Association
750 First Street, NE
Washington, DC 20002
https://www.apa.org

Order Department
https://www.apa.org/pubs/books
order@apa.org

Typeset in Charter and Interstate by Circle Graphics, Inc., Reisterstown, MD

Printer: Sheridan Books, Chelsea, MI
Cover Designer: Anthony Paular

Library of Congress Cataloging-in-Publication Data

Names: Jaffe, Janet, Ph. D. | American Psychological Association.
Title: Reproductive trauma : psychotherapy with clients experiencing
    infertility and pregnancy loss / by Janet Jaffe.
Description: Second edition. | Washington, DC : American Psychological
    Association, [2024] | Includes bibliographical references and index.
Identifiers: LCCN 2023043355 (print) | LCCN 2023043356 (ebook) | ISBN
    9781433841453 (paperback) | ISBN 9781433841460 (ebook)
Subjects: LCSH: Infertility—Psychological aspects. |
    Childlessness—Psychological aspects. | Miscarriage—Psychological
    aspects. | Psychotherapy.
Classification: LCC RC889 .J325 2024 (print) | LCC RC889 (ebook) | DDC
    616.6/92—dc23/eng/20240119
LC record available at https://lccn.loc.gov/2023043355
LC ebook record available at https://lccn.loc.gov/2023043356

https://doi.org/10.1037/0000400-000

Printed in the United States of America

10 9 8 7 6 5 4 3 2 1

In loving memory of my parents.

Let me fall if I must fall.
The one I will become will catch me.

—the Baal Shem Tov

Contents

Introduction

The Past, Present, and Future of Reproductive Challenges and Opportunities

As I reflect on how much has changed since the first edition of *Reproductive Trauma* was published in 2011, I am also struck by how much has stayed the same. To begin with, what has changed? Advances in new technology in reproductive medicine have continued to develop at lightning speed. Early on, when Louise Brown was born in 1978, assisted reproductive technology was considered miraculous; since that time, millions of children who would otherwise not exist have been born using this technology. As discussed in Chapter 2, genetic testing of embryos can provide more information than ever before, an exciting development that can also lead to complicated and risky decisions. The preponderance of companies like 23andMe doing DNA testing has also proved overwhelming; people are learning of biological ties that were previously unknown and secret. This newly gained knowledge can be both shocking and distressing; more and more mental health practitioners will be called on to help sort out complex feelings about family and identity.

In addition, there have been advances in cryopreservation, allowing people of all genders to save their gametes for use at a later time. This allows patients with life-threatening medical illnesses, such as cancer, the opportunity to have biological children. It also provides the possibility for women to lessen the pressure of their biological clock and delay childbearing; advances in the technology of freezing and thawing oocytes make this a viable option. Likewise, transgender men and women have the ability to freeze their gametes before transitioning. Throughout this edition, these developments will be highlighted and discussed.

The world has also changed in significant ways. Not only has a pandemic of life-changing proportions altered our world but concerns about climate change have escalated also. The fears are existential, leading some to question whether future generations will survive. Social and cultural constructs continue to evolve that also have a direct impact on reproductive choices. At the time of this writing, the United States Supreme Court has overturned the landmark *Roe v. Wade* (1973) decision, casting a pall over a woman's reproductive right to choose. Although recognition of some of the reproductive rights of the LGBTQ+ community has expanded, it is also in peril, given the current political climate in the United States. As is discussed in this volume, it is imperative for clinicians to understand the impact this will have not just on abortion but also on the potential disruption to fertility care in general. Likewise, we need to recognize the economic and social disparities in access to reproductive care throughout the United States and around the world. Choices about family building, mental health care, and women's health care are greatly affected by where one lives, racial inequities, and economic and social constraints.

Last, since the first edition of this book, I have changed as well. From my clinical work, as well as my more in-depth investigations into trauma and how to heal from it, my interest and belief in the importance of the therapeutic dynamic has grown. I view it as more critical to the healing process than any particular theoretical orientation. As therapists, we bring so much of ourselves into the clinical room that we might not pay attention to how our personalities and life experiences shape the dynamic between our patients and ourselves, but this is of primary importance. This therapeutic dynamic is present not just with mental health practitioners but also with physicians, nurses, medical staff, embryologists, geneticists, sonographers, attorneys, donor and surrogacy agencies, and adoption agencies—basically anyone who works with and counsels reproductive patients.

In the first writing of *Reproductive Trauma*, focus on providers occupied a single chapter. It has now been expanded to encompass Part II of this edition, with Part I focusing, as before, on the needs of the patient. More emphasis on self-awareness—where we are in our own reproductive journey, for example—is thoroughly discussed. How clinicians present difficult information (perhaps announcing their own pregnancy or loss), discuss heartbreaking news about a patient's pregnancy (if tasked with addressing a fetal anomaly, for instance), and cope with patients' feelings about us are subjects that have exponentially grown on my radar screen. How much we tell, how we tell it, what we have to tell, and what is okay to withhold while continuing to provide empathy can be challenging. Through case examples, we, as clinicians, will gain skills to help cope with our anxieties in doing this work. This edition will also explore the need for self-care, how to avoid burnout, and what to do if we feel traumatized by our work.

While so much continues to change, many things have remained the same. Our thoughts about what it means to have a family and raise children remain fundamental to our core sense of self. As discussed in the first edition, a unifying theme for all patients dealing with reproductive issues is the notion of the *reproductive story*: the conscious and unconscious hopes, dreams, and assumptions about becoming a parent (see Chapter 1). Even if we conclude that having children is not for us, contemplating the story of our lives follows a similar path: "What will it be like?" For those experiencing a reproductive trauma along the way, this inner narrative has gone completely awry, leaving individuals and couples—heterosexual, same sex, or otherwise—feeling that the world is no longer safe and predictable. As discussed, reproductive trauma can be defined as any event that disrupts the hoped-for pathway to pregnancy, childbirth, and parenting. It includes a wide swath of negative reproductive occurrences, including infertility, miscarriage, ectopic pregnancy, stillbirth, traumatic birth, premature birth, neonatal loss, and postpartum reactions. With updates in research and new case examples[1] throughout, this new edition expands on ideas about trauma, emphasizing the difference between what happens when core beliefs are shattered—an internal experience—and the experience created by an externalized trauma resulting in posttraumatic stress disorder (PTSD).

What is of primary importance is the understanding that having fertility struggles, pregnancy losses, or other challenges on the road to parenthood trigger the same emotions as they always have. No matter what the circumstances, reproductive trauma elicits emotional pain, depressed mood, anxiety, insecurity, and despair. As explored in Chapter 4, grief does not change, but our interpretation of it does. While there have been so many advances in reproductive technology, with more avenues to parenthood than ever, they also bring more decision making, difficult choices, and sometimes unrelenting heartache. Educating patients about grief is often the first step in healing; letting them know that "No, you are not going crazy" helps to normalize the process.

This revised edition examines the psychological upheaval of people struggling to become parents but also considers the emotions of the donors and surrogates who offer their gametes and/or their wombs to carry a child.

---

[1] The case examples throughout this book have been modified to disguise the identities of the patients and protect their confidentiality.

They, too, have feelings, not only about their reproductive story but also about the outcome of the people they are hoping to help. Likewise, the stories of birth parents who relinquish their child for adoption are often overlooked in the discussion of reproductive trauma. Their struggle is included in this new edition as well.

Like a stone thrown into a pond, the ripple effect of a reproductive story gone awry touches so many; understanding the impact of this trauma on patients, their extended family, friends, and those of us who work with them is the goal of this edition. Helping patients—and ourselves—cope, heal, and recognize the potential growth that a crisis can foster is the ultimate objective.

WHO WILL BENEFIT FROM READING THIS BOOK?

This book is intended for any and all mental health professionals—budding or seasoned—who want to expand their knowledge of the crises that can affect clients of reproductive age. This includes psychologists, psychiatrists, psychiatric nurse practitioners, social workers, marriage and family therapists, professional counselors, and pastoral counselors. Although the focus of the book is on psychotherapy, other medical practitioners and students, such as reproductive endocrinologists, obstetricians and gynecologists, perinatologists, nurse practitioners, family medicine doctors, emergency room doctors, and pediatricians, would benefit from reading this volume to understand the psychological distress of these patients fully. Nurses—especially those working in hospital emergency rooms or labor and delivery, those on the front lines of treating reproductive trauma—will find useful tools to apply in support of patients. Genetic counselors and sonographers may also find themselves on the front lines, needing to deliver bad news about an impending miscarriage or other genetic anomaly. In addition, this book is aimed at anyone who works with, counsels, and advises reproductive patients, including attorneys, donor and surrogacy agencies, or adoption agencies. Gaining knowledge, sensitivity, and insight into the many losses reproductive clients experience will undoubtedly enhance their work.

A NOTE ABOUT TERMINOLOGY AND DIVERSITY

Throughout this edition, masculine and feminine terms may be used for simplicity. This by no means discounts the recognition that gender is a continuum; not all individuals capable of bearing children identify as female.

It should be noted that much of the literature and research on reproduction has studied cisgender women and men, again influencing the use of gender binary terms throughout the book.

While I believe that the reproductive desires of the LGBTQ+ community, as well as single parents by choice, should be integrated into reproductive medicine and psychology and not be thought of as separate entities, there are unique issues they face that are addressed as such in this volume. Likewise, people of color often contend with unequal access to services and increased risk of maternal mortality, adding to the trauma they experience. Although many of the concepts addressed in the book are universal to all people, awareness of the reproductive issues that non-White and marginalized people contend with is essential for clinicians of all backgrounds to take into account.

OVERVIEW OF THE BOOK'S CONTENTS

The following are brief summaries of each chapter. It should be noted that it is beyond the scope of this book to address all the medical reasons for infertility and pregnancy loss. Rather, the focus is on the psychological and emotional consequences when traumatic events occur on the journey to parenthood.

The chapters in Part I collectively examine patients' experiences of reproductive trauma. Feelings about parenthood are a universal and core component of one's identity, regardless of gender, sexual orientation, or whether one wants children or not. Chapter 1 introduces the theoretical construct of the reproductive story: the contemplation of possibly becoming a parent someday, the origins and influences on that story, and what happens when the story of our dreams veers off course.

Advances in reproductive medicine have occurred rapidly over the past several decades, offering ever-new possibilities in ways to create families. While the technology has changed, the emotional and psychological tolls on people remains the same. Chapter 2 not only explores medical advances, including cryopreservation but also addresses the emotional and ethical concerns that clients are confronted with.

Chapter 3 addresses the empirical literature regarding PTSD and reproductive losses and expands the definition of trauma to include the disruption of basic core beliefs. It delves into assumptions about pregnancy and parenting that crumble when reproductive trauma occurs.

When a baby dies, or a wished-for baby fails to occur, the loss is unlike any other. There are few, if any, rituals to facilitate grief, and many reproductive patients are in the throes of mourning while at the same time actively pursuing attempts at pregnancy and holding on to hope. Chapter 4 explores grief in general but also focuses on the distinct challenges of mourning infertility and pregnancy loss.

Multiple case studies are presented in Chapter 5 from various theoretical perspectives, including narrative, psychodynamic, and cognitive therapies. In addition, controversies over the causal relationship between stress and reproduction are discussed. Regardless of the therapist's theoretical orientation, listening to a patient's reproductive story and guiding them in writing different endings to their story—whether that ultimately includes children or not—is the goal.

As clinicians, we not only counsel the recipients or intended parents of third-party arrangements, but we also assess the donors (of gametes or embryos), surrogates, and birth parents who relinquish children for adoption. Chapter 6 focuses on the assessment of third-party participants and their psychological needs. It also addresses the unique challenges of the recipients, especially in disclosure to their offspring.

Chapter 7 focuses on additional treatment options that patients may pursue other than traditional psychotherapy. These can include online or in-person support groups, eye-movement desensitization and reprocessing, Traditional *Chinese* Medicine, acupuncture, yoga, and/or changes to diet and lifestyle.

The phenomenon of posttraumatic growth (PTG), which refers to the potential for positive change following a major catastrophic life event, is addressed here. Chapter 8 focuses on PTG in general and how it can develop in reproductive trauma patients.

The book then turns to Part II, where the emphasis shifts from clients' needs to those of the clinician. Chapter 9 explores an overall discussion of therapist self-disclosure, including its risks and benefits. A deeper dive into the complexities of therapist self-disclosure with reproductive patients is presented, focusing on the ever-present question that patients pose: "Do you have any children?"

When a therapist becomes pregnant, it can unleash myriad emotions—not just for clients but for the therapist as well. Chapter 10 reviews the literature on pregnancy and psychotherapy in general. It describes how therapists can use their personal reproductive stories in the service of clients.

Chapter 11 builds on the last by addressing the even more intense emotions that can emerge when the therapist is pregnant and working with reproductive clients. The therapeutic alliance, the bedrock of the relationship, can vanish in an instant. Again, a multitude of feelings can erupt; how to manage the ensuing therapeutic ruptures is explored.

Therapists and other professionals working in the field of reproductive psychology are caregivers, and as so often happens, caregivers put their own needs at the end of the to-do list. While there is much satisfaction in this work, Chapter 12 describes the emotional pitfalls that can occur when working in the field of reproductive trauma, including burnout, compassion fatigue, and vicarious trauma. It also lists self-care strategies to avoid these risks, such as mindfulness, balance, and finding meaning in one's practice and life.

The book concludes with an epilogue that emphasizes how important it is for us as therapists to help patients give voice to their reproductive stories while maintaining awareness of our reproductive stories.

Acknowledgments

I am thankful to so many for their support and encouragement in making this second edition a reality. A special appreciation goes out to Martha and David Diamond for all our work together over the years. In particular, I would like to acknowledge Martha Diamond for her contributions to the first edition of this book. Who could have predicted that the birth of the reproductive story all those years ago would grow and develop as it has? Their clinical wisdom and devotion to the field of reproductive psychology are truly valued.

Others who deserve recognition are Julie Bindeman, Laura Covington, and Loree Johnson for their early reading of this volume and incredible feedback—thank you so much! Much appreciation also goes to Kendra Schaa, genetic counselor supreme, who taught me so much about the inner workings of genetic testing. I also want to thank the members of the San Diego Reproductive Psychology Study Group: Carol Bateman, Katherine Ellis, Karen Hall, and Shira Keri. You are all so dear to me and have provided so much insight, understanding, and support for—can it really be—close to 2 decades!

I am deeply indebted to all at the American Psychological Association for believing in this book and pressing for this new edition. None of this would be possible without the editorial wisdom and support of Susan Reynolds and David Becker. Your critical advice and vision have pushed me to make this updated edition fill so many important gaps.

It goes without saying that my family and friends deserve thanks. I treasure your ability to listen and support me always. Glo—you are my rock! And Daniel, Michelle, and Jules—I can't imagine life without you. Words can't express what you mean to me. Love you always.

Reproductive
TRAUMA

PART **I** THE PATIENT'S VIEWPOINT

1
THE REPRODUCTIVE STORY
Parents' Possible Selves and How Things Should Have Been

Sometimes I think I have organized the inner crowd. For a brief, breathtaking moment, I feel completely whole. I understand that I am composed of many selves that make up a single chorus. To listen to the music this chorus makes, to recognize it as music, as something noble, varied, patterned, sublime— that is the work of a lifetime.

–Dani Shapiro, *Hourglass: Time, Memory, Marriage*

We all have stories to tell. Many of our stories are about the past, our culture and family of origin, and the events and experiences we have lived. As you read this, imagine introducing yourself to someone new. The "story" you tell will highlight pieces of your past and present, and perhaps future plans. We do this without effort—our stories are so ingrained in who we are, in our sense of self, that we tell them with ease.

Narrative researchers suggest that turning the events of our lives into stories is what makes our lives meaningful (Hydén, 2010). Not only do stories emerge out of our past, but we also create stories about our future, especially as children. Remember being asked what you wanted to be when you grew

https://doi.org/10.1037/0000400-001
Reproductive Trauma: Psychotherapy With Clients Experiencing Infertility and Pregnancy Loss, Second Edition, by J. Jaffe

up? Undoubtedly, the answer you gave back then has morphed and evolved over time. Our ability to imagine our adult selves and all the possibilities that lie ahead of us can be thought of as cognitive representations of our hopes and fears, our fantasies and worries about life (Bak, 2015). Markus and Nurius (1986) noted that our "possible selves" include ideas of what we may become and what we would like to become, as well as what we may be fearful of becoming; they labeled the positive as *hoped-for selves* and the negative as *feared selves*.

By definition, our possible selves begin with an assessment and knowledge of our current selves. Children, for example, may view their possibilities as limitless, with projections of themselves as adults. They may be aware of what they cannot achieve at the moment (their current self-concept) and what they need to do to achieve their dreams (their motivation). The repertoire of these possibilities "can be viewed as the cognitive manifestation of enduring goals, aspirations, motives, fears and threats" and is the "essential link between the self-concept and motivation" (Markus & Nurius, 1986, p. 954). Whatever one aspires to be or achieve, there are steps along the way to attain that goal. It goes without saying that stories about the future change and evolve: My 4-year-old who wanted to be a "tennis player on TV" did take tennis lessons and still plays as an adult, but his professional aspirations changed with time. As will be discussed, the interplay of our self-evaluation and desire for change is the essence of psychotherapy (Bak, 2015). It also has implications for reproductive patients as they assess their stories and how they might evolve over time.

WHAT IS THE REPRODUCTIVE STORY?

One story that is universal is that of parenthood. Everyone has ideas and thoughts about what it might be like to become a parent—whether one has or wants children, this story exists for all. This is a possible self that is deeply ingrained into our core; indeed, reproduction is one of the most fundamental elements of life. The desire to become a parent is not limited to normative heterosexual couples. Indeed, individuals who want to parent solo and couples in the LGBTQ+ community all have reproductive stories. Likewise, the reproductive story is not bound by any particular race, culture, or religion; it is a phenomenon that is present in all human beings. Even if we decide we do not want children, our thoughts about it take the form of the question, "What will it be like?" This contemplation of the possible self as a parent provides the theoretical basis for the concept of the *reproductive story* (Jaffe, 2017; Jaffe & Diamond, 2011; Jaffe et al., 2005). Whether we are conscious of it or not, the reproductive story is that part of ourselves that thinks about parenthood. It is integral to our adult identity and, consequently, to the narrative of our lives (McAdams et al., 2006).

What is the reproductive story, and how does it develop over time? As we discussed, the concept of possible selves—the reproductive story—for those of us who want children, consists of all the hopes and dreams of having a family and the fears that it may not happen. We talk later about those of us who do not want children and how their reproductive story unfolds, but for now, the focus is on the desire for children. The story consists of fantasies about creating a family with or without a partner, the visions of what our children will be like, and how we see ourselves as nurturing, loving, and teaching parents. The story can be detailed: It is not uncommon for people to pick out names long before conception or pursue career choices that are amenable to family life. Sometimes, the narrative is more like a picture book, with snapshots of a future with kids playing or family holiday traditions continuing into the next generation. Often, though, the story remains murky, more an intangible "knowing" that having a family of one's own will happen one day. The notion that having children will not happen may be so feared that it may not even be considered a possibility.

HOW DOES THE REPRODUCTIVE STORY DEVELOP?

Observe any preschool setting, and you will witness the beginning of the reproductive story. Children absorb and imitate their experience of being parented. They may tuck a toy into bed, pretend to breastfeed, or scold it for hitting. While it may be easier to identify parenting themes in the play of young girls, little boys also engage in these nurturing activities. Their play with monsters and superheroes can be interpreted as providing protection; they may have a "family" of toy trucks that get fed, bathed, or go on outings, mimicking the events of their lives. Playing house or donning adult's oversized shoes and clothing is a way that children convey their interest both in adults and in being adults, and in this way, the child's parental identity begins to form. We can see how the threads of possible selves, adult identity, and the reproductive story intertwine in the minds and activities of young children.

Many other factors can influence the early development of the reproductive story, including trauma that may have occurred in the family of origin, socioeconomic status, relationship with siblings, and/or conflicts with parents.

For example, one client, Caitlin, had four older siblings and a depressed, alcoholic, and overwhelmed mother.[1] "My household was utter chaos. I never quite knew when my mother would be nurturing or when she would fly into a rage," she stated. "I was so frightened of turning into my mother. I do not want to have a child experience what I did." Another client, Kai, who identified as nonbinary, wanted to become a parent, but their desire was overshadowed by their father's suicide when they were a young child. They echoed Caitlin's fears of turning into their parent but also felt they did not have a good parental role model to follow.

While many ideas about future selves coexist, those that endure will likely define possible selves and dictate one's behavior (Markus & Nurius, 1986). The potential-self-as-parent is one such stable thread; the reproductive story evolves and matures as one does, with changes occurring depending on the stage and circumstance of one's life. As the story develops, it incorporates not just the internalized sense of self and early family-of-origin relationships but also the society, culture, ethnic background, religious affiliation, and peer group norms in which one lives (Vignoles et al., 2008). These kinds of environmental influences have a direct and powerful impact on self-concept, behavior, and, in turn, one's reproductive story. For example, there is a strong expectation among Arab migrants in the United States to have children immediately after marriage (Grocher & Gerrits, 2022).

While family history and cultural expectations may encourage parenthood at a particular age, one's peer group may have an influence as well. My grandmother, for example, expected that I would meet my spouse during college, become a teacher, and immediately start a family; this was a very different story than what I had in mind. My peer group put off having children until our mid-to-late 30s. While the timeline of my reproductive story did not match that of previous generations, the possible-self-as-parent for me was still quite strong.

For most people, the imagined story of pregnancy and childbirth goes something like this: "We'll stop using birth control, and voila! We're pregnant, and without a hitch, we'll have a happy, healthy baby in our arms." This is the hoped-for self. After all the years of worrying about an unwanted pregnancy, it will happen easily and perfectly. Some may worry about things going wrong, but being young, healthy, smart, and resilient, they believe that the feared self cannot possibly happen to them. The shock and trauma of when it does not go as it should have—whether due to fertility issues, miscarriage,

---

[1] All case examples in this chapter have been modified to disguise the patients' identities.

stillbirth, premature birth, needing to terminate a desired pregnancy for medical reasons, giving birth to a child with disabilities, or other postpartum struggles—is emotionally overwhelming and ego crushing. Because the reproductive story is such a fundamental piece of one's identity, any disruption can be perceived as an enormous narcissistic blow, a trauma to the self that can affect all aspects of one's life. The farther away from reality one's imagined narrative is, the more intense the shock and the more traumatized patients become.

People who choose not to become parents have reproductive stories as well. Being child free by choice is clearly different from disrupting the self with involuntary childlessness. Nevertheless, in deciding not to have children, the same question occurs: What will it be like? While possible selves commonly address new elements of identity, it is also likely that people are motivated by the fear of what will happen to existing parts of themselves (Vignoles et al., 2008). In other words, fear of losing qualities of their lifestyle may drive the desire not to have children.

Having a child-free life has been considered aberrant behavior and is frequently associated with being selfish and nonconformist, especially for women (Mollen, 2006; Rubin, 2002). Women may be criticized as being unfeminine and self-centered; men may be disparaged for being unmanly. There is, however, growing worry about the sustainability of our planet's resources; the phenomenon of climate change anxiety, defined as "negative cognitive, emotional, and behavioral responses associated with concerns about climate change," is growing (Schwartz et al., 2022, p. 1). A study of adult students (ages 18–35), those at or approaching childbearing age, found that worry over bringing "kids into a world that is currently on a climate clock" was paramount to their concerns (Schwartz et al., 2022, p. 9). Feeling helpless, they considered not having children as a way of taking action against contributing to climate change.

SINGLE PARENTS AND LGBTQ+ FAMILIES

Much of the literature and research on infertility and pregnancy loss focuses on normative heterosexual couples, but the yearning to become a parent and potential reproductive trauma and loss applies to single parents by choice as well as the LGBTQ+ community. These two categories of parents-to-be share much in common. They may not be infertile and yet will likely need assisted reproductive technologies (ART) or to go down the path of adoption to pursue their dreams. While a single woman can "accidentally" become pregnant outside of a committed relationship, for most, the desire to create a family comes with clear intention. Likewise, in the LGBTQ+ community, the decision to have and raise a family is discussed, researched, and approached with purpose.

There have been barriers, however, to reproductive care in the LGBTQ+ community in the United States, despite the Supreme Court decision in 2015 to make same-sex marriage legal in all 50 states (*Obergefell v. Hodges*, 2015). One reason for this is the outdated definition of infertility: the failure to achieve pregnancy after a year of unprotected sexual intercourse. A new definition has been proposed for single individuals and LGBTQ+ couples: *social infertility*. To this point, the American Society for Reproductive Medicine (ASRM) Practice Committee has issued a new definition of infertility. The new definition characterizes infertility as "the inability to achieve a successful pregnancy based on a patient's medical, sexual, and reproductive history" (ASMR, 2023, para. 3) and notes that reproductive challenges can be caused by many reasons. "This revised definition reflects that all persons, regardless of marital status, sexual orientation, or gender identity, deserve equal access to reproductive medicine" (ASRM, 2023, para. 5). Indeed, this population may not struggle with physical infertility at all but need to use ART to create their family. If insurance for in vitro fertilization (IVF)—when it exists—only covers physical infertility, it completely excludes single people and the LGBTQ+ community (Neyra, 2021).

Other barriers exist as well. Questions have been raised about the suitability of single or same-sex couples becoming parents: Do the children in these families suffer? There is growing evidence that the mental well-being of children raised in these types of families does not differ from more traditional family configurations (Gates, 2015; Golombok et al., 2016, 2021). Research on single-mothers-by-choice suggests there is lower mother–child conflict than in two-parent families (Golombok et al., 2016). Any differences in children's well-being have been found to have more to do with circumstances, such as divorce, than the gender identity or sexual orientation of their parents (Raja et al., 2022).

Single Parents by Choice

The motivation to become a solo parent is often based on considerations of age and biological clock; people often feel that they do not have time to wait for the right partner. Before embarking on this path, they consider the network of family and friends that can support them emotionally and help with childcare (Jadva, Badger, et al., 2009). Their decision is well thought out.

People who become single parents because of divorce, separation, or the death of a spouse often struggle more, dealing with the loss of a relationship as well. In contrast to those who parent solo due to divorce, single parents by choice have reported fewer financial concerns (Volgsten & Schmidt, 2021).

While there has been a great deal of research on women becoming single mothers, there is much less on single fathers by choice. As with women, men, whether heterosexual or gay, choose to become single parents with great consideration, citing the desire to reproduce and not wanting to wait for the right relationship. They tend to be well educated and financially secure. A study comparing single mothers by choice and single fathers by choice found that their reasons for pursuing solo parenthood were similar; they accessed the same types of social support, and there were no differences in their overall mental health. The gender assumption that women have a stronger craving than men to become a parent was challenged; this study concluded that both men and women have great desires to become parents (Jones et al., 2022).

In the first study to explore single men using surrogacy and egg donation, Carone et al. (2017) found that men's stories were similar to those of single women who used donor sperm to conceive. Like single mothers by choice, these men were concerned about their increasing age and finding the right partner. Regardless of sexual orientation, these men all had to overcome societal expectations that a female caregiver is essential for child development. It is interesting to note that the researchers asked participants when they first thought of having a child, and a heterosexual father replied, "It's just a core part of who I've always been," while a gay father stated, "It's been a dream since I was a child myself, as an adult. Even if I didn't know how it would materialize, the wish was always there, very strong" (Carone et al., 2017, p. 1876). In their quotes, we can hear their reproductive stories loud and clear.

Single parents-to-be may desire to preserve their gametes for future use (fertility preservation is discussed in Chapter 2). They may wish to use them later with the right partner, or they may not be ready to have children. If they are hoping to conceive immediately, however, it will be necessary to use donor gametes. A challenge these patients face—as all people do when they use donors—is how to choose the donor. The first question is whether the donor should be an anonymous, "nonidentified" donor[2] or someone who

---

[2] The term "nonidentified donor" has replaced "anonymous donor" with the understanding that anonymity is becoming less possible, especially due to the increased use of DNA testing.

is a known "directed" donor (Raja et al., 2022). A thorough discussion of how patients choose a donor and the plusses and minuses of these choices is addressed in Chapter 6, but suffice it to say that donor selection can come with much anxiety. It is, after all, a decision that will significantly affect the parent's life and the life of their child.

LGBTQ+ Family Building

With shifts in the social and legal status of same-sex marriage, the diversity of family configurations has grown. There has become more acceptance of using ART with the LGBTQ+ community. Although adoption has been a traditional pathway to create same-sex families, ART has allowed gay and lesbian couples to use their own gametes to become parents. As of 2016, 68% of same-sex couples were bringing up biological children (S. K. Goldberg & Conron, 2018). While less is known about the transgender-nonbinary (TGNB) community and their desire to have children, research is growing. One study reported that over half of the transgender men surveyed wanted to have children (Wierckx et al., 2012). It is important for mental health providers and clinicians to understand the unique needs and challenges that same-sex and transgender individuals have in their pursuit of family building.

Same-Sex Cisgender Female Couples

Lesbian couples need to use donor insemination (DI) of sperm to conceive. The first step in the process is deciding whether to use a known donor or an anonymous donor from a sperm bank (see Chapter 6 regarding pros and cons). A decision must also be made as to who will carry the pregnancy. For some couples, the decision is clear-cut because of one partner's age, fertility, health, or the desire to experience pregnancy and birth. Some couples decide that the older partner should attempt pregnancy first, followed by another pregnancy for the younger partner. Another option is for the couple to do reciprocal or co-IVF. This is a procedure whereby one member of the couple undergoes egg retrieval, which then gets fertilized and transferred to the other partner's uterus (Raja et al., 2022). Although this is more costly and invasive than doing DI, it provides a psychological advantage; they can both feel they are contributing jointly as biological (one genetic and one gestational) parents in the creation of their child (Dondorp et al., 2010). It lessens the risk of jealousy or competition that could develop if there are unequal biological ties to the child(ren). Indeed, one study found less jealousy in couples that adopted or used IVF to co-mother than in couples that conceived with DI (Pelka, 2009).

If one of the partners discovers fertility problems in attempts at conception, a reasonable solution might be for the other partner to become pregnant instead. The grief and loss for the infertile partner can be overwhelming, watching their partner grow with the pregnancy. After the birth, the non-biological mother may feel as if she is not a "real" parent, leading to feelings of disenfranchisement (Hadley & Stuart, 2009). It is important for mental health practitioners to be aware of the potential disruptions in the relationship over parental roles and help the couple focus on the best interest of the child(ren).

Same-Sex Cisgender Male Couples

The choices for gay men who want to become parents are much more limited. In the past, the only option open to them was adoption or fostering, but with reproductive advances in medicine, they are also able to become parents by using an oocyte donor and a gestational surrogate. Same-sex male couples have considerations identical to those same-sex women go through regarding choosing a donor, whether nonidentified or directed (see Chapter 6). They must also contract with a surrogate at great financial and emotional cost. A note about surrogacy: Gestational surrogacy is similar to IVF—it requires an egg donor and a procedure to harvest her eggs, fertilize them with sperm, and then transfer them to a woman genetically unrelated to that child. Traditional surrogacy differs in that the woman who carries the pregnancy uses her own oocytes to conceive, thus becoming the genetic mother with legal rights to the child in most states in the United States (Bewkes, 2014). Traditional surrogacy is not recommended by ASRM (Raja et al., 2022).

For many same-sex male couples, the reasoning for using a surrogate rather than adopting parallels the feelings of heterosexual couples. They want a biological connection with the child and want to maintain a sense of control. Like same-sex female couples deciding on whose gametes to use, which partner provides sperm comes into question. Sometimes, decisions have been made based on age, the desire for genetic parenthood, and whose genes were deemed to be better. For some couples, the solution was to alternate between using sperm from one partner and then the other on each insemination attempt or to use the sperm from both in a single IVF cycle (Friedman, 2007). Another possibility for equal paternity was for each to fertilize separate eggs from their donor and then transfer one embryo from each to the surrogate. Yet another solution was to choose an egg donor who had similar physical features to their partner (Murphy, 2013).

In a study that explored gay men's narratives about parenthood, similar themes were found with men who pursued single fatherhood by choice. While some dismissed the possibility of becoming a parent because of the socially accepted idea that gay men should not be fathers, others expressed an innate desire to become one. One participant said, "Well, I guess it's a, it's fulfillment of a dream come true. I always wanted to have children, always said I'd have children. Didn't know how I'd actually go about it, but it was always my intention in life" (Murphy, 2013, p. 1110). As previously stated, everyone has a reproductive story. The more mental health practitioners recognize and explore the deep-rooted feelings that patients have, regardless of gender or sexual orientation, of what parenthood means to them, the more we can help them achieve their dreams.

Transgender Parenthood

An estimated 1.6 million people living in the United States identify as TGNB; 38.5% are transgender women, 35.9% are transgender men, and 25.6% identified as gender nonconforming (Herman et al., 2022). The assumption that TGNB people do not want to have children is false. Many studies have shown that, on the contrary, having biological children is important to them (Cheng et al., 2019). It should be noted that many transgender people were parents with a partner before transitioning. Those who pursue parenthood after transitioning, including patients who transitioned before puberty, may face many barriers: accessing care, misunderstanding and/or discrimination by providers, and coping with fertility challenges due to hormonal gender-affirming therapies and surgeries. For mental health professionals and reproductive caregivers, it is vital to understand the issues that TGNB people have to tackle in their pursuit of parenthood.

Before the transition process, people may consider preserving their gametes for future use (see Chapter 2). For trans women, the most viable option is to cryopreserve sperm; for trans men, cryopreservation of oocytes or embryos is the best option. It may be unrealistic to form embryos, however, because trans men, especially those who transition during adolescence, may not be ready to think about parenting. Cryopreservation of ovarian or testicular tissue, as discussed in Chapter 2, continues to be developed (James-Abra et al., 2015). Although it is recommended that fertility preservation be discussed with all patients before transitioning (E. Coleman et al., 2012), there is mixed evidence as to whether the pediatric population is appropriately counseled (Raja et al., 2022).

For the pediatric transgender population, hormonal treatment can prevent the development of secondary sex characteristics; this can be gender-affirming and reduce psychological distress. Gender-affirming hormonal treatment can, however, impact fertility. For those assigned female at birth, testosterone can suppress ovulation and menses; for those assigned male at birth, estrogen can cause decreased spermatogenesis (Cheng et al., 2019; Raja et al., 2022). Temporarily stopping hormonal treatment has been shown to reverse some of these changes and allow TGNB patients to have biologically related children. While the goal of having children might be successful, the temporary cessation of hormonal therapy may cause physical changes that cause psychological distress. Knowledge of and sensitivity to the dysphoria that TGNB patients may experience is necessary for all health care providers to help them through this period.

Another barrier to parenthood for TGNB people is access to care, with some arguing that TGNB people are mentally unfit to parent (Cheng et al., 2019). While this type of thinking persists, it is outdated, not based on evidence, and discriminatory (Ethics Committee of the ASRM, 2015). A study highlighted the difficulties that trans individuals and their partners experienced when they sought services through ART and how clinics and providers can better accommodate trans patients (James-Abra et al., 2015). Their recommendations include better education and training for physicians, nurses, and mental health providers, as well as adjusting intake paperwork to indicate what pronouns and names patients prefer. The researchers also suggest using gender-neutral language. For example, trans men who are able to carry a pregnancy may not label themselves as "mothers," and people who contribute sperm do not necessarily think of themselves as "fathers" (James-Abra et al., 2015). Listening to TGNB individuals' reproductive stories and their shift from their gender assigned at birth to the gender they identify with can allow mental health providers to support them on their journey to parenthood.

LISTENING TO PATIENTS' CURRENT REPRODUCTIVE STORIES

As noted, everyone has a reproductive story—whether we have children or not, whether we want children or not, regardless of gender or sexual orientation. As discussed, the development of the reproductive story is deep-rooted, starting when people are children themselves. When reproduction goes awry, their present story is clearly "not the way it was supposed to be"; patients tell us this all the time. Without necessarily asking them directly how it was supposed to be, therapists can listen for their reproductive stories, and they will say,

- "I was supposed to have my babies 2 years apart."
- "I was going to be 'that dad' who coached all the games."
- "I thought I'd have my kids by the time I was 30."
- "No one in my family ever had a problem getting pregnant."
- "My frozen embryos are all boys."
- "Both of us come from big families."
- "My younger sister had a baby before me."
- "I did everything 'right': married—check; career—check; house—check. But no baby."

These are snippets—clues, so to speak—of reproductive stories gone awry and core assumptions patients have about themselves and parenthood. Undoubtedly, the anguish stems from the loss of a would-be baby, but underneath that trauma are the many other losses that patients experience. While some features of an individual's story might seem insignificant to providers, they are quite real to patients and can be used to work through grief and trauma and lead to growth.

Just as important as paying attention to a patient's current trauma, exploring a person's reproductive history, even if they are well beyond reproductive age, can give us insight into what has brought them into therapy. One woman in her early 50s began therapy with me to deal with her soaring anxiety. She described herself as being distracted all the time, having difficulty sleeping, and suffering from migraines. She also spoke about her difficulty in parenting her son, age 15. Many thoughts and hypotheses came to my mind: was this something organic, or was it about her son pulling away from her? When I asked her about her reproductive history, she revealed that she had dealt with infertility and used a donor to conceive her son. As it turned out, she had never spoken to anyone about her situation or her son's birth origins. Did I think this could be behind her agonizing anxiety? She was afraid to tell him about his conception, afraid of what he might think of her.

Before therapists label patients' reproductive stories as such, our job is to take note of the stories of the immediate crisis as well as their backstories. These stories help clinicians understand the meaning that parenthood holds for individuals and couples. As devastating as patients' experiences are, we must hold their stories in our hearts to help them move out of the pits of despair. As Markin (2017) so poignantly stated, "The depth of a parent's grief is also the heights of his or her capacity to love a child he or she never knew or will get the chance to meet" (p. 371).

REWRITING THE STORY: IMAGING THE FUTURE

The concept of the reproductive story conveniently lends itself to therapeutic interpretations. When patients seek medical and/or psychological help, it is clear that their story has not unfolded as expected or hoped. We see them in the middle of their story, the middle of their trauma, where they may feel completely and irreversibly stuck. Insight into how their story went off track and how they thought it should have been provides us with the opportunity to validate, console, educate, and eventually open new ways of thinking about the trauma and loss.

The use of the reproductive story in treatment is based on cognitive therapy, narrative therapy, and psychodynamic interventions. The job of the clinician is to listen for pieces of the story reflected in the current crisis as well as in core beliefs that have been shattered. Reflections on "how it should have been" help patients acknowledge their past, present, and future ideas about themselves and parenting. For some, it is only after a reproductive trauma that they realize they had a story to tell. The story and the telling of it make conscious what may have been assumed; as will be explored in subsequent chapters, once the story is aired, it sets the stage for grieving and the possibility for growth.

All stories have a beginning, a middle, and an end. Most often, clinicians see patients in the middle of their reproductive story when it has taken an unexpected and emotionally devastating plot twist. How will it end? The beauty of introducing the idea of the reproductive story to clients is that they can imagine different future possible selves and different ways of becoming a parent or not and control the process of getting there. Patients can "try on" different endings by imagining how particular options feel: "What would it feel like to use an egg donor? What would it feel like to adopt? Should we remain a family of two?" It also can be helpful for them to imagine what it might be like in 5 or 10 years, to see beyond their current reproductive crisis into the future. Even if a decision cannot be made immediately—it certainly deserves time to weigh all the options—just knowing that other paths exist can provide reassurance and relief.

SUMMARY

The Oxford Learner's Dictionaries (Oxford University Press, n.d.) defines *story* as "an account of past events or of how something has developed" (Definition 3). Stories help us make meaning and sense of life's ups and downs. One universal storyline is that of reproduction. Beginning in child-hood, the reproductive story naturally grows and develops over time. This story often remains unconscious, especially if one easily transitions into adult life and parenthood. It is often only when a reproductive crisis occurs, when the reproductive story hits a traumatic snag, that it becomes apparent. We understand it was there all the time, and we realize what we are afraid of losing, what is at stake. All of us who work in reproductive health have heard many patients' stories that have gone awry. Through our listening with care and understanding, we can help them gain insight, grieve, and find new meaning in their ongoing story, whether they are able to have children or not.

2 DEVELOPMENTS IN REPRODUCTIVE TECHNOLOGY
Ethical Concerns and Emotional Constants

It has become appallingly obvious that our technology has exceeded our humanity.

—Albert Einstein

The focus of this chapter is on the incredible advances and opportunities afforded by reproductive medicine over the last several decades. The fast pace of these scientific developments often surpasses our ability to process their meaning because they offer new possibilities to consider in patients' reproductive stories. An exploration of ethical dilemmas that may arise is reviewed. It is not surprising that decisions about what technology to use, if any, continue to take the same emotional and psychological tolls on people of all genders as they have in the past. As is discussed, these feelings remain constant as more choices become available.

https://doi.org/10.1037/0000400-002
Reproductive Trauma: Psychotherapy With Clients Experiencing Infertility and Pregnancy Loss, Second Edition, by J. Jaffe

NEW AND IMPROVED ASSISTED REPRODUCTIVE TECHNOLOGY

In the "old days," people who struggled with infertility had three choices: keep trying, adopt, or remain child free. Similarly, the potential for having a healthy baby when parents had a genetic disorder (e.g., Huntington's disease or cystic fibrosis) was left to a roll of the dice. Times have changed, allowing more people to become parents and have healthy children. After reviewing its beginnings, this section explores the extraordinary developments of assisted reproductive technology (ART) over time.

A Brief History

It all began in 1978 with the birth of Louise Brown, the first in vitro fertilization (IVF) baby conceived and born in England (Edwards, 2001). Since that time, the advances in ART have allowed more and more heterosexual couples, unable to have children the "old-fashioned way," to become parents. In the early days, implantation rates were less than 5% per transferred embryo; now, it is greater than 50% (de Ziegler & Toner, 2022). Live birth rates have drastically improved as well, from less than 10% per cycle to more than 50% for women under 35 (Eskew & Jungheim, 2017). IVF has also broadened its scope to reach not just those struggling with fertility issues but also those concerned about transmitting certain diseases, those who choose to become single parents, and those in same-sex relationships. ART continues to expand its reach as more people who identify as nonbinary or trans begin families.

A brief overview of the history of IVF informs us how reproductive medicine has changed. Early on, a fertility workup would likely include a record of a woman's basal body temperature to monitor ovulation, a postcoital test to evaluate how well sperm swim through cervical mucus, and a hysterosalpingogram to assess the shape of the uterus and health of the fallopian tubes. In addition, a laparoscopy may have been performed to try to treat problems with fallopian tubes or endometriosis. Although these tests are still in use, they have generally been replaced by more modern techniques. Uterine and tubal issues, for example, can now be assessed with ultrasound. Likewise, the diagnosis of endometriosis with ultrasound and magnetic resonance imaging has replaced surgical explorations (de Ziegler & Toner, 2022; Pirtea et al., 2022).

Drs. Patrick Steptoe and Robert Edwards performed the first successful IVF pregnancy with the birth of Louise Brown. In her case, a single preovulatory oocyte was retrieved laparoscopically in a natural menstrual cycle from her mother, was fertilized in vitro, and then transferred back to her mother's uterus (Kamel, 2013). In the 1980s, women began receiving injections with human menopausal gonadotropin to induce multiple ovarian follicles to yield multiple oocytes instead of just one. While this controlled ovarian stimulation improved pregnancy rates, it was not without risks. One serious complication of IVF is ovarian hyperstimulation syndrome (OHSS). As its name implies, the ovaries can become stimulated to excess with symptoms that range from mild abdominal discomfort to renal failure and death. With increased monitoring of women and the use of gonadotropin-releasing hormone agonists, OHSS is now better controlled.

In the hopes that there would be a greater chance of a pregnancy, multiple embryos were often transferred in the past, resulting in a greater likelihood of twins or an even higher order of multiple fetuses. These were high-risk pregnancies with the potential for pregnancy demise, premature birth, and low birth weight. If babies did survive, they were often subject to long-term neonatal intensive care and/or long-term health problems. Innovations in cryopreservation and improvements in culture media have increased the quality of embryos, allowing them to progress to the blastocyst stage before transfer. Because of this, current practice usually limits the number of embryos transferred to one (single embryo transfer), thus reducing both maternal and neonatal morbidity caused by multiples (Eskew & Jungheim, 2017; Komorowski & Feinberg, 2022).

The Revolution of Genetic Technology

One technological advance in IVF is preimplantation genetic testing (PGT). Before 1990, the options to determine genetic defects were chorionic villus sampling (CVS) and amniocentesis, both invasive procedures, which increased the risk of miscarriage. If an anomaly was found, women and their partners had to decide whether to terminate or continue the pregnancy. CVS was performed between 11 to 14 weeks of pregnancy, while amniocentesis was done between 15 to 18 weeks, with little time to consider terminating the pregnancy. These tests are no longer routinely performed, and as will be discussed, PGT has significantly revolutionized IVF; the technology is changing so rapidly that what is current at the time of this writing may be outdated by the time of publication. As with most technological advances, questions emerge about what they mean practically for patients.

Preimplantation genetic testing is a procedure done on an embryo created through IVF. Several cells are removed from the developing embryo and then sent to a lab to assess the number of chromosomes present. PGT can be broken down into various components:

- preimplantation genetic testing for aneuploidy (PGT-A)[1]
- preimplantation genetic testing for single gene or monogenic conditions (PGT-M)
- preimplantation genetic testing for structural rearrangements (PGT-SR)[2]

Preimplantation Genetic Testing for Aneuploidy
PGT-A screens an embryo for chromosomal abnormalities when there are no known genetic disorders. It analyzes biopsied cells from the embryo to determine if an embryo is euploid (chromosomally normal) or aneuploid (an embryo with an abnormal number of chromosomes, either too few or too many). An aneuploid embryo is less likely to lead to birth and has a higher chance of causing a miscarriage. PGT-A has been found to improve live birth rates for patients over 35 years old (Simopoulou et al., 2021). PGT-A is also indicated for recurrent miscarriage, recurrent implantation failure, and severe male factor issues (ESHRE PGT Consortium Steering Committee et al., 2020).

It would be simple if the results of PGT-A were black and white, with good embryos and bad. Advances in genetic testing, including next-generation sequencing and comparative genomic hybridization, have detected a variety of chromosomal abnormalities, creating a gray area called mosaicism. The Preimplantation Genetic Diagnosis International Society (2016) has classified PGT-A results as follows:

- Embryos with 20% to 80% abnormal cells are mosaic,
- < 20% are considered euploid, and
- > 80% are considered aneuploid (Garvin et al., 2019).

Mosaicism refers to the number of chromosomes in a cell. Most cells in the body have 23 pairs of chromosomes. As an embryo develops and cells divide over and over through mitosis, mistakes in replication can happen. Some cells may have one more or one less chromosome, which may lead to a variety of disorders. How, then, do we advise patients who receive results in this gray area?

Counseling can become challenging in cases of mosaicism, depending on the specific results. Mosaicism can involve any of the 23 pairs of chromosomes

---

[1] PGT-A was formerly known as PGS or preimplantation genetic screening. The rapidly changing technology changes the terminology we use as well.
[2] PGT-M and PGT-SR were formerly classified as PGD.

and can include the entire chromosome, part of the chromosome, or multiple chromosomes. The percentage of mosaicism can vary significantly in an embryo, and the level of mosaicism can vary by tissue type. For example, if 30% mosaicism is identified in the sample sent for testing (which may include cells from an embryo biopsy or amniotic fluid from an amniocentesis), this does not necessarily translate to 30% mosaicism throughout all the cells in a fetus. Depending on the specific chromosome involved and the percentage of mosaicism identified, counseling about postnatal outcomes varies significantly, from the possibility of a life-limiting diagnosis to a healthy live birth. Due to a lack of long-term outcomes on children born from mosaic embryos, some degree of uncertainty is often present, which may or may not be acceptable to a patient.

—K. Schaa, personal communication, June 18, 2022

Preimplantation Genetic Testing for Single Gene or Monogenic Conditions

PGT-M is used if there is a known genetic mutation in one or both biological parents. If, for example, there is a risk of cystic fibrosis, Tay Sachs, or sickle cell anemia, Preimplantation Genetic Diagnosis (PGD) can be performed to ensure that only embryos that are not affected by that single gene are used. In this way, PGT-M can prevent transmission of the disease to offspring (ESHRE PGT Consortium Steering Committee et al., 2020).

Preimplantation Genetic Testing for Structural Rearrangements

PGT-SR is another genetic test of the embryo that looks at chromosomal structural rearrangements. In other words, the chromosome is present but is in a different place than usual. While this does not affect the health of the would-be parent, it can increase the risk of pregnancy loss. Selecting embryos that are not affected by structural rearrangement is more likely to lead to a live birth (ESHRE PGT Consortium Steering Committee et al., 2020).

Psychological Impact of PGT

From clinical experience, it is clear that patients see PGT as the definitive answer for themselves, believing that the results will be irrefutable. Because they have been through so much and would like reassurance, they consider PGT a guarantee for a healthy baby and are willing to extend themselves financially for this sense of comfort. However, the assumption that PGT will guarantee a positive outcome is false. As can happen, a so-called "perfect embryo" that fails to implant creates profound heartache and confusion. Likewise, receiving results from PGT-A with all embryos considered "bad" is devastating. What continues to be under investigation is the level of self-correction that may occur in an embryo and how these findings may or may not affect the child (Esfandiari et al., 2016; Garvin et al., 2019). Esfandiari et al. (2016) pointed out the difference between the inner cell mass (ICM), which develops into the fetus, and the trophectoderm (TE) of the embryo, which forms the placenta. The cells that are tested are from the outer layer (TE) of the blastocyst. It may be that these abnormal cells move to the developing placenta, leaving the ICM, or fetus, normal. It is possible that mosaic embryos will self-correct and develop into healthy live births (Popovic et al., 2020).

Although many clinics will not transfer mosaic embryos because of the potential for an adverse outcome, it is important to remember that before the development of PGT, embryos were transferred all the time without knowing if they were mosaic or not (Komorowski & Feinberg, 2022). It may be that we all have some amount of mosaicism but not enough to cause disease. Genetic counseling is critical in helping patients make decisions about using or discarding embryos. As often happens, technology outpaces scientific and psychological understanding of its results; clinicians are left in a position of trying to advise patients on a case-by-case basis as to the risks involved in transferring a mosaic embryo. If no "normal" embryos are available, should mosaic embryos be transferred?

Carla,[3] 40-years-old, was on her last IVF attempt and desperately hoping for good results from PGT. Unfortunately, out of the five embryos that had been fertilized and tested, three came back as aneuploidy, and two were identified as mosaic. Because this was her last chance of having a pregnancy using her own gametes, she was faced with an unnerving decision: Was it better to do a transfer than not at all? She sought the advice of a genetic counselor, her reproductive endocrinologist, and a mental health practitioner to weigh the options. She questioned how it might affect her life, her relationship with her spouse, and the life of the child: Were they prepared to raise a child who might have health issues? Was it selfish of them to want a biological baby?

Ultimately, the decision was for Carla and her partner to make, weighing the positive (having a biological child) against the negative (risk of miscarriage or having a baby with health issues). Experts agree that mosaics should be considered only when there are no euploid embryos to transfer. As this was the case for Carla and because there is a growing body of evidence that mosaic embryos can result in healthy babies (Abhari & Kawwass, 2021),

---

[3] All case examples in this chapter have been modified to disguise the patients' identities.

she and her partner decided to transfer the better of the two mosaic embryos. The resulting pregnancy was filled with anxiety, but an amniocentesis confirmed that there were no genetic anomalies with their baby. No doubt, as more research on mosaicism and its variety of classifications become known, it will help clinicians to better guide clients on these life-altering decisions.

ADVANCES IN FERTILITY PRESERVATION: CRYOPRESERVATION

Cryopreservation has been used to help save peoples' gametes for use at a later date. There are many reasons for considering cryopreservation: medical, convenience, and/or social. Medically, no one anticipates that their reproductive story will be derailed by a life-threatening illness like cancer. Being presented with a diagnosis of cancer, with treatment that can cause infertility, is overwhelming, to say the least. Patients often have no time to consider their future fertility and may need to make rapid decisions about it while dealing with fears about their disease. Advances in cancer treatment have led to long-term survival rates, with cure rates of over 90% in women and girls (Donnez et al., 2013). Thus, the issue of quality of life after recovery is essential to consider. Preserving fertility in children diagnosed with cancer who are prepubescent is a special case and is explored here as well.

Cryopreservation for nonmedical, social reasons is increasing in demand. With the trend in many Western countries to delay childbearing, women may choose to cryopreserve their eggs for use at a later time. They may wish to postpone family building for a variety of reasons: educational pursuits, career pursuits, financial reasons, or lack of a partner. Those who are transitioning from female to male may also decide to freeze their eggs for use in the future. Advances in the technology of freezing and thawing eggs are making this a viable option. Likewise, males transitioning to female have the opportunity to freeze sperm before their transition.

Cryopreservation for Cisgender Males and Transgender Women

Two methods of cryopreservation are available for cisgender males and transgender women: freezing sperm and freezing testicular tissue.

Freezing Sperm

Lazzaro Spallanzani, an Italian scientist, performed the first successful artificial insemination (AI) of a dog in 1784. Fast-forward 100 years, and AI was being used to inseminate horses, cattle, sheep, swine, and poultry (Foote, 2002). It was not until the middle of the 20th century that artificial insemination in humans began, a treatment that increases the possibility of conception with a higher density of sperm at the fertilization site. Another significant development was the use of frozen sperm; the first human pregnancy with frozen sperm occurred in 1953 (Ombelet & Van Robays, 2015). The sperm bank industry was thus inaugurated. Now, frozen sperm (which is washed to remove dead or nonmotile sperm) is routinely used by single women or lesbian couples for intrauterine insemination and IVF. Heterosexual couples may also use frozen sperm, either a donor's or the partner's.

In addition, men facing cancer treatment or men who are transitioning to female may choose to preserve their gametes for later use by freezing their sperm. The standard method of fertility preservation for postpubertal males is collection by masturbation before chemotherapy or radiation. The emotional strain of the diagnosis and performance pressure may make it difficult to obtain sperm samples. An alternative strategy is to surgically retrieve and cryopreserve sperm from the testes (Practice Committee of the American Society for Reproductive Medicine [ASRM], 2019).

Freezing Testicular Tissue

In the past, boys who had not yet reached puberty, had not produced sperm, and were diagnosed with cancer had no options to preserve their fertility (Valli-Pulaski et al., 2019). Testicular tissue cryopreservation (TTCP) is under development as an alternative preservation method. The procedure consists of taking a biopsy and then freezing testicular tissue. As recently as 2013, TTCP was not available for these young patients (Ho et al., 2017). Since that time, TTCP has provided hope that, at some time in the future, frozen tissue will be able to be used to generate sperm and children. This technique is still considered experimental in humans, although animal research has demonstrated its feasibility (Practice Committee of ASRM, 2019).

Cryopreservation for Cisgender Females and Transgender Men

Cryopreservation for women is more complicated than it is for men. While freezing human sperm has been available for fertility preservation and conception since the 1950s, cryopreservation of female gametes is only now becoming more established.

Freezing Eggs

As of 2006, egg freezing was still considered experimental (Jain & Paulson, 2006). In 2013, however, both the Practice Committees of the ASRM and the Society for Assisted Reproductive Technology (SART) concluded that the freezing of oocytes should be made available to preserve the fertility of women undergoing chemotherapy and radiation (Angarita et al., 2016). Advances in the actual freezing and thawing process have also made it possible to consider freezing eggs for social reasons.

In addition to fertility preservation with oncology patients, freezing eggs is gaining in use for other reasons: loss of fertility with age, ovarian insufficiency, or female-to-male gender transition (Ethics Committee of ASRM, 2018b). It provides women with more options for their future: The worry that their biological clock is ticking can be eased, they can wait until they have found a suitable partner, and they can focus on other pursuits until they are ready for parenthood (Rosen, 2015; Seyhan et al., 2012). Likewise, transgender men can preserve their oocytes by freezing them and using them at a future time if they wish to. Many see oocyte cryopreservation as their last chance of having a genetically related baby and wait until they are over 35 to do so, at which point the potential for age-related fertility due to poor egg quality becomes a primary issue (Rosen, 2015). To avoid this decline in fertility, it may make sense to freeze eggs a decade earlier. Paulson (2021) suggested that a single oocyte cryopreservation cycle, performed when a woman is in her 20s, will likely produce enough eggs for two or more live births.

Several factors complicate oocyte freezing:

- the age of the patient: Prepubescent girls do not qualify but may be candidates for ovarian tissue cryopreservation, discussed in the next section;

- the need to undergo an IVF cycle, which may not be covered by insurance;

- the potential for delay in the start of chemotherapy or radiation treatment with cancer patients—depending on the patient and diagnosis, this may not be possible; and

- the challenge of freezing and thawing oocytes—the freeze–thaw process is complicated due to the concentration of water in the cell, making it susceptible to damage.

It has been well established that fertility preservation is a key survivorship issue for people of all genders, and counseling cancer patients about the risks to their fertility is essential before treatment (Angarita et al., 2016). A natural consequence of the aging process for those born with ovaries is the decline in the quality and quantity of reserved eggs. With chemotherapy and/or radiation, this decline is sped up, leading to primary ovarian insufficiency (POI). Because younger patients have more ovarian reserve, the damaging effect is less severe than for older patients (Seyhan et al., 2012). For example, the risk of POI for teenagers undergoing cancer treatment was increased by a factor of four, while for patients 21 to 25, the risk increased by a factor of 27 (Larsen et al., 2003). Clearly, gamete preservation should be addressed and performed before the start of these toxic treatments whenever possible. However, the diagnosis will determine if cancer treatment can be delayed to stimulate the ovaries and retrieve the eggs without risking the life of the patient.

A challenge to oocyte cryopreservation is the technology involved with freezing and thawing the eggs. There have been two main freezing methods: slow freezing and vitrification. Slow freezing, as its name implies, uses a technique in which the temperature is lowered gradually but increases the risk of producing damaging ice crystals. Cryoprotectants have been used to correct this and safeguard the egg. Slow freezing is time consuming and expensive, requiring special programmable freezing equipment. A newer freezing method is vitrification, which uses rapid cooling by plunging the oocytes into liquid nitrogen. This converts the intracellular water into a vitreous condition, transforming it from a liquid to a solid, glass-like state, thereby preventing damaging ice crystals from forming (Angarita et al., 2016; Casillas et al., 2015; Donnez et al., 2013; Jain & Paulson, 2006; Porcu et al., 2022). Two different meta-analyses found that vitrification was a superior method of freezing oocytes compared with slow freezing (Cil et al., 2013; Rienzi et al., 2017). Studies have demonstrated that outcomes have improved when using vitrification; survival rates of oocytes after freezing and warming were reported between 90% and close to 100%, with fertilization and implantation rates similar to using fresh oocytes (Seyhan et al., 2012).

Freezing Ovarian Tissue

An exciting development in reproductive technology is ovarian tissue cryopreservation (OTC). For prepubescent girls and women who cannot delay the start of chemotherapy, the only option to preserve fertility is to freeze ovarian tissue. This is accomplished by surgically removing one whole or part of an ovary, sectioning it, freezing it for later use, and eventually transplanting it back into the patient after completion of her treatment or when she is ready to start her family (Yding Andersen et al., 2019). The patient's age needs to be considered because ovarian reserve diminishes by the mid-30s; anti-Mullerian hormone (AMH) and antral follicle count (AFC) have been used to determine selection for this procedure in adults (Donnez et al., 2013; Moolhuijsen & Visser, 2020). It should be noted that AMH is a good estimate for oocyte quantity, but neither AMH nor AFC can predict oocyte quality or chance of pregnancy (Cedars, 2022).

For preadolescent children, however, the only choice is OTC. Although OTC in humans has only been in practice for a couple of decades, it has been estimated that more than 10,000 patients have undergone OTC, and while only about 500 patients have had the tissue transplanted back at the completion of their treatment, nearly all regained ovarian function. In addition, as of 2019, more than 130 children have been born using OTC (Yding Andersen et al., 2019). As improvements develop over time, OTC may become more widely used "because the functional unit of the ovary is stored, not only oocytes, which enable restoration of both fertility and the endocrine function" (Yding Andersen et al., 2019, p. 28).

Freezing Embryos

Embryo cryopreservation is still considered the gold standard for fertility preservation because it offers the best chance of having a live birth (Angarita et al., 2016). Embryos formed in an IVF cycle grow to the blastocyst stage, at which point they may be frozen for future use. This was a remarkable development in reproductive medicine; a couple could potentially complete their family from a single IVF procedure using a frozen embryo transfer at a later date. Combining advances in genetic testing with improved cryopreservation techniques, it has become common practice in many clinics to freeze all blastocysts, subject them to genetic testing (PGT-A), and then transfer usually a single frozen embryo, based on testing results (Bortoletto, 2020).

While it makes sense for heterosexual couples undergoing IVF to freeze embryos for use in the future, for other patients, freezing embryos may not be feasible. The only way to create embryos is through IVF, but this is not a viable option for everyone. Some religions, for example, ban the use of ART (see Table 2.1). IVF may be prohibitively costly, and only a minority of the population in the United States has access to treatment, even if they have insurance coverage for it. Regardless of socioeconomic status, fertility services have been disproportionally underrepresented in Hispanic and non-Hispanic Black women (Quinn & Fujimoto, 2016).

Pursuing IVF for cancer patients may also not be viable because the time it takes to undergo ovarian stimulation and retrieval to create embryos may interfere with the start of life-saving treatment. Genetic testing of embryos is also costly, and as mentioned previously, testing of embryos may not provide definitive answers; it may, in fact, create more decisions and dilemmas in its wake.

Another complication of cryopreserving embryos is reflected in the sheer number of frozen embryos that are being stored. It is not uncommon for more embryos to be produced in one cycle of IVF than can be used. In 2003, it was estimated that there were at least 400,000 cryopreserved embryos in the United States (Hoffman et al., 2003), with thousands more stored in Europe and Australia (Newton et al., 2007). In an analysis of data from SART, researchers calculated that during the years between 2004 and 2013, over 1,950,000 embryos were frozen in the United States alone, and only 717,345 were transferred (Christianson et al., 2020).

At the outset of IVF treatment, producing as many embryos as possible may seem like a measure of success, but when childbearing is completed, the disposition of remaining embryos can create yet another reproductive trauma. While patients may have felt one way at the start of fertility treatment, they may be forced into ethical territory they never anticipated at the end. The disposition choices available for patients are to

- save frozen embryos for a future child,
- donate them to scientific research,
- donate them to another intended parent,
- thaw and discard them,
- store them indefinitely, or
- compassionately transfer them.

Compassionate transfer is an option proposed by the Ethics Committee of the ASRM (2020). This refers to embryo transfer at a time in the menstrual cycle when pregnancy is not likely to occur. For some, this feels like a more natural way of using surplus embryos no longer intended for reproduction, but as will be discussed, it is not without its own set of ethical issues.

Indeed, the increase in the number of embryos in storage and what to do with them is a conundrum not just for patients but for IVF clinics as well. Complicating the issue is the current state of reproductive rights in the United States. As of this writing, the Supreme Court has overturned *Roe v. Wade* (1973), eliminating a national right to seek an abortion and giving states the authority to make their own decisions about it. Many states have instituted near-total bans on abortion and define the beginning of life starting at conception. How this might apply to the hundreds of thousands of embryos on ice is currently unknown. An investigation into the moral and ethical concerns regarding embryo disposition and other complicated reproductive decisions follows.

ETHICAL CONSIDERATIONS

Providing services and offering counseling to fertility patients can place reproductive counselors in the middle of multiple ethical dilemmas. At the forefront are fundamental beliefs about when life begins, who "owns" gametes, and religious, cultural, and legal tenets. The personal opinions of counselors must be kept in check to help patients wrangle with multiple choices and decisions. It is imperative for practitioners to stay abreast of medical advancements as new technology often presents new ethical predicaments. It is also vital to stay abreast of current legal issues where one practices and their impact on reproductive rights. The following presents some ethical conundrums that advanced ART may present. Before delving into specifics, however, the four basic bioethical principles, originally developed by Beauchamp and Childress in 1979, should help guide our thinking (Lawrence, 2007).

- **Autonomy:** Respect the patient to make their own choices.
- **Nonmaleficence:** Do no harm to the patient.
- **Beneficence:** Take care of the well-being of the patient.
- **Justice:** Treat patients fairly and equitably.

There are situations when these principles may conflict. Using ART when multiple parties are involved and the autonomy of one is at odds with the autonomy of another is one such case (Galst & Horowitz, 2015). Surrogacy, for example, may pit the autonomy of the surrogate against the needs of the parents-to-be. Similarly, beneficence to one may mean that harm befalls another: The issue of abortion rights comes into play because saving an unborn child may come at the risk of a mother's life or vice versa. Does an embryo hold the same status and rights as a living person? Autonomy also needs to be considered in this case: Does a woman have autonomy over her body, or does religion and/or the state hold authority? Paltrow et al. (2022) contended that all pregnant women, not just those seeking abortion, will be affected by the overturning of *Roe v. Wade* (1973): "In undoing Roe, it will in effect be establishing that when a person is pregnant their Constitutional rights—to things such as bodily autonomy and liberty—may be denied" (p. 3). The principle of justice, that all patients be treated fairly and impartially, is also problematic in the use of ART. Because the industry is not regulated, and most procedures are not covered by insurance, costs prohibit people of low socioeconomic status from its use; in the United States, this often translates to people of color.

Ethical Dilemma: Surplus of Frozen Embryos

Patients share the news of how many eggs were harvested and how many were fertilized with either excitement or utter dismay. After the physical, financial, and emotional toll of IVF, it may feel as if they are back in school being graded on an assignment, although now with much higher stakes. Did they ace it, or did they fail? At the onset, having many embryos on ice may be reassuring; it represents the possibility of a family that they might not have thought possible. Their focus is on getting pregnant; they are not thinking about disposing of the embryos they are trying so hard to attain (Lyerly et al., 2006). However, once family building is completed, the fate of supernumerary embryos can become a major ethical dilemma (Christianson et al., 2020).

When patients begin the process of IVF, they need to understand the potential ethical problems that may occur; standard practice includes detailed informed consent discussing excess embryos. As sometimes happens, though, people feel different about their embryos at the beginning versus the end of treatment; patients often change their minds over time (Newton et al., 2007). Approximately one third of patients will not return to make a decision regarding disposition (Christianson et al., 2020); some patients "abandon" the embryos by not paying the storage fees (Mihai et al., 2017). The burden then falls to the fertility clinic; ASRM suggests a 5-year cutoff to discard the embryos if contact with the patient fails (Ethics Committee of ASRM, 2013a). In reality, however, a majority of IVF centers continue to keep abandoned embryos frozen, with concerns that their owners may return; thus, these embryos accumulate (Gleicher & Caplan, 2018).

Gleicher and Caplan (2018) proposed that abandoned embryos be used for research purposes rather than destroyed. They argued that neither the maintenance of abandoned embryos nor their destruction exhibits respect to human embryos. The disposal of embryos that could contribute to research "that enhances fertility and reduces the impact of diseases represents, in contrast, a purpose exemplifying a solid moral foundation" (Gleicher & Caplan, 2018, p. 140). Some feel that embryos should be treated with the same ethical and legal rights afforded to living human beings. This is at the heart of the abortion debate in the United States: What is the status of an unborn child? If embryos have the same standing as living human beings, their destruction for the sake of scientific research would not be acceptable. However, donating them to advance medical knowledge allows patients to feel their excess embryos are not going to waste (McMahon et al., 2003; Zweifel et al., 2007).

As noted, embryo cryopreservation offers the best chance of having a live birth (Angarita et al., 2016). Because the definition of personhood is so controversial, freezing oocytes may be more palatable. Most governments and religions have less of an issue disposing of unfertilized eggs versus fertilized embryos. In cases of separation or divorce, ownership of frozen oocytes would not be under dispute. Some patients may even choose to limit the number of oocytes to be inseminated in an IVF cycle to limit the number of spare embryos produced (Jain & Paulson, 2006; Tucker et al., 2004).

Ethics of Embryo Donation

How patients conceptualize embryos appears to be key to their feelings about donating them to another individual or couple with fertility issues (Christianson et al., 2020). One study showed that almost 90% of patients viewed their frozen embryos as "siblings" to their existing children (Stiel et al., 2010). Because of this view, donating to another couple felt wrong, akin to relinquishing a child for adoption. These patients were also concerned about the possibility of consanguine relationships developing and loss of control if their genetic embryo(s) were to be raised in another family. As such, these patients were more likely to destroy excess embryos than donate them (de Lacey, 2007; Nachtigall et al., 2005).

Others, who think of their embryos as simply biological material (cells or tissue), viewed embryo donation positively. Wanting to help other infertile individuals or couples was a huge motivator. Their view of family was based on relationships rather than genetics, defining the "real" parents as the ones who raised and nurtured the child. These parents were more likely to donate their embryos than destroy them (de Lacey, 2007).

Culture and religion play a large part in the ethical decision-making process regarding embryo donation as well. While all major religions promote family and the need to procreate, there are varying views on the role of ART in building a family. Christianity, comprising primarily Catholics, Protestants, and Greek and Roman Orthodox, has the most membership of all religions worldwide and, in general, is opposed to ART. In Catholicism, for example, all forms of ART are unaccepted because it separates reproduction from the sexual union of a married man and woman, whereas Protestants may support IVF but only with embryos to be used by the married couples that created them. Although the Orthodox church supports the protection of embryos, it considers embryo donation akin to adultery. In Judaism, views regarding ART tend to be more supportive. Jews are instructed by the Torah to "be fruitful and multiply" and see ART as a means to an end. When it comes to embryo donation, however, most Rabbis strongly discourage it. Likewise, in Islamic law, ART is allowed as long as the sperm and egg are those of the married man and woman, and the resulting embryo is transferred to that woman only (Dombo & Flood, 2022; Mihai et al., 2017; Sallam & Sallam, 2016). Table 2.1 summarizes the views of various religions and cultures on ART.

Although patients may desire to help other intended parents by donating embryos, they may have moral conflicts based on religious tenets. As providers, it is essential not to assume how their background may influence their decision but to learn from them what their belief system supports.

TABLE 2.1. Summary of Assisted Reproduction Techniques Allowed by Various Religions and Cultures

Religion or culture	IUI	IVF/ICSI	PGD	Surrogacy	Gamete donation	Fetal reduction
Catholic	No	No	No	No	No	No
Orthodox	Yes	No	No	No	No	No
Protestants	Yes	Yes	No	No	No	No
Anglicans	Yes	Yes	No	No	No	No
Coptic	Yes	Yes	Yes	No	No	No
Judaism	Yes	Yes	Yes	Yes	Yes	Yes
Sunni Islam	Yes	Yes	Yes	Debating	No	Yes
Shi'a Islam	Yes	Yes	Yes	Yes	Yes	Yes
Hinduism	Yes	Yes	Yes	Yes	Yes	Yes
Buddhism	Yes	Yes	Yes	Yes	Yes	Yes
Japan	Yes	Yes	Yes	No	Sperm only	Yes
China	Yes	Yes	Yes	No	No	Yes

Note. IUI = intrauterine insemination, IVF/ICSI = in-vitro-fertilization/intracytoplasmic sperm injection, PGD = pre-implantation genetic diagnosis. From "Religious Aspects of Assisted Reproduction," by H. N. Sallam and N. H. Sallam, 2016, *Facts, Views & Vision in ObGyn*, 8(1), p. 47. Copyright 2016 by Facts, Views & Vision. Reprinted with permission.

Ethics of Compassionate Transfer

Compassionate transfer is a way of disposing of supernumerary embryos by transferring them into the woman's uterus at a time when it is unlikely a pregnancy will result. For some, compassionate transfer is more morally palatable than destroying embryos, donating them to research, donating them to other intended parents, or leaving them frozen indefinitely. The argument for compassionate transfer is that the experience would be more like a miscarriage and that it provides an autonomous choice (Lee, 2017). The ethical principle of autonomy refers to a patient's right to make decisions about their life. However, this principle is nuanced, and many feel that if there is an alternative that provides a greater good, autonomy may be limited. In the argument against compassionate transfer, many feel that because it is not a medically necessary procedure, practitioners' time should be spent in more constructive ways for the greater good (Lee, 2017; Mihai et al., 2017).

Ethics and Genetic Testing

Preimplantation genetic testing of embryos has greatly improved the live birth rate and decreased the miscarriage rate by selecting the best embryo(s) to transfer. Patients can transfer embryos that are not affected by specific genetic disorders. More controversial is testing for conditions that are polygenic in nature. Diseases such as diabetes, hypertension, breast cancer, and schizophrenia are complex, often with adult onset and not based on a single gene. PGT allows embryo selection based on polygenic scores (ESPS).

Some have suggested that all patients undergoing IVF and PGT should select embryos based on these scores, prioritizing those with the lowest risk of disease. Ethically, this is in line with the principle of autonomy, allowing patients to make their own decisions. The Ethics Committee of the ASRM (2018c) concurs.

Others see limitations in using ESPS because environmental factors may influence the development of these medical conditions and give a misleading sense of assessment (Treff et al., 2022).

Another ethical dilemma that arises with PGT is when results are mosaic. As previously discussed, the risk of an adverse pregnancy outcome has caused many clinics to refuse to transfer these embryos. Do patients have the autonomy to make this decision? Is it ethical for a clinic to withhold treatment, especially if this is a last-chance attempt at a pregnancy? Other questions plague reproductive ethicists: As the technology becomes more refined, will PGT extend to include other nonmedical traits (intelligence, height, gender)? Should reproductive rights include these choices at the risk of creating designer babies? As we advise patients and help them work through these complicated questions, it is not our responsibility to answer them but to discuss them with patients so they can make the best decision for themselves.

NEW TECHNOLOGY, SAME OLD FEELINGS

When people prepare themselves to have a baby, their thoughts are not necessarily on the technological advances that have been made in reproductive medicine. What they do focus on are their feelings and the dreams and hopes about what it will be like—in other words, their reproductive story. Excitement combines with anxiety as they consider this change in their lives. It is a time of tremendous growth; the sense of self may dramatically alter. No longer is the focus on one's own needs but on the care of another totally dependent human being. "With parenthood, the focus of concern shifts inexorably from responsibility for one's self to responsibility for others" (Arnett, 2000, p. 473).

These changes in thinking happen well before conception. This may be when one's reproductive story becomes conscious in a new way, with one's identity as a parent beginning to take root. Thus, one becomes a psychological parent well before becoming a physical or biological one. This is extremely important to keep in mind because psychological upheavals in one's sense of self can create growth as well as feelings of vulnerability. Like the developmental crises of separation–individuation in childhood (Mahler et al., 1975) and adolescence (Blos, 1967), Colarusso (1990) described parenthood as the third individuation stage. As such, reproductive patients, before any loss or trauma, are already in a susceptible state. With infertility, when repeated attempts to produce a child are unsuccessful, the narcissistic blow can overwhelm any positive self-worth. Likewise, with a pregnancy loss or the discovery of a genetic anomaly, there is a sense of personal failure that can overcome the ego. Feelings of depression, anxiety, isolation, and grief have not changed; no technology can take away these normal reactions to the pain patients feel.

Losses on Multiple Levels

Using a biopsychosocial framework to understand the depth and breadth of reproductive losses is helpful. The following are many of the losses that can occur:

- loss of experience of pregnancy and childbirth
- loss of feeling healthy and normal
- loss of control over one's body and/or plans
- loss of self-esteem
- loss of belonging
- loss of relationships (e.g., partner, family, friends)
- loss of sexual intimacy
- loss of financial freedom
- loss of trust in belief systems

Not every patient will encounter every one of these losses, but as we listen to their narratives, it can be helpful to delineate and point out to patients the physical and emotional injuries they have faced. Often just realizing how many losses they have experienced is validating: Patients can recognize why they feel anxious, depressed, and grief stricken. The following case illustrates that no matter what ART is used, patients' underlying feelings are the same.

Julia and Peter: Viewing Infertility Through a Biopsychosocial Lens

Julia, an elementary school teacher, was 36 years old, and Peter, who worked in sales for a pharmaceutical company, was 38. They had been trying to have a baby for a little over a year on their own. They had reservations about seeking medical help—they knew how costly it could be—but ultimately, they consulted with a reproductive endocrinologist. They were delighted to learn that some of the costs would be covered by insurance and felt assured that they had a good chance of a successful outcome. They came in for counseling after their attempt at IVF was unsuccessful.

They both looked shell-shocked when they began counseling. Peter did most of the talking at first, continuously looking to Julia as if for approval, not wanting to get details wrong. He spoke about how physically difficult the hormonal stimulation was for her but that she persevered, keeping the end goal in sight: "I kept coaching her along—she's strong and a fighter— I knew she'd be all right." He went on to say that her anxiety soared when it was time for the retrieval—again noting his supportive role: "I think all of it would have been put behind us if the results were different. But they were only able to get three eggs, and none of them fertilized. Julia thinks it's all because of her, but maybe it was because of me." Julia slowly shook her head as she joined in the conversation: "They checked you out beforehand. You are fine. It has to be me—I'm probably just too old." Peter chimed in, "You are not too old. These things happen. We can try again."

As Julia and Peter illustrate, biology is at the heart of the issue: Patients' sense of being healthy and normal disappears. Pregnancy is a complicated anatomical and biochemical process that can get derailed at any point. While it may seem to patients that "everyone can do this," it is, in fact, remarkable that healthy babies are ever born. Self-blame is one of the most common reactions when reproductive trauma occurs; whether it is a failed IVF, a miscarriage, or other perinatal loss, finding fault with oneself is a way of channeling the grief. Peter was doing his best to reassure Julia and have her regain her confidence. He was attempting to eliminate the grief process and move forward for her as well as for himself. This dynamic can be seen in many patients—where one person in the dyad tries to boost the other while trying to ignore or deny their own feelings. It was essential for them to both grieve, even in the midst of trying again. The balance between grief and moving on with one's life can be precarious, but both processes can and should go on simultaneously.

As they spoke more about themselves and their relationship, it became clear just how much having a family meant to them. They met 3 years earlier. Julia commented that they were "late to the game"—another indicator of self-blame. They started trying soon after their wedding with the hopes of having two children "before it was too late"—that theme repeating itself over and over. As their therapist, I noted their reproductive story and wondered to myself if their bond would be strong enough to withstand this blow. Had they come together knowing this was potentially a last chance at having a family? Was there enough glue to hold them together through this crisis?

Psychologically, the loss of the reproductive story can have profound effects on one's sense of self, one's relationship, and one's belief system that the world is safe and just. The narcissistic blow and loss of ego can be enormous; patients lose sight of who they are. As can be seen in Julia, she downgraded her view of herself to someone who is incompetent and a failure. I wondered if her feelings of being "late" had deeper roots in her past; this was on my radar to explore over time. I also wanted to explore Peter's need to be her caretaker; could this be a pattern from other relationships and/or family-of-origin dynamics?

As I listened to their story unfold, I knew the stakes were high for their relationship. Reproductive trauma puts a strain on one's feelings about one's partner and sexual intimacy. Baby making often takes over sexual sponta-neity, and because Julia and Peter started trying soon after meeting, what should have been romantic had turned into work. They were no longer in control of their storyline, so they anxiously had to hand it over to a medical team. Julia's shame and self-blame dominated her self-worth. One of my goals was to help her differentiate the part from the whole, to compartmen-talize her reproductive organs from her feelings about herself.

Both of them spoke about friends and coworkers who all seemed to be pregnant or have young children. Both commented on how unfair it was and how left out they felt. Julia tearfully described an incident where she could not answer a phone call because she "just knew it was a friend wanting to share her good news." Peter had a similar experience at work when a coworker announced her pregnancy: "Of course, I was happy for her. Work used to feel like a place where I could escape from all this, but not anymore."

Not only were they concerned that at any moment they would hear about yet another person's joy and success but their social standing also felt like it was on shaky grounds. Where did they fit in? We talked about how they were psychological parents: They had begun to weave another person (a child) into their story (their life), but the absence of a baby led to feel-ing alienated and misunderstood, not only with friends but also with their families. "One thing that really got to us," Peter said, "was not being invited to my nephew's birthday party. When I confronted my brother about it, he said he didn't think we'd feel comfortable. Right?! But it sure doesn't feel comfortable being excluded either." While it is true that in social situations, others often ask, "Do you have any kids?" or "How many kids do you have?" not to be included can make couples feel like they are pariahs.

SUMMARY

The case of Julia and Peter illustrates the devastating impact that negative reproductive events can have on all aspects of a person's life. Thinking about the reproductive story from a biopsychosocial theoretical point of view can help frame these cases. It cannot be overstated that whatever reproductive technology patients pursue, when it does not work, there is a period of mourning over the trauma they have experienced and the depth of what has been lost. Would Julia and Peter consider other reproductive interventions in the future? What would they be comfortable with? What could they afford? While ART and its associated technology offer many incredible opportunities to create a family, it is not for everyone. Regardless of future decisions, they were coping with the loss of their reproductive story, how it should have been, which is at the core of what continues to deeply affect patients, as it always has. As we follow Julia and Peter in the next chapters, working through the trauma and grief of these losses helps patients to cope and heal.

3 PATIENTS' REPRODUCTIVE TRAUMA EXPERIENCES

"Our World Is Falling Apart"

He steeled himself for another attempt; she grieved. And this was the difference between them, that he saw hope, still, some feeble, skeletal hope, where she saw loss.

—Gish Jen, *Who's Irish?*

Whatever your morning routine, today was probably a lot like yesterday; tomorrow will undoubtedly be similar to today. The alarm goes off, the coffee goes on, and you ready yourself for the day. There may be differences in the details of each day, but the routine will likely stay the same. The predictability of one's life may seem tedious at times, but, in fact, we take comfort in it. Whether we are conscious of it or not, being able to envisage, make plans, and have our ideas come to fruition brings great satisfaction.

Trauma occurs when our ability to predict our future and feel safe in the world is no longer possible. This chapter focuses on how patients experience reproductive trauma: events that may be a one-time horrific experience, such as a miscarriage or stillbirth, or experiences that are long-lasting, such as the chronicity of infertility. Unfortunately, many clients experience both fertility

https://doi.org/10.1037/0000400-003
Reproductive Trauma: Psychotherapy With Clients Experiencing Infertility and Pregnancy Loss, Second Edition, by J. Jaffe

issues and pregnancy loss; these patients report the highest levels of distress (Schwerdtfeger & Shreffler, 2009). This chapter also examines core assumptions and beliefs that patients often have about pregnancy, which may exacerbate these traumatic experiences.

When a traumatic event occurs, our vision of the world shifts; what we thought we could count on does not exist anymore. It is as if a rug has been pulled out from under our feet—everything is flying in the air, and we do not know if, when, where, or how things will settle into place again. Trauma not only rocks one's external understanding of the world but it also has a huge impact on one's internal world and sense of self. It causes patients to feel dramatically off-kilter, with questions about their sense of purpose, relationships, and even the meaning of life. The unraveling of their reproductive story, with no new narrative to hold on to, leaves patients with a profound sense of loss (Jaffe, 2022).

WHAT IS TRAUMA?

According to the diagnostic criteria for posttraumatic stress disorder (PTSD) in the *Diagnostic and Statistical Manual of Mental Disorders* (5th ed.; American Psychiatric Association, 2022), trauma is defined as "exposure to actual or threatened death, serious injury or sexual violence" (p. 1266). PTSD is often associated with a single dreadful event: an accident, a shooting, or an earthquake. Other long-lasting situations, such as exposure to crime, poverty, the threat of violence, or war, can also induce PTSD symptoms. The distress caused by PTSD is considerable: Symptoms include flashbacks, depression, anxiety, sleep disturbance, irritability, and/or social isolation.

Perinatal loss, whether it is a miscarriage, ectopic pregnancy, or stillbirth, falls under this category and can cause not only grief but also PTSD symptoms (Białek & Malmur, 2020). A large epidemiological study found that bereaved mothers had four times greater odds of depression and seven times greater odds of PTSD than parents who did not have a perinatal loss (Gold et al., 2016). Reproductive patients who fit the criteria of PTSD have been described as having a triad of symptoms: (a) persistent retriggering (ongoing doctor appointments, seeing pregnant women); (b) avoidant behavior (avoiding social interactions, especially baby showers); and (c) hyperarousal (anxiety and guardedness; Bartlik et al., 1997).

Not all fertility and pregnancy loss patients fit the full criteria for a diagnosis of PTSD, yet they are still traumatized by their experiences. A broader definition of trauma is helpful, considering trauma as an event or series of events that overwhelms and shatters basic core beliefs and assumptions (Cann et al., 2010). This concept of trauma is not only based on events that may happen to a person but also describes what happens internally to the sense of self. The catastrophic demise of one's internal world, the distress of losing one's way, and the trauma of losing one's story are the issues at hand. This more fully captures the experience of reproductive patients coping with fertility issues and pregnancy demise. These events challenge individuals' adaptive resources, ability to cope, and understanding of the world and how they fit into it.

CORE ASSUMPTIONS AND BELIEFS

We all rely on general core beliefs about how life should be; these assumptions guide our actions and decision-making processes, help us understand cause and effect, and provide us with an overall sense of meaning to our existence. Some universal assumptions have been suggested, including "benevolence, predictability, and controllability of the world" (Tedeschi & Calhoun, 2004, p. 5). *Benevolence* refers to the belief that the world is essentially a good place with kind and caring people. It allows us to form bonds with other people and create a sense of mutual dependence. *Predictability* refers to consistency. Most people thrive on structure in their lives; being able to count on one another to follow through on a commitment brings a feeling of well-being and trust. In attempting to make sense of and predict the "bad things" that happen in life, we would like to believe that justice prevails. We hold onto the belief, even if erroneously, that good things happen to decent, upright people while misfortune occurs for the ethically corrupt. There is a tendency to blame the victim, not because we are cruel but out of a psychological attempt to have the rules of right and wrong prevail. We can then be protected if we do not engage in the same behavior. This sense of control over our environment, our lives, our hopes, and our dreams runs deep. Think of a person who has been in a car accident—were they just unlucky, or were they not being careful? If they were inebriated or distracted, we can feel vindicated in the knowledge that we can control our actions and will not be involved in an accident. The belief that we can control what happens allows us to make meaning of the world. It is more difficult to believe that random events happen with no ability to predict and protect oneself from misfortune (Janoff-Bulman, 1992).

When universal assumptions are shattered, the resulting trauma has been likened to an earthquake. Tedeschi and Calhoun (2004) suggested it is "a psychologically seismic event that can severely shake, threaten, or reduce to rubble many of the schematic structures that have guided understanding, decision making, and meaningfulness" (p. 5). In the following sections, specific core beliefs about pregnancy and childbirth are discussed. If these are compromised, negative assumptions about oneself and the world get activated, and the ability to navigate through the trauma becomes severely compromised. Patients with preexisting negative core beliefs about themselves or the future are at even higher risk for poor self-esteem and mood disorders.

Reproductive core beliefs are fundamental to one's reproductive story. When compromised by infertility or pregnancy loss, disintegration not just of the would-be pregnancy but also of one's entire inner world occurs. It affects every aspect of one's life, including feelings about one's self, one's purpose in life, worries about the future, and relationships with one's partner, family, and friends. The narrative patients once held is no longer tenable. Just as the reproductive story may be unconscious until it disintegrates, so too are the underlying core beliefs, the building blocks, on which the story is constructed. Take a block or two away, and the sense of self in a just world crumbles. Understanding how these beliefs impact patients and how we can help them rebuild a solid sense of well-being is fundamental to helping them heal (Jaffe, 2019).

The following are some assumptions about pregnancy, which are described in more detail next. Although not every client will make all these assumptions or may label them differently, they illustrate just how pervasive people's thinking is when it comes to reproduction.

- "I thought this would be easy."
- "I'm healthy and strong."
- "Everyone else is pregnant; I should be too."
- "I'm in control of my life."
- "Good things happen to good people."
- "Life is just and fair."
- "Just work hard, and you'll succeed."

Assumption 1. "I Thought This Would Be Easy"

Because reproduction and the biological imperative are fundamental throughout the world, it can come as a shock that creating a family takes work—both biologically and psychologically. Some patients know there will be challenges on the road to parenthood; anyone with a diagnosis of endometriosis or polycystic ovary syndrome, for example, knows that this journey will be difficult. Likewise, members of the LGBTQ+ community are aware that challenges and biases exist. For many, however, the myth remains that having children is straightforward and uncomplicated.

Reproductive patients usually begin therapy either after a loss or after several months (and many times much longer) of "trying." With the development of birth control pills in the 1960s, women were given a greater sense of control over their reproductive lives. The power not to conceive may have erroneously led patients to believe they had control over when they would conceive; all they had to do was stop using birth control, and voila, a pregnancy would happen! The fear of unwittingly getting pregnant was so instilled in people that they believed it would occur on the first try. Even if they are aware that it is normal to take several months to conceive, they believe it happens to other people, not them. After spending years diligently trying not to conceive, they arrive in our offices depleted and depressed, with their assumptions about how easy it should be to get pregnant squelched.

Assumption 2. "I'm Healthy and Strong"

Most people do not think of pregnancy as a risky medical condition. The overall assumption is that because it is so universal and "natural," any woman who wants to have a baby should be able to do so, especially if she is young and healthy. As discussed in the case of Julia and Peter in Chapter 2,[1] Peter assumed that Julia was physically fit and healthy and did not believe, as she did, that she was too old. Ask any physician about pregnancy and childbirth, though, and they will likely acknowledge that no matter what the woman's age or fitness, getting and staying pregnant and giving birth can present challenges. While it is true that the odds are in a woman's favor that all will go as it should, there is no predicting the course of a pregnancy if the woman is able to conceive at all. While some may worry about conceiving or having a miscarriage, a cornerstone of most reproductive stories is that the woman will be able to get pregnant when and as she chooses, as if this were something within her control. The idea that men will have reproductive issues is also not something they usually consider. They might joke about "shooting blanks" and have some underlying anxiety about it, but how could it happen to them? Likewise, unease about a fetal anomaly may enter an individual's or couple's consciousness, but these concerns are often set aside when they consider their vitality and health.

Not only are there medical challenges related to conception but pregnancy can also have negative effects on the patient's overall health. Gestational diabetes, for example, is one of the most common medical complications

---

[1] The case of Julia and Peter has been modified to disguise the patients' identities.

of pregnancy; if untreated, it can cause a baby to grow too large, making a C-section birth more likely. It may also increase the risk of a premature delivery or stillbirth. For the pregnant person, it can raise the risk of hypertensive disorders (McIntyre et al., 2019). Preeclampsia is yet another related disorder of pregnancy, implicated in approximately 46,000 maternal deaths and 500,000 perinatal deaths annually around the world. Preeclampsia is associated with high blood pressure, usually after 20 weeks of pregnancy. There may also be higher levels of protein in the urine, with implications of kidney damage. Most cases of preeclampsia resolve after delivery, but early delivery of the baby or termination of the pregnancy may be necessary for the health of the mother. There are several risk factors for preeclampsia, including being a member of a minority racial or ethnic group or using assisted reproductive technologies (Magee et al., 2022).

Racial discrepancy is prevalent in access to fertility care, with the astronomical cost of treatment (Galic et al., 2021; Richard-Davis & Morris, 2023), but this extends to maternal mortality and morbidity as well. The assumption that because a Black woman is healthy, she will easily have a baby has been proven false. In fact, Black women are two to three times more likely to die because of pregnancy-related circumstances (J. K. Taylor, 2020). One study found that childbirth is deadlier for Black mothers even when they are in top income brackets. It was found that out of 100,000 births, 173 high-income White women die before the baby's first birthday compared with 350 low-income White women. For Black women in the highest income bracket, 437 died, while for low-income Black women, 653 died (Kennedy-Moulton et al., 2022). That means that high-income Black women had a higher mortality rate than the lowest-income White women. Clearly, it is not just socioeconomic status that is a determinant here but also likely systemic injustices in health care (Richard-Davis & Morris, 2023). Similar results were echoed in another study that compared different regions of the United States as having higher or lower maternal vulnerable areas. It was found that Black mothers lived in disproportionally more vulnerable regions than White mothers (Valerio et al., 2023). Research has suggested that race concordance may mitigate these effects, increasing trust, communication, and birth satisfaction (Bogdan-Lovis et al., 2023).

Regardless of race or socioeconomic status, when a pregnancy does not happen as anticipated, one can go from feeling "healthy and strong" to being thrust into a medical world that feels anything but normal. The American Society for Reproductive Medicine (2017) stated that "infertility is not an inconvenience; it is a disease of the reproductive system that impairs the body's ability to perform the basic function of reproduction" (para. 1).

Infertility or pregnancy loss may be the first major medical crisis that an individual or couple may face. The identity shift from "physically healthy, normal" to "physically impaired patient" is another blow to identity and self-worth. One patient said, "I put on that flimsy medical gown, and I felt like I was erased." Taking on the identity of "damaged goods," patients often forget that they are much more than that, in their work and hobbies, as a partner and friend. Feelings can range from incompetent ("My body has betrayed me") to diminished ("I am worthless") to frightened ("What will happen next?"). These feelings fuel new negative assumptions about the self. In these instances, the part often becomes the whole; rather than thinking about a part of the body that is not functioning well, the entire self is reduced to a weakened and broken state.

Assumption 3. "Everyone Else Is Pregnant, I Should Be Too"
"A few years ago, everyone I knew was getting married," remarked one patient. "Now they're all starting to have kids. I feel totally out of sync; I don't feel like I fit in anymore." The wish to have a baby at the same time as a friend or family member is not uncommon and can be seen as one of the pieces of the reproductive story. When people are left behind on the assumptive timeline of having children, it can add to the feelings of trauma and loss. As the case of Julia and Peter illustrated, patients become psychological parents as soon as they start trying to conceive. Would-be parents find themselves in a state of limbo—they are not card-carrying members with the proof of a child, nor do they fully fit in with single friends or other child-free couples. Where do they belong if they have experienced a miscarriage or a failed in vitro fertilization (IVF)? They have made the psychological shift in their identity to become a parent without the physical reality of having a family.

Feeling off-kilter and out of step with others can promote isolation and avoidance. At a time when support and understanding are needed, patients often withdraw from peers and family. They may avoid all gatherings where the focus is on children: holidays, birthday parties, and especially baby showers. As Julia and Peter experienced when they were not invited to their nephew's birthday party, the community may not know how to handle these situations either, reinforcing the feeling of not fitting in. Even "adults only" get-togethers can feel like minefields with conversations about babysitters, day care, and the various other topics that consume parents of young children. The assumption that "we'd be in this together" falls away, leaving patients struggling to find a place where they belong.

This sense of marginalization is even more acute in non-White and non-heterosexual communities. For example, transgender men who have ovaries and a uterus often face discrimination when it comes to reproduction. Although able to become pregnant, they may struggle with their sense of identity and body dysphoria if they temporarily stop gender-affirming hormone use to pursue biological pregnancy. A study of transgender men's experiences of pregnancy found that social support within the community varied from feelings of isolation to overwhelming support. In addition, it was critical for some to be addressed by male names and pronouns, while others were not upset by being mistakenly gendered. To "fit in," some intentionally acted as cisgender women to increase feelings of safety from transphobic hostility and violence (Hoffkling et al., 2017). It is important for mental health professionals to recognize the social constructs affecting all patients on their quest for a family and not assume heteronormative values.

Assumption 4. "I'm in Control of My Life"
While realistically, we know we are not in control of many aspects of our lives, we still believe we can set forth plans and have them come to fruition. The predictability and controllability of the world and our lives are two of the most fundamental core beliefs deeply ingrained in our psyches (Tedeschi & Calhoun, 2004). So many patients have spoken about their pregnancy plans: "If I get pregnant in [fill in the month], I'll have the baby by the holidays or in time for summer vacation or by the time I'm [fill in the age]." This is central to their reproductive story. Rationally, it is easy to see the fallacy of making this assumption; nonetheless, it happens all the time. A planned pregnancy that does not go as planned can shake the premise of control over reproduction.

It is important to consider that the trauma may not be caused by being unable to conceive or by a loss, but it can be traumatic if the timing or the way it occurs is not according to plan. One patient spoke of her intentions of having her children 2 years apart. When she saw the time passing—and her fantasy fading—she became completely distraught. The loss of control over reproduction elicited a tsunami-like fear of losing control over everything. It was difficult for her because she felt no one understood, especially her husband. He was annoyed with her obsessively talking about it and felt pressure to perform. One of the first interventions in psychotherapy was taking her concerns seriously, validating how frightened she was, and labeling her experience as traumatic; feeling heard helped her rein in her anxiety.

Another way to gain control is to blame oneself, thinking, "If I am not getting pregnant, or if I have had a pregnancy loss, I must have done something to cause it." This is akin to the myth of Santa Claus. Regardless of one's religious beliefs, it is embedded in our culture that if you are "a good little girl or boy," Santa will reward your behavior. If you do not get the desired gift—in this case, a baby—it must mean that you have done something wrong. As flawed as this thinking may be, the control lies in being able to not perform that behavior—or even have negative thoughts—next time around. One patient was convinced she had a stillbirth (it was a boy) because she had really wanted a girl. Her grief was compounded by self-blame, as if her negative feelings about having a boy caused the pregnancy's demise. Another patient blamed her miscarriage on carrying heavy groceries and decided to be much more careful if or when she got pregnant again. While it is not always rational and almost always inaccurate, it may be more reassuring to blame oneself rather than believing the trauma to be a random event.

One assumption that adds to self-blame is the notion that fertility issues are caused by stress. So often, patients are told to "just relax," as if reproductive issues were not medical dysfunctions but psychological in nature. Indeed, past beliefs about pregnancy loss and infertility were based on the psychogenic theory, which postulated that a woman's unresolved emotional issues caused procreative problems. In particular, it was thought that a woman's conflict with her mother was the root of the problem (Benedek, 1952; Deutsch, 1945; Leon, 1990). This theory has become virtually obsolete with advances in medical understanding of fertility and pregnancy losses; it is now widely believed that stress is not the cause of these issues but rather the result of the trauma and loss. Even so, an analysis by Negris et al. (2021) indicated the strong power of self-blame and stress in finding a causal relationship for fertility problems. Negris and her colleagues surveyed over 1,400 women seeking fertility care, with results clearly indicating the belief that stress plays an active role in reproductive issues. Nearly 30% of the women in the study believed stress caused infertility and/or miscarriage; 69% believed stress would negatively impact fertility treatment, while less than a quarter believed that emotional stress had no impact on fertility (Negris et al., 2021). This points to a need for increased psychoeducation for reproductive patients as well as the general public. Informing them that there is no proven biological cause and effect between stress and reproduction may mitigate some of their negative emotional baggage.

Sometimes, patients review their past to blame themselves and make sense of their current reproductive trauma. They may worry about former relationships, conflicts, or perceived past indiscretions (Wilson & Kopitzke, 2002). Perhaps they focus on the partying they did in college or promiscuous behavior. Clinicians can provide reassurance that there is no scorecard keeping track of these kinds of behaviors. If there has been a history of trauma, such as drug abuse, poverty, or an unstable home environment, patients may be more prone to assuming they are to blame. Survivors of sexual abuse may be especially vulnerable to this sense of responsibility (Hamama et al., 2010). Conducting a thorough history, especially as it relates to sexual abuse, can help providers understand the extent of its effects on a patient's reproductive story and sense of self. Providing a rational reframing of perceived wrongdoings may help to reduce or eliminate negative self-blame.

An unwanted pregnancy resulting in an abortion poses many questions about women's autonomy and is rife with political implications. Some research has suggested that women who have an abortion are at risk for subsequent mental health problems (Bellieni & Buonocore, 2013; P. K. Coleman, 2011; Cougle et al., 2003), but these claims have been largely refuted. In fact, research indicates that women suffer more long-term negative consequences when abortion has been denied (Miller et al., 2020). In the United States, the Turnaway Study (Rocca et al., 2020) collected data over 5 years on women who desired an abortion. The study analyzed nearly 1,000 women from 30 abortion facilities across 21 states. Although all participants were seeking to abort, some were "turned away" because they were above the facility's gestational limit, while others were within the limit and, therefore, able to move forward with the procedure. For those receiving the abortion, there was no evidence of negative emotions or regret over the decision; in fact, the most salient emotion at the 5-year mark was relief (Rocca et al., 2020). In comparing the two groups, those who were turned away were more likely to be struggling, with higher rates of needing public assistance, higher poverty rates, and worse health (Miller et al., 2020). In addition, children born out of abortion denial were more likely to have poor bonding with their mothers and higher rates of psychiatric hospitalizations (Abrams, 2022). These studies indicate that significant, long-term social and psychological problems can occur when abortion is restricted.

Having an induced abortion does not increase risks to mental health for most women, nor does it contribute to fertility problems or pregnancy complications (American College of Obstetricians & Gynecologists, 2015). What happens, though, if a woman who has had an abortion has subsequent difficulty in getting pregnant? Is there emotional fallout and self-blame when one struggles with fertility later? If an unwanted pregnancy results in relinquishment for adoption, are there emotional consequences if a subsequent desired pregnancy fails? Would the reproductive decisions that had been in their control in the past create misgivings when their current reproductive ability seems so out of control? There is virtually no empirical literature on this, but anecdotally, patients have wondered if the aborted pregnancy was their only chance at becoming pregnant. The current reproductive crisis, whether sparked by infertility, pregnancy loss, or both, seems to be a time of reflection on what might have been. From clinical experience, it does not seem to evoke regret but more of a consideration of "what if?" Future research may shed a better light on the complexities presented here.

Assumptions 5–7. "Good Things Happen to Good People," "Life Is Just and Fair," and "Just Work Hard, and You'll Succeed"
Although described in different ways, these last three assumptions focus on the same fundamental core belief: the deep sense of right and wrong. How often reproductive patients cry, "This is so unfair! Everyone else can do this—why not me?" Whatever one's religion or spiritual beliefs, we recoil when things seem unfair, whether they be minor incidents (someone pushing in front of you in line) or more significant events (witnessing the daily horrors of inequality around the world). We may react to unfair circumstances by taking action; if we just work harder, we are bound to be successful and make positive changes. Other times, the injustices and hardships in society and the world can leave us feeling helpless, confused, and depressed. The inequities in reproductive medicine are a case in point. As discussed, even when financial privilege is taken out of the equation, Black women are at a higher risk for maternal mortality (Kennedy-Moulton et al., 2022). Likewise, members of the LGBTQ+ community struggle with access to health care in general for fear of discrimination. They may even avoid perinatal care, especially trans pregnant people, to circumvent negative experiences (Hoffkling et al., 2017; Parker et al., 2022).

Many patients do try to work harder at overcoming reproductive obstacles; they research all possible paths open to them, sometimes obsessively. They may pursue just one more IVF, even though statistically, the odds are against them. If an iota of hope is held out in front of them, they eagerly grab it. Unfortunately, unlike other things one may strive for, achieving parenthood is not something that one can attain by sheer will. For people who are used to achieving their goals, running into the brick wall of fertility exacerbates these fundamental beliefs. Therapists are often put in a tricky situation when patients zealously take action and pursue treatment. While there may be an inherent desire on the part of the counselor to support their patient's pursuits, it is also important for counselors not to collude with them. Patients need to come to terms with the potential loss of their dreams.

While some patients take action to quell their anxiety, other patients may feel helpless, hopeless, and feel like giving up, especially in marginalized communities. It is also not uncommon to feel both anxiety and depression at the same time. Hopelessness comes in the form of pondering, "How can this be happening to me? This only happens to other people!" This idea of right and wrong or good and bad can be a severe and somewhat simplistic way of viewing oneself or one's situation. Life is far more complex and nuanced than that, yet its unfairness stirs up many feelings. One Latina patient reflected on her ne'er-do-well cousin, who, despite a history of drug and alcohol use, got pregnant unintentionally and had a healthy baby. "How is it," she cried, "that I did everything 'right,' and she has a baby? This makes no sense!" As previously discussed, the effort to grasp some sense of control and find the cause for these reproductive losses stems from this sense of inequity.

JULIA AND PETER: A TRAUMA PERSPECTIVE

In Chapter 2, we viewed this case from a biopsychosocial stance; here, we examine it through the viewpoint of trauma. These different theoretical perspectives, of course, are not mutually exclusive. Considering cases from multiple angles allows clinicians to meet the needs of clients as they process the events of their lives. We will continue to revisit Julia and Peter to illustrate how to use many points of view at once in the therapeutic setting.

In the initial session with Julia and Peter, it was clear that they had been traumatized by the IVF experience. They had already felt off-kilter after having tried unsuccessfully on their own, only to become even more vulnerable when the IVF cycle did not work. The assumption that becoming pregnant would be easy was no longer possible to hold on to. When Peter described Julia as "strong and a fighter," he had not calculated just how susceptible the hormones and shots had made her feel. She was clearly depleted and depressed—no longer feeling "healthy and normal"—and he was doing his best to lift her spirits. He wanted her to know that they would get through it and try again, while she was plagued with insecurities about herself. The assumption that if "you just work hard at something, you will succeed" was driving his optimism, but hers was shaken.

They both expressed how distressed they were hearing news that friends and coworkers were able to get pregnant. Why was it so easy for everyone else? Here again, they felt traumatized by the unfairness of the situation where seemingly everyone else was pregnant. As Peter said, work no longer felt like an escape. What they had trusted in—that the world was safe, predictable, and fair—was no longer true. Overriding all was the loss of control over their reproductive life, sense of autonomy, relationships with others, and ideas about the future. The reproductive events they experienced rattled the internal sense of themselves. These were the emotional consequences of having the rug pulled out from under them. Their ability to trust, predict, and feel a sense of control were the things that were flying through the air, seeking a place to land and return to order. Labeling this as trauma was a first step in validating their distress.

SUMMARY

With reproductive trauma, patients experience not only the loss of the would-be pregnancy but also the disintegration of many core beliefs, all at the same time. These are the fundamental building blocks, usually not in one's conscious awareness, which form the foundation of one's sense of self. Trauma occurs when the blocks come tumbling down. As is discussed in the following chapters, healing and growth for reproductive patients happen when they can identify and label the core beliefs that have been shattered, grieve what has been lost, and build a new understanding of the self.

4

GRIEVING AN UNBORN CHILD

Pain and Hope

With the many unwelcome losses of life—of people, places, projects and possessions in seemingly endless succession, we are called on to reconstruct a world of meaning that has been challenged by loss, at every level from the simple habit structures of our daily lives, through our identities in a social world, to our personal and collective cosmologies, whether secular or spiritual.
—Neimeyer et al., 2014, p. 486

Grief is a profound emotion all of us experience in our lifetime. As a reaction to loss, it can occur with the loss of employment, the loss of housing, a romantic breakup, or the death of a loved one. In this chapter, we focus on the grief experienced when a baby has died or when the wished-for baby is unattainable. In general, the closer the bond to the person who has died, the more intense the grief; feelings can range from sadness to anger, devastation to anxiety. When experiencing loss, some people withdraw into themselves, while others need to interact with people for support. Although there are no rules for how to grieve a loved one, rituals and memories create pathways to mourning. The loss of a baby, the loss of a pregnancy, or even a menstrual

https://doi.org/10.1037/0000400-004
Reproductive Trauma: Psychotherapy With Clients Experiencing Infertility and Pregnancy Loss, Second Edition, by J. Jaffe

cycle that passed without fertilization creates unique challenges because there are few, if any, rituals and virtually no positive memories. How does one grieve a baby that never was? How does one mourn a death when there should have been life? How does one grieve while at the same time holding out hope for the next attempt at pregnancy? There are so many intangible losses that occur that they shake the very foundation of one's identity. It is not just the loss of a would-be child; not being able to become a parent can be seen as the inability to transition into adulthood (Loftus & Andriot, 2012). How does one grieve the loss of adult development and sense of belonging?

This chapter discusses grief in general and focuses on the distinct trials of mourning a reproductive loss. Identifying the multiple losses associated with infertility and pregnancy loss is crucial for patients: It allows them to recognize the trauma, repair damage to their self-worth, and make decisions about future family planning.

MODELS OF BEREAVEMENT

Theories of grief and mourning in Western culture have evolved since Freud in 1917 first proposed the need to hypercathect and then decathect the image of the deceased (Rothaupt & Becker, 2007). Freud's model proposed that after an initial period of emotional discharge and acknowledgment of the death, mourners needed to sever bonds with the deceased to build new relationships. Here, the ultimate goal of grieving was to free oneself from the emotional attachments to the deceased.[1] Lindemann (1944), expanding on Freud's ideas, discussed the concept of *griefwork*: acknowledging the person's absence, feeling the loss, and adjusting to life without the loved one. Lindemann also noted that grief can be delayed or reemerge long after the death and may depend on the attachment and relationship to the deceased.

Stage theories of grief are based on the notion that grief follows a particular progression over time and that one stage must be completed before moving on to the next. Kubler-Ross (1969), in her seminal work with terminally ill patients, developed a five-stage theory: denial ("This can't be happening

---

[1] In Freud's personal experience with grief, he admitted that severing bonds with a loved one was not truly possible. He profoundly stated,

> Although we know that after such a loss the acute state of mourning will subside, we also know we shall remain inconsolable and will never find a substitute. No matter what may fill the gap, even if it be filled completely, it nevertheless remains something else. And actually, this is how it should be, it is the only way of perpetuating that love which we do not want to relinquish. (E. L. Freud, 1960, p. 386)

to me"), anger ("Why is this happening?"), bargaining ("If I promise to do better, this will not happen"), despair or resignation (a loss of hope; "There is no way to stop this from happening"), and finally, acceptance ("It has happened"). Kubler-Ross's work has been generalized to encompass all grief, not just for those who are dying, but the model does not necessarily fit for those living with grief.

One of the drawbacks to the stage theory model is that people do not necessarily grieve in a set order, nor do they totally complete one stage before entering the next. There is no timeline for grief. It is not uncommon for people, especially reproductive patients, to experience all the stages in a short time and then repeatedly return to prior stages. Stage theories of grief imply that it is a disorder from which one needs to recover (Wada & Park, 2009). In framing grief as an illness, stage theories have been criticized as too rigid and strict. If the stages are taken too literally, the bereaved may feel as if they are doing something wrong and not grieving "correctly," further diminishing their ability to cope (Stroebe et al., 2017). As discussed later in the chapter, this can be especially difficult for couples when one partner is at a different stage from the other or thinks the other "should be over it."

The question of whether one can truly detach from the deceased has led to more recent theories that more adequately match the clinical experience of parental bereavement. The notion of a continued emotional bond between the bereaved and the deceased has emerged. Before this wave of research, the task for the bereaved was to disengage emotionally from the deceased. In fact, for much of the 20th century, it was considered a sign of pathological grieving if a person had continued bonds with the deceased (Klass, 2006). However, researchers have shown that mourners do have a continued sense of connection with the deceased—by having positive memories, feeling their presence, talking about (or to) them in one's mind, or saving meaningful belongings—all this can bring comfort to the bereaved. Rather than breaking bonds, a new and transformed relationship with the deceased can emerge, one in which the survivors learn to live without the person and find comfort in their memories (Capitulo, 2005).

Non-Western cultures' views of death have shaped this current thinking. In Japan, for example, where Buddhism influences many ideas about mourn- ing and ritual, it is not uncommon to have home altars where ancestors are honored and consulted for advice (Arnason, 2012). Death is not viewed as the endpoint of life but rather as a cycle of birth, death, and rebirth, a con- tinuation of the connection with the deceased. Neither severing bonds nor rigidly holding on to the loss promotes healthy coping (Wada & Park, 2009). If we think of loss on a continuum, it can be helpful to consider how grief changes over time. With the passing of time, feelings of sorrow may resurface (as on an anniversary date), but the strength of emotions and thoughts about the loss will change. As life goes on for the survivor, perspectives on the loss evolve to include their current life circumstances. It is not possible to "just get over it"; the mourner is changed by the experience, and the change reflects an ongoing, new relationship with the deceased.

CONTINUED BONDS, ATTACHMENT, AND THE REPRODUCTIVE STORY

Before 1970, grief following a miscarriage or stillbirth was not readily acknowledged. In fact, these losses were treated as nonevents; families were routinely told to simply get on with their lives and not dwell on them (Brownlee & Oikonen, 2004). Stillborn babies were routinely whisked out of sight to protect parents from distress. Although the advice was well-intentioned and offered by family and friends as well as the medical community, bereaved parents were left feeling confused and unsupported. To grieve "properly," they had to disregard their emotions—an impossible task. One woman in her mid-70s was heartened to learn about a support group for perinatal loss. "There was nothing like that when I had my miscarriage," she said. "Nobody talked about it; it just got shoved under the carpet. But it's not something that goes away. I still feel upset whenever I think about it." This was after over 50 years had passed.

Rather than thinking of reproductive losses as nonevents, therapists have more recently come to view them as potentially devastating and traumatic for the bereaved individual or couple. Attachment exists between parent and child long before the infant's birth. Indeed, as heard in the telling of patients' reproductive stories, the parent–child bond begins far earlier, before conception, and for many, even before a committed relationship. This is a deep, internalized bond that may not be recognized as having existed until it is broken. With infertility or when a pregnancy fails, the loss is not only perceived as a loss of connection with the hoped-for child but also as a personal failure, the loss of part of the self.

A key factor in understanding grief is the meaning the loss holds in both the internal and external world of the bereaved; meaning making is not just an intrapsychic phenomenon but is culturally and socially shaped (Valentine, 2019). In fact, the process of finding meaning is thought to aid in regaining a sense of control and purpose for the bereaved (Gillies & Neimeyer, 2006).

The search for meaning—for why this loss has happened—is a central element of the grief process. It occurs by creating individual narratives that try to make sense of it; added to that are narratives from within the community that include oral and written accounts to process the death (Neimeyer et al., 2014). The ritual of a eulogy at a funeral or memorial service is one such phenomenon. As painful as it is to lose a loved one, mourners can find meaning in taking account of the life and contributions their loved one had in their family and society. Although rituals vary from culture to culture, most involve family and friends coming together to remember and honor the deceased. Reminiscing about the person—recalling the good times and the bad—is a natural phenomenon that aids and enhances the mourning process. The bond can, therefore, be continued and can contribute to successful mourning (Rothaupt & Becker, 2007).

But how does one make sense of a loss, as with infertility or pregnancy demise, when there are no memories or only painful ones? Memories may consist of hospital procedures, seeing the pained look on a sonographer's face, medical emergencies, or just the crushing disappointment of a negative pregnancy test. As discussed in Chapter 3, core beliefs—the underpinnings of understanding oneself, others, and the world—can crumble when faced with a reproductive loss. Making sense of the loss may feel impossible for patients, especially considering the connection to the longed-for child.

Thinking back to the narrative of the reproductive story can play a vital role in helping to grieve a reproductive loss. Not only is it healing to tell the story as it was originally perceived but it is also necessary to incorporate and communicate the story of the loss itself. Neimeyer et al. (2014) described this process as twofold: telling the *event story* (the actual loss and impact on one's life) and the *backstory* (the relationship one has with the deceased). Telling the story of the trauma, in all its details, and exploring how it should have been allows would-be parents to maintain a sense of their hopes and dreams, clearly not in the way originally anticipated. By finding different possible endings to their story, they can establish a sense of continuity between what was, how it is now, and how it might be in the future. Exploring various reproductive technologies that may have been previously dismissed are stories of the future. One patient who would "never consider egg donation" found herself reconsidering it as a viable option when all else failed. Future stories may even include the possibility of remaining child free. These types of explorations in therapy allow would-be parents to maintain a sense of attachment to their past dreams, grieving that which is lost while at the same time replacing the trauma with hope.

One misconception about reproductive losses is that the duration of the pregnancy determines the amount of attachment and intensity of grief. It is, however, far more complicated than that. Reactions can be affected by many variables: whether the pregnancy was desired, if there had been previous perinatal or other losses, the difficulty and length of time it took to conceive, the amount of outside intervention necessary for conception, whether there are any living children, the nature of the couple's relationship, and the woman's age (Bennett et al., 2005; Conway & Valentine, 1988; Lasker & Toedter, 2000). A woman who had an early miscarriage, for example, may experience similar feelings as a woman who had a third-trimester perinatal loss. The bond that forms may be just as significant, and the grief reaction may be just as intense; in both cases, her baby has died. Attachment can take place even without a pregnancy. One couple was elated when their doctor told them that their embryos looked perfect; when implantation failed to occur, they experienced it as a death. Symptoms of grief after a failed in vitro fertilization (IVF) have been described as mirroring those of women suffering a pregnancy loss, with the woman's attachment to the anticipated pregnancy as the predictor of her reaction (Greenfeld et al., 1988).

Attachment can also predict differences based on the meaning of the pregnancy. A pregnant teen with ambivalence toward motherhood at her age may have a different response to a miscarriage than a 38-year-old woman who has had several years of infertility. Although both have a reproductive story that has gone awry, it is fair to assume that their focus is completely different. The teen may have had thoughts about having children "someday," and may be relieved that she miscarried, whereas the 38-year-old is likely to be devastated by the event. Their responses have less to do with the point in their pregnancy than the point in their life. In assessing patients, clinicians must factor in the meaning of the pregnancy, their readiness and wish to take on the responsibility of parenting, and the extent and intensity of the attachment. "Accurate assessment of the degree of attachment is a critical factor" in understanding patients' reactions (Robinson et al., 1999, p. 265.)

Regardless of the type of reproductive loss, clinicians need to understand the unique meaning the pregnancy or the hoped-for pregnancy has for each patient. Assessing their core beliefs as they pertain to pregnancy and the degree to which they have been shaken can help the practitioner understand the impact of these losses. By recognizing that attachment may begin far earlier than conception, clinicians can help families through the grief process by validating their emotions, helping them develop rituals, and using the reproductive story to continue their relationship with the would-be child.

HOW DOES ONE GRIEVE PERINATAL LOSS AND INFERTILITY?

Most of us have a core belief that generations follow a certain pattern: Grandparents predecease parents who predecease their children. As painful as it is when a loved one dies, if it happens in the "correct" sequence, it makes sense in a universal orderliness. Grieving an anticipated loss, although painful and sad, is made that much easier by the structure of culture, societal norms, and/or religion. When the order is reversed, however, and a child dies, it is crushing and goes against all our values of right and wrong. It just should not be.

Helping patients through the grief process is a large part of what we do as reproductive mental health providers. We encourage patients to talk about their stories and how they went awry—over and over again. Sometimes, patients are reluctant to talk about the frightening parts of it, concerned about how it might impact the therapist. The safer they feel discussing all aspects of their trauma, the better. We encourage them to sit with their feelings, tell us about them all, and validate the significance of their loss. Like a splinter that will fester and become infected if it is not removed, so too are the feelings patients hold onto. It is often only once the story is out that healing can begin.

We help clients make memories and continue the bonds with their longed-for baby by finding meaningful rituals for them. This is hard work for both patients and providers. As addressed in Part II of this volume, these heart-wrenching stories of loss can be emotionally taxing and can have a negative impact on clinicians as well as patients. Dealing with death on an ongoing basis, especially those losses that are out of order, is not for the faint of heart. However, witnessing and having a part in the healing process of patients can be enormously rewarding.

While the reproductive story is a presence throughout all these events, the following sections differentiate between how therapists help patients manage and mourn stillbirth or other perinatal death and early miscarriage or infertility.

Grieving a Stillbirth or Infant Death

As noted earlier, before the 1970s, well-meaning medical practices thought it best for parents of a stillborn baby not to see, hold, or bond with their baby. The emptiness and aching this left behind was profound and devastating. Hazen (2006), having gone through a perinatal loss herself, interviewed women about the "silence" of their experience. Not only did they feel silenced by others but women also silenced themselves about their loss. Feeling that this most devastating trauma was not acknowledged by hospitals, by friends and family, or in the workplace, they believed what they had gone through was unspeakable.

Hazen (2006) also noted how women's experiences have changed over the decades since that time. There are now a number of socially sanctioned practices following a death after a premature birth, stillbirth, or other neonatal demise. It is common practice for hospital staff to encourage parents to see and hold their baby (Hazen, 2006). Some controversy exists in the literature about this practice, with some research suggesting deleterious consequences for women who held their stillborn baby (higher rates of mental health and relationship problems; Hughes et al., 2002; Redshaw et al., 2016). Other research, however, has suggested positive outcomes for those who had contact with their baby, with fewer symptoms of anxiety and depression and an appreciation for seeing and holding the baby even if they were initially reluctant to do so (Kingdon et al., 2015).

Although parents may at first reject the idea of spending time with their stillborn baby, many have described how appreciative they were to do so, finding it helpful in coming to terms with their loss. Women who chose not to see or hold their baby or were unable to because of medical complications described feeling robbed of their only chance to connect with their child (Kingdon et al., 2015). Seeing their child can bring relief; the fantasies of what they look like are often much worse than the reality. It has been reported, for example, that mothers who did not see their deceased baby dreamt their child was a monster (Kroth et al., 2004). The choice is clearly the parents' to make, but knowing there are options is important for hospital health care workers to convey.

One recurring theme is that parents want something tangible to memorialize their child. Parents may be encouraged to name their child unless it is not a cultural norm to do so. If they do name their baby, therapists should refer to the baby in kind. The baby then becomes real—not a phantom or a ghost. Likewise, having photographs of the deceased infant is a concrete way of remembering the baby; sharing the photos with others, including with their therapist, is another way of validating the loss. One couple described their experience of having photographs taken in the hospital: "We were hesitant to have this other person in the room as we held our daughter. But they were so discreet that, at a certain point, we forgot they were there. And now we have the most amazing pictures of our beautiful little girl." Holding and/or naming the baby can help make the child and the experience genuine, which facilitates the grief process. Bakhbakhi et al. (2017) stressed the importance of memory making. Hospitals may help concretize the loss by creating memory boxes, which, along with photographs, may include locks of the baby's hair, handprints and footprints, hand or foot casts, or a hospital name bracelet. Some patients take comfort in writing letters to their baby or may choose to include a meaningful poem in the box. These tangible remembrances provide some solace.

Even when there is a body to grieve over, as with a stillborn baby, grief can feel invisible. Until recently, parents who had a stillbirth in the United States were given a death certificate but not a birth certificate. In a grass-roots effort, many parents pushed for legislation to receive a birth certificate as a symbolic acknowledgment of their child, and now several states have enacted laws to issue such certificates (Lewin, 2007). The disturbing juxta-position of death when a new baby is expected is something everyone would prefer to ignore, but by not legitimizing the experience, parents are left even more at a loss in their grief.

Many parents choose to have a funeral or memorial service for their baby. Not only is this a validation of the loss but these rituals themselves, religious or not, also serve to create memories for the surviving family. Some families choose to visit the gravesite of the deceased baby on a regular basis, bringing flowers, gifts, or even food. One family asked friends and relatives to meet at a beach and write a personal note to their baby. They then placed her ashes in a canister with the messages and "sent her spirit out to sea." Another family held a private ceremony: Each parent attached a letter to the baby to a helium balloon and sent it off. The parents continue to do so every year on the date their son died, creating stories and memories with each passing year. Yet another woman chose to plant a flowering bush that blooms each year on the anniversary of her baby's birth and death.

These rituals and symbolic remembrances are in keeping with the continuing bonds theory of bereavement. Rather than withdrawing emotional energy from the deceased, a connection continues and gets woven into the fabric of the family's life (Côté-Arsenault, 2003). It can help parents regain a sense of control and can potentially facilitate growth by creating memories and connections with their baby. Mental health professionals can help parents by validating the need for this link, suggesting meaningful rituals, and eliciting concrete ways to ensure that the child will not be forgotten.

Grieving Miscarriage or Infertility

As much as stillbirth or perinatal loss has been enshrouded in silence, the void in recognizing bereavement for a miscarriage or infertility is even more palpable. Mourning is more complicated, given the absence of religious or socially validated grieving rituals. These losses, although not less meaningful, are less tangible, less recognized by society at large, and have no prescribed ceremonies to guide parents through bereavement. As devastating as a still-birth or neonatal death is to parents, the mourning process is facilitated by the reality of the baby's body (McGreal et al., 1997). When there is no actual body to grieve over, as in a miscarriage, in an ectopic pregnancy, or with infertility, grief may feel illegitimate. Doka (1989) defined this phenomenon as *disenfranchised grief*, which refers to grief that is not publicly recognized or acknowledged and, therefore, minimized by society at large. If a relationship does not meet the unwritten rules of a sanctioned loss, the survivors may feel deprived of their grief. Many situations fall into this category, such as the loss of a former spouse, the loss a birth parent experiences when relinquishing a child for adoption, or the loss experienced with an elective abortion. Parents who experience infertility and/or miscarriage are at risk for disenfranchised grief. There are no rules for how these losses should be mourned and no models to follow for the bereaved or their close relations.

The well-meaning advice people often give can complicate grief: "You can have another," "It was for the best," or "Just relax." These recommendations totally miss the mark. Although this guidance is given in an effort to soothe the bereaved, it is also because the "comforters" feel awkward: They just do not know what to say. It often falls on those who are suffering to educate others that a simple "I'm so sorry" can be the most supportive thing to say. The impulse to want to try and "fix it" can leave the bereaved feeling more alone with their loss and completely misunderstood. The desire to find a solution for these losses is strong and may be present for mental health professionals as well. As discussed in Part II of this book, awareness of one's reactions is critical in providing the best care to patients.

The invisible losses of infertility and/or miscarriage leave people feeling alone with their feelings, and, many times, they are alone because the only people who may be aware that a significant trauma has occurred are the individual or couple or perhaps their medical team. Consider an early miscarriage: The woman may feel every twinge and ache as she experiences changes in her body while pregnant—the pregnancy and growing baby are very real to her. When there is a miscarriage, there is no tangible evidence that the baby existed, and the grief can be misunderstood and unrecognized.

Fertility treatments can evoke similar feelings. Injecting hormones in the privacy of one's home, for example, can cause an extremely emotional process to become invisible. While it can be all-consuming to the individual or couple, few, if any, other people may know about it. If there is no positive pregnancy as a result, acknowledgment of the loss may be minimized. One patient described her frustration: "If I told my boss I needed to attend my aunt's funeral, the time would readily be granted. But if I told him that I was grieving because I got my period again this month, he would think I was nuts."

As with grieving other perinatal losses, creating meaningful rituals can validate the significance of the experience. One couple agreed to have dinner out after each unwanted menses, not as a celebration, but as a way of staying connected. They acknowledged that even if they did not focus directly on "the baby issue," these dinners provided a catalyst for communication. It forced them to focus on what they did have rather than on what was missing. Other ways of memorializing these losses are to go out in nature, buy flowers, light candles, or journal one's feelings. Considering the need to make memories, these kinds of rituals mark the passage of time and generate concrete remembrances of an ethereal but significant trauma. Given that these losses can create chronic feelings of helplessness, partaking in a ritual can help individuals and couples feel more in control and like they are doing something. Creating a ritual for a pregnancy or baby that never was validates the reality of a loss that is so intangible.

Julia and Peter: Grieving Together

In working with Julia and Peter,[2] it was important to address the trauma of infertility—the repeated disappointments of trying on their own and the erosion of their hopes and dreams—but also the significant loss when their IVF cycle utterly failed. As we got to know each other better and they felt more comfortable in therapy, we focused on the process of their grief using a combination of psychoeducation and catharsis. Neither of them had ever experienced a major loss until this point—their parents were all doing well. Julia's maternal grandparents, although elderly, were still alive, Peter had a surviving grandmother, and their other grandparents had either died when they were young or before they were born. Because it is easy for a reproductive loss to be dismissed as a nonevent, it was important to establish with them that what they were feeling was normal and to be expected. It was equally important that they understood there was no right way to "do it" and no set timeline for grief.

---

[2] All case examples in this chapter have been modified to disguise the patients' identities.

They knew about Kubler-Ross (1969) and her stage theory because it is so ingrained in our culture, but they were puzzled about what stage they were in. Julia felt that they somehow missed the mark and were not grieving right. "Am I a failure at this too?" she asked. I assured her she was not "failing grief" and used an analogy of a super ball to describe the nonlinear aspect of the stages: "It's like this ball is bouncing in your head. It hits one spot, bounces off that and hits another, and just keeps going. Each time it hits, emotions get triggered—and then they get retriggered. This is all normal and the way grief works. It doesn't function in a neat and orderly way. Sometimes you'll feel okay; the next moment you may be crushed with emotion. That's normal." We also discussed that each of their super balls would hit different emotional spots at different times. "Don't be surprised if one of you is in tears," I continued, "while the other is in a state of self-blame and anger. Or if one of you needs to talk and the other needs not to talk. Try to treat each other with understanding and kindness. You are both trying to sort a lot of things out."

Peter noted that the issue of when and how to talk with each other had come up just recently: "What's the best way to navigate this? I was trying to engage Julia the other day about dinner plans, and she was just shut down. I felt like she wanted nothing to do with me—I was angry and hurt. Maybe this wasn't the best way to handle it, but I just stormed off into the other room." This was a great opening for us to analyze and deconstruct what might have been going on. Often, what seems to be a minor conversation—dinner plans—is couched in layers of other emotions that erupt. Approaching this from a grief perspective would allow them to understand each other better. "You are both on tenterhooks. That's totally understandable, given what you've gone through," I began. "It's difficult for you to know what's going on inside the other at any given moment. My guess is your inner distress makes each of you withdraw at times or explode at others." I paused, letting it sink in. "If we could do an instant replay of that conversation, what might you consider doing differently?"

Julia had tears in her eyes. "He's the last person in the world I want to push away." She turned to him and said, "I'm so sorry." With that, Peter immediately softened, and the anger dissipated like air being let out of a balloon: "I guess I could try to be more understanding. We really are going through a lot—and the pressure to figure out what's next is constantly on my mind." He turned to look at her, "It's got to be on your mind as well." I asked them if there was a way to let the other know what their internal self was coping with at any given moment: Could Julia have said, "I just need a few minutes before I can talk about dinner"? Could Peter have asked,

"Is this a good time to talk?" Knowing that they were both feeling fragile and raw, could they have kept that in the forefront of their minds as they approached each other?

This intervention helped them realize they were not each other's enemies, but in the same battle together. They might be in different places in their grief, and the intensity of emotions may hit them at different times, but they were both grieving. The conversation also set the stage for further exploration into yet another potential minefield: "What do we do next?" This was a conversation that would unfold in time.

When Couples Grieve Differently

While previously stated, it bears repeating: It is the meaning of the would-be child that determines the extent of the trauma and subsequent grief. Within each person's reproductive story are the clues that can help the patient and clinician decipher this meaning. Just as each member of a couple may ascribe a different meaning to a pregnancy, each will cope and grieve differently to a reproductive loss; this may be due to individual differences in cognitive, emotional, or personality styles. In addition, there is no one right way to grieve, especially in the context of disenfranchised grief. What can cause tension in the relationship, however, is a misunderstanding of responses that each individual may have, whether in a heterosexual, same-sex, or other relationship. As illustrated with Julia and Peter, feelings of impatience, resentment, or frustration may emerge when one member of the couple struggles with their feelings in a different way than the other or expresses them in a way the other does not understand.

Diane and Liz: Taking Turns With Grief

When a couple shares a reproductive trauma, whether a pregnancy loss or infertility, they may assume that their own reaction will be the same as their partner's. It should be noted, however, that partners often will literally "take turns" expressing their grief. The tables can completely turn as the feelings of each partner switch.

Diane and Liz, an interracial, married, lesbian couple, knew exactly who would be the partner to attempt pregnancy. Diane, who identifies as Black, had no desire to carry a pregnancy or give birth, while Liz, who is White, was all in. They both agreed that the sperm donor would be Black so their children would be biracial. Their interactions with their fertility specialist went well; they both felt heard and respected. Unfortunately, this was not the case when they arrived at urgent care with symptoms of a miscarriage, where their relationship was questioned. Not only was Liz experiencing vaginal bleeding and cramping but she also had to insist that Diane be allowed to accompany her. Explaining that Diane was her wife while going through a miscarriage added to the trauma.

"Liz has been so despondent after our loss, I felt I had to be positive and uplifting," Diane said. "Yes, the experience at urgent care was maddening—we've weathered this kind of racial and homophobic discrimination before—but the important thing was that Liz got good care, which she did. And yes, we lost a pregnancy, but I knew we could try again."

Liz was depressed and was having difficulty focusing. She described herself as going through the motions of doing her job at work, with those feelings continuing for her at home. Diane tried to counter Liz's grief by diving back into life: "I have been pushing for us to see friends and socialize. I want to start trying again, not just trying to get pregnant but trying to go on with our lives. Clearly, Liz is not on the same page."

Liz was confused by what she perceived as Diane's insensitivity: "I don't understand how Diane could be back to normal. Did this baby mean nothing to her?" Diane was equally frustrated: "Of course, I'm sad about losing this pregnancy, but we have to go on." They began couples therapy with me because they were not on the same page.

I was able to normalize that how they perceived the loss was different for each of them and that this was a common occurrence with couples. I noted that even the language they used when describing the loss was dissimilar: Liz referred to losing a baby, while Diane spoke of losing a pregnancy. Did they each feel different about it because Liz was the pregnant partner, and it was her eggs they were using? Research has suggested that birth (biological) mothers react differently than social (nonbiological) mothers; birth mothers felt they could openly grieve, while social mothers felt the need to be strong for their partners (Craven & Peel, 2014; Wojnar, 2007). Although Liz and Diane shared their eagerness to have children, it was possible that Liz felt more attached to the unborn baby than Diane. Not only did she experience all the physical sensations of the pregnancy as well as the miscarriage, but psychologically, she also felt different about herself. Liz stated, "This baby was part of me. I'm not sure that Diane can understand that a part of myself feels like it disappeared." In the calm setting of therapy, Liz was able to articulate the multiple losses she felt. When Diane was probed about her feelings, she continued to focus the attention on wanting Liz to get the care she needed.

As time went on, however, Liz started to feel better; she was more ready to reengage with the world and possibly try for another pregnancy. This was when Diane's feelings of anxiety and sadness began to surface. I noted the shift and gently brought the emotional focus onto Diane instead of Liz. "With Liz so upset, there was no room for my own feelings," she realized. "All my energy was spent on suppressing my pain and trying to prop her up."

This emotional "flip-flop" is common between grieving partners; it is not unique to cisgender heterosexual couples but happens to people of all genders, sexual orientations, and cultural identities. It often occurs when a decision needs to be made, in this case, whether Liz and Diane were ready to attempt another pregnancy. The couple essentially splits the ambivalence, with one person taking one point of view ("Let's get going") and the other taking the opposite ("I'm not ready"). If one person changes their position, the other may change as well, as if to keep a balance between them like a seesaw. It can take time and continued negotiation for them to come to the middle and make a shared decision. Misunderstandings like this can cause strife within the relationship and leave one person feeling as if they are not grieving "right." It is rarely the case that a couple will grieve in the same way and at the same time. They will not only have contrasting styles of grief but will also deal with different issues at different points in the process (Avelin et al., 2013; Gilbert, 1996).

Stroebe et al. (2013) described this common way of coping with grief as partners engaging in *partner-oriented self-regulation* (POSR). In an effort to protect each other, they may avoid talking about the trauma and try to remain strong for each other. Unfortunately, rather than the intended relief, this seems to amplify grief instead. If one member of the couple tries to suppress their feelings (as Diane did), it may signal to the other (in this case, Liz) that the expression of grief is not acceptable. Stroebe et al.'s findings highlight the paradoxical nature of the couple's attempts to help each other. The idea of holding back one's feelings can have the opposite effect: Not only does it increase their partner's grief but their own as well. POSR can cause the misinterpretation of "no apparent grief for no actual grief, which could lead to such thoughts as 'my partner is not suffering as much as I am,' 'my partner is callous and forgetting our child,' and 'I am alone in this'" (Stroebe et al., 2013, p. 400). One man confessed that he would cry alone in his car. He was afraid that if he cried in front of his wife or even talked about their infertility, it would make her more upset. The irony was that she was upset because he had not been talking about it; she wondered if he cared and was no longer sure he even wanted children anymore.

The more Liz and Diane engaged in understanding their individual emotional reactions to the miscarriage and how it affected their relationship, the more they were able to come together again. This highlights the need for clinicians to help couples process their individual grief, as well as understand the interpersonal processes of grieving and the impact on their relationship.

Are There Gender Differences in Grief?

On the surface, it appears that there are gender differences in how people of different genders express their grief but, when analyzed, the dissimilarities across genders are not clear-cut. The studies noted in this section are based on cisgender norms; more research regarding the differences in categorization, if any, in noncisgender or nonbinary people is needed.

The commonly held idea of how grief is conveyed—through tears, sadness, and depressed mood—is considered a feminine model. Characteristics of the feminine style of bereavement include emotional expression of the loss and a need to talk about and "process" it (Rando, 1985, 1986). Those who follow the more masculine model, however, bear the stereotype of not showing their emotions; typecast in the role of the stoic partner, they typically deal with their reactions through thought, not feelings. They are less likely to talk about the trauma (DeFrain, 1991), avoid emotional displays, and use cognitive, problem-solving strategies to cope with the loss (Rando, 1985, 1986).

Stroebe and Schut (1999) recognized gender-related differences in grieving and proposed a dual-process model, with each person having varying degrees of both loss-orientation and restoration-orientation styles of coping. *Loss-orientation* refers to the more traditional notion of grief, with concentration and rumination on the loss and trauma, whereas *restoration-orientation* coping focuses on the things that need to be dealt with when a loss occurs to build one's life without the loved one. For successful coping, there needs to be a balance between (a) expression of feelings and contemplation of the past and (b) accepting the reality of the changes in one's life. This is another type of seesawing between partners when grieving reproductive loss. Not only do they attempt to balance each other but they must also balance the grief over what was lost while simultaneously looking forward, with hope, to their next procedure and their next pregnancy. At the same time they are grieving the loss, they are attempting to rewrite their reproductive story to restore meaning and hope for the future.

Studies have shown that there are differences in how men and women grieve, but not necessarily in stereotypical ways. In comparisons of men and women following a pregnancy loss, scores on the Perinatal Grief Scale (PGS; Toedter et al., 1988) indicated that women's grief is more intense immediately following the loss ("active grief") while men have delayed effects, as measured by two subscales of the PGS: Difficulty in Coping and Despair

(Puddifoot & Johnson, 1999; Stinson et al., 1992). The Despair subscale is the most serious; it reflects an internalized response to the grief and has implications for long-term emotional effects (Toedter et al., 2001). Men may return to work, try to restore a sense of order and control, and may seemingly get back to normal, but by no means does this imply that they do not have intense grief reactions. As Stroebe et al. (2013) described in their work on POSR, men's need to regulate and suppress expressions of grief is often attributed to societal expectations. Men are culturally expected—and expect themselves—to be strong and to protect and support their partners (Rinehart & Kiselica, 2010). They often take on the job, especially following pregnancy demise, of informing the family of the event and making the funeral arrangements. With infertility patients, men tend to take on the "coach" or "cheerleader" role, providing comfort and suggestions for solutions for the future. Although they may appear to be functioning well, they are more than likely masking their devastation. It is not unusual for men to act out on their feelings: They may work more, drink more, or physically throw themselves into working out more.

Anger is another way of expressing grief and may be more socially acceptable for men than voicing their feelings through tears. Returning home from the hospital after a stillbirth, one man took a sledgehammer to their kitchen, much to the horror of his wife. Although they had previously discussed plans to renovate, it was the furthest thing from her mind at that moment; she became furious with him and felt he was being completely insensitive. In conjoint therapy, the meaning of his actions became clear to them both. He was able to understand his unconscious need to "do something" about their loss: Ripping off cabinet doors and smashing countertops was a way of coping with his sadness. In addition, building something new allowed him to overcome feelings of helplessness; unlike the pregnancy, he could create something he had control over. Discussing this in therapy, he realized how disconcerting the kitchen project was to his wife, and she understood his actions in a different light. Clinicians need to remember that there are many ways to cope with grief and that its expression may reveal itself in a multitude of ways.

Doka and Martin (2011) recommended thinking of grief outside typical gender stereotypes. They offered two styles of grieving that are related to gender but not necessarily determined by it: intuitive and instrumental. *Intuitive* grievers are characterized by their expression of feelings; outward displays of crying and lamenting reflect what they are experiencing internally. They may have difficulty concentrating, feel disorganized or confused, and feel physically exhausted as a result. In contrast, *instrumental* grievers display less intense feelings, with thinking being the dominant characteristic. Most important for instrumental grievers is the ability to master the situation. Rather than talk about feelings, these grievers rely on problem-solving strategies to regain a sense of control. Instead of focusing on stereotypical gender norms, this "blended" pattern incorporating both intuitive and instrumental styles moves away from gender-based terminology. The continuum from intuitive to instrumental may vary by individual, depending on their particular need and loss (Doka & Martin, 2011; T. L. Martin & Doka, 2000).

CULTURAL CONSIDERATIONS

Having children is an expectation that crosses all cultures, and the anguish caused by infertility and perinatal loss knows no boundaries. There are, however, cultural and religious differences in the meaning of these losses and how they are expressed. The pressure on women to produce offspring varies across cultures, as does access to care, and the consequences for people who cannot have children differ around the globe. Knowledge of the cultural norms of a particular patient is crucial for practitioners in determining the course of treatment.

Understanding the difference between two cultural frameworks—collectivist cultures versus individualist cultures—provides insight (Hynie & Burns, 2006). *Collectivist cultures* stress the importance of family and community over personal goals and the well-being of the group over individual needs. Arranged marriages may prevail by merging two families rather than two individuals. Children then represent the continuation of the culture's lineage and can establish social status and rank within the community. Childlessness, however, becomes not just a traumatic experience for the couple but also a crisis for the entire group (Buluc-Halper & Griffin, 2015). Often, the woman is blamed for the inability to have children, whether it is her "fault" or not. There may be serious consequences for childlessness in these cultures, including divorce, physical and/or emotional abuse, or infidelity. Places that score high in collectivism include China, India, Middle Eastern countries, South and East Asian countries, and African nations (Hynie & Burns, 2006).

An *individualistic culture*, by contrast, focuses more on an individual's goals and less on the norms of the group. Children are seen as an extension of the couple rather than that of the group. Childlessness through this lens can be seen as a personal failure and a narcissistic blow. Loss of self-esteem and inability to achieve this highly sought-after goal shake the foundations of one's worldview, creating high levels of depression and anxiety. The United States is predominantly an individualistic culture, especially among White, middle-class Americans; other nations where individualism is also pronounced include most European countries, Canada, and Australia (Hynie & Burns, 2006).

Knowledge of cultural norms and a woman's social role in her culture is crucial for the clinician in providing treatment and helping individuals and couples through the grief process. Although the course of psychological treatment may not alter, mental health providers should be sensitive to cultural expectations and how perinatal loss is interpreted. In addition, it is important not to make assumptions about a patient's belief system based solely on their race or ethnicity. Children of immigrant parents are bicultural, with their feet in two, sometimes opposing, worldviews. How much they have acculturated and blended into their new social structure varies from person to person. They may alternate between beliefs, falling on family traditions in one instance while pursuing convictions from their new culture in other circumstances.

Contradictions in the patient's belief system may become apparent when the desire to use reproductive technologies clashes with religious or cultural norms. Although most societies see childlessness as an aberration, not all religions support the use of assisted reproductive technologies to create life (see Table 2.1, this volume). Couples may find themselves caught between the pressure to procreate and the prohibitions of their value system. The desire to have a child may override whatever religious bans against technology exist, but this can add a layer of guilt and anxiety to an already stressful situation. How should a Catholic patient manage frozen embryos? Is destroying them equivalent to abortion, which is taboo in the Catholic Church? How can an Islamic couple reconcile their wish to use egg donation when their religion dictates that procreation is only acceptable if it involves the genetic material of both the husband and wife? These present terrible quandaries for those who are committed to their faiths yet desperately want a child.

Termination for medical reasons (TFMR) occurs when continuing the pregnancy would risk the health or life of the mother or when there is a chromosomal, genetic, or structural defect in the fetus. This is one of the most painful situations for individuals or couples to address. Currently, because of restrictive abortion laws in some states in the United States, such terminations have become more difficult to procure, causing increased emotional distress in an already painful circumstance. In a review of multiple studies on TFMR, the emotional responses of women are, in many ways, not surprising: They feel anxiety, depression, shock, guilt, shame, and fear that it could occur again. In addition, one of the studies found that women were thankful for having the choice to terminate (González-Ramos et al., 2021; Guy, 2018), not wanting to bear a child who would not survive.

For some, pregnancy termination may conflict with cultural or religious doctrine. For example, in the ultraorthodox Jewish community, pregnancy termination is forbidden after the 40th day. In most cases in the Muslim Arab community, it is not allowed after 120 days (Zlotogora, 2002). In Catholicism, termination of a pregnancy is prohibited under any circumstances. The journey these parents take can be agonizing: Not only are they in shock that their reproductive story does not include a healthy pregnancy but they must also reconcile medical realities with fundamental beliefs about life and death as well as religious doctrine. The decision-making process includes thinking about the life of the affected child, the welfare of other children in the family, and concerns for one's partner and oneself (Korenromp et al., 2007). Clinicians should understand that regardless of culture or religion, women who choose TFMR grieve just as intensely as those who spontaneously lose a pregnancy (Zeanah et al., 1993).

JULIA AND PETER: GRIEVING THE STORY THAT WAS

As Julia, Peter, and I worked through the trauma of their failed IVF, the topic of what to do next was ever present. We talked about the many options that reproductive medicine offered and the plusses and minuses of each. They were acutely aware of their slim chances with another IVF cycle using Julia's gametes, but the idea of using an ovum donor was at first rejected: "If this baby can't be ours . . . what's the point?" Here was another layer of grief: They had already mourned having a baby "the old-fashioned way" in their shift to doing IVF. If they were going to consider using third-party reproduction, it would require mourning the loss of using their own gametes.

Some believe that once a baby is born, all concerns of how they came to be will vanish. While this may be true for some, it is certainly not true for all. The literature on pursuing nongenetic parenthood has studied adoption as well as gamete donation, both of which typically follow the trauma of infertility (Imrie et al., 2020). In adoption, studies have highlighted the pain of losing the imagined genetically related child. In addition, the research has stressed the worries adoptive parents have about being able to love a child who is genetically unrelated to them (Daniluk & Hurtig-Mitchell, 2003). Clinical observation suggests some adoptive parents struggle with imposter feelings: "Do I really have the right to parent this child?" Working through this process has been termed *parental claiming*—the emotional and intellectual work adoptive parents do to claim the right to a child that is not genetically their own (Sandelowski et al., 1993).

Do parents pursuing gamete donation undergo similar thoughts and feelings? Research has suggested that some women feel as if they are not the "real" mother (Kirkman, 2008). One patient who used a donor egg and a surrogate stated, "I feel like this baby belongs to my husband and not me. I had no part in it." As she and I worked through these feelings in therapy, she was able to feel bonded to her daughter but sadly felt "like I lost the first 2 years of her life due to my own insecurities."

Other research has suggested that once a woman finds out she is pregnant, even without a genetic connection, she "instantly" bonds with her baby in utero and at birth (Applegarth & Riddle, 2007). One study proposed that egg donation mothers use a similar process of parental claiming as adoptive parents (Imrie et al., 2020). In this study, the researchers found that the emotional work of attachment began even before conception and that thinking about relationships with nongenetic close family (i.e., stepsiblings) allowed women to believe that they could establish a strong parental bond with their children. They also found that bonding was not necessarily instant but developed over time. These findings echo the experience not only of adoptive parents but also of genetically related parents: Affection, bonding, and feeling like a "real" parent develops with engagement with an infant through nurturing and care (Figueiredo et al., 2007; A. E. Goldberg et al., 2009; Koniak-Griffin et al., 2006).

It was logical for Julia and Peter to consider egg donation, given Julia's poor response to IVF. Their doctor had recommended it when the IVF failed, but it had been too soon for them to even think about it. Over time, I was able to introduce it as a viable possibility. I was cautious not to try to sell them on it, but I also did not want it to go unheeded. It was important not to make assumptions but to find out exactly what their fears were. Some of what troubled Julia, in particular, was that the baby would not look like her and that people would make comments to that effect. She also worried that she would not be able to bond with the baby and, likewise, the baby would not bond with her. I acknowledged her worries as real but also pointed out that genetics did not automatically and instantly create a bond. Pointing to the empirical literature and the evidence presented, she and Peter began to feel better about this process. We discussed that moving on with egg donation would not erase their losses and that there may always be a sore spot knowing that their story had to shift in this way but that a lot of healing could happen as they pursued this avenue to parenthood. They knew there were no guarantees, but they felt reassured that they could be good parents no matter what.

SUMMARY

A reproductive loss is one of the most difficult experiences for an individual or couple. Not only has a real or wished-for child been lost but feelings of hope and dreams of the future must also be reshaped. Grieving is essential, but how one grieves is determined by many factors, such as feelings of attachment, ethnicity, religion, social mores, and gender. As clinicians, we can help patients grieve by validating their experience as traumatic. Giving patients the opportunity to talk repeatedly about their infertility or perinatal loss and reflect on the meaning of the loss in the context of their lives is a large part of the healing process. Also essential is understanding the different but equally legitimate ways people express their grief. The one-size-fits-all notion of grief is harmful because it implies there is a right and wrong way to manage and cope with this trauma. Just because someone does not show their feelings in traditionally expected ways does not mean they are not grieving. Normalizing patients' reactions, giving them "permission" to take the time they need to process their losses, and establishing ways to communicate with their partner will enable them to find their bearings again, find meaning again, and discover the potential for growth from the trauma.

5
HELPING PATIENTS COPE WITH REPRODUCTIVE LOSS
Treatment Options

To have one story is the most reassuring situation of all. Everything is perfectly clear. To be suddenly left without any story is terrifying. Nothing makes any sense.

—Yuval Noah Harari, *Sapiens*

Parents-to-be seek psychological help when their reproductive story has gone off course. Their fundamental assumptions about creating a family have been shattered; they are traumatized and grieving but, at the same time, hold out hope that the next cycle, the next round of medical interventions, will prove successful. It is a time of enormous psychological upheaval.

We wear many hats as mental health professionals when we treat reproductive patients. As discussed in Chapter 6, one of our roles is to make assessments regarding third-party participants. We are called on to do psychoeducational consults to ensure all parties involved can give full informed consent. In other words, we use our wisdom and clinical knowledge of the possible pitfalls in third-party reproduction to protect all involved for the best possible outcome.

https://doi.org/10.1037/0000400-005
Reproductive Trauma: Psychotherapy With Clients Experiencing Infertility and Pregnancy Loss, Second Edition, by J. Jaffe

This chapter addresses our therapeutic work with parents-to-be. While much of reproductive medicine is focused on heterosexual patients, reproductive technology has opened pathways to parenthood for single parents by choice and gay and lesbian couples as well. It has also given the transgender population opportunities to become parents using their own gametes. As discussed, clinicians should understand the unique challenges that single parents and the LGBTQ+ community experience in creating families.

Given what we know of how trauma and loss can unsettle patients' lives, clinicians need to take note of patients' reproductive stories and understand the meaning of the disruptions in their stories. Using a combination of narrative, psychodynamic, and cognitive therapies, therapists can help reconstruct clients' lives, whether they have children or not at the end of the story. Psychodynamic explorations can help patients deepen their understanding of their childhoods and how that has affected the development of their reproductive story. Being attuned to the assumptions that patients make about "how it should be" can guide clinicians in reframing their stories. Psychoeducation can help normalize and validate the reactions they are experiencing.

Regardless of technique or theoretical approach, reproductive patients enter therapy feeling depleted and demoralized—physically, emotionally, and financially. They have been through any number of tests, procedures, and/or surgeries; they may have experienced or witnessed a medical emergency; or they may have spent enormous sums of money as well as time in pursuit of their dream. They are likely feeling fragile, their defenses brittle and worn. Added to this, they may feel isolated and alienated because infertility and pregnancy loss are often unrecognized by society and considered an "invisible disability" (C. H. Shapiro, 2009, p. 142). Under normal circumstances, pregnancy can be considered a developmental upheaval (Benedek, 1952; Bibring, 1959; Colarusso, 1990; Leon, 1990). A reproductive crisis within the normal developmental challenges of the transition to parenthood is often what causes individuals or couples to seek psychological help (Applegarth, 2000). It can be thought of as "a crisis within a crisis"; instead of moving into the next phase of development (parenthood), a "developmental interference occurs" (Leon, 2001, p. 150).

While patients may seek psychological support at any point in their struggle, clinical observation points to key times when they are more likely to reach out:

- at the time of diagnosis or first visit to a reproductive specialist
- during stressful in vitro fertilization (IVF) procedures
- after multiple IVF attempts and failures or when beginning yet another cycle
- after a pregnancy loss (miscarriage, stillbirth, ectopic pregnancy, multifetal reduction, termination for medical reasons)

- on reaching a crossroads in deciding about other available family-building options or when they decide to stop treatment altogether
- when couples differ in these choices
- if they are planning to use third-party reproductive technology (donors and/or surrogates)
- when they struggle with the disposition of unused embryos

As in all psychological treatment, a thorough assessment of each person's needs is necessary to fully understand the depth and meaning of what has been lost. Meeting patients "where they are at" provides support at a time when their emotions are raw; so often, they crave validation and understanding— asking, perhaps directly but more often indirectly, "Do you get me?" Because patients present with a wide variety of symptoms that may overlap with multiple diagnoses, no single treatment plan is adequate to address their needs. They do not enter therapy to make fundamental changes to their personality; rather, they come to repair their sense of self and return to feeling whole again (Leon, 1996). An eclectic style of treatment is therefore recommended, combining psychoeducation with various other techniques to reduce emotional distress, augment self-esteem, allow for catharsis, and increase communication and understanding between partners.

As discussed in the following sections, the initial focus of treatment needs to center on the immediate trauma and loss, dealing as one would in a crisis intervention. Over time, a more in-depth history will naturally unfold as the therapist listens for, looks for, and asks about a number of themes. These include:

- the reproductive story
- the meaning of pregnancy and family, including family of origin history
- medical information
- symptoms of depression, anxiety, posttraumatic stress disorder, and/or obsessive-compulsive disorders
- differences in partners' coping and grief styles
- patterns of communication and couple dynamics
- previous trauma and loss, whether reproductive or not

THE INITIAL APPOINTMENT(S)

Regardless of theoretical orientation, our job is to listen. In the first session(s), clinicians need to allow patients to pour out their hearts in some combination of words, tears, frustration, and pain. If we are seeing a couple, sometimes one person is the designated "talker" while the other is just present in their grief. We need to pay attention to their trauma; these accounts are painful to hear as we witness the loss of a baby, whether a neonate, a blastocyst, or a failed cycle. The intensity of the emotions can be overpowering; it is important for providers to stay present, listen without judgment, and not try to "fix" the problem.

By listening to the details of their trauma, clinicians give patients permission to air negative thoughts and feelings. Patients crave emotional support as they navigate difficult medical procedures and losses on many levels. As basic as this may seem, patients have complained that some medical providers have not been supportive, sometimes due to scheduling constraints; sometimes due to their focus on physical symptoms, not emotional ones (Öztürk et al., 2021); and sometimes due to a minimization of these losses in general (Geller et al., 2010). One study of women who had experienced a miscarriage found that dissatisfaction with health care services predicted more persistent grief symptoms (deMontigny et al., 2017). This may be especially true in the LGBTQ+ community and communities of color. Queer individuals are more likely to experience bias and less understanding when seeking reproductive health care (Carpenter, 2021). People of color often face similar disparities in health care, with higher rates of miscarriage (Quinn & Fujimoto, 2016) and increased mortality (Valerio et al., 2023).

Patients have also reported feeling misunderstood by mental health professionals who do not have training in reproductive crises. Indeed, a major concern of reproductive patients seeking psychotherapy is that their provider does not understand the full extent of what they are going through (Hart, 2002). Therapists need training and clinical guidelines to know the best ways to work with this population; otherwise, opportunities for patients' healing and growth may be missed (Markin, 2017).

The rug has truly been pulled out from under these patients. This can make them feel as if they are going crazy; their foundation has been shaken. They have been thrown an unexpected left hook that hits at the core. Having a therapist normalize and validate their feelings brings an enormous sense of relief. A simple statement from a therapist, such as, "Of course, you can't think straight. You've just had all your hopes and dreams shattered," can place their reactions in the realm of "normal." Acknowledging this in the initial appointments helps to release the patient's anxiety, reduce their stress, and ameliorate feelings of isolation.

THE REPRODUCTIVE STORY IN TREATMENT

At some point early in therapy, educating patients on the concept of the reproductive story can be extremely useful. Patients readily "get it"; it helps them understand and identify the multiple losses they have sustained. They can also view their reproductive trauma in the broader context of their lives. Not only does this work expand their understanding about themselves—their childhood and role within the family of origin, their self-concept as an adult, and their coping strategies under pressure—but it also reveals the intricacies and nuances of their most intimate relationships. There is often an "aha" moment when the pieces of the puzzle, the deepening of their self-awareness and their relationships, come together. The following sections provide case examples of how the reproductive story can be seen from different theoretical orientations.[1] While discussed separately here, most of the time, a combination of different theories and points of view come together when treating reproductive patients. All are used in the service of working through their trauma and grief.

A Narrative Perspective

"I thought we should start trying years ago, but Eric wasn't ready. He wanted to finish his PhD and get settled in a professorship, but now it may be too late," Anita, a 39-year-old special education teacher, began. Her rage was palpable. "It's not like I don't value his career—or my own—but I always wanted to be a mom." She turned to him, "You knew that! And now you've made it nearly impossible!"

Her reproductive story was clear: Her identity was deeply connected to becoming a parent. As it is for many people, she held a deep-seated cultural expectation that people should and will have children. There was something about their dynamic, however, that I was sensing as Eric silently took her verbal punches: What was his reproductive story, and how was it affecting their relationship?

It was soon revealed that Eric had an older brother who had died in infancy, several years before Eric was born: "It always felt like there was a phantom that I was competing with in our house." There it was: His story was unfolding right before our eyes. It was not that Anita did not know about this part of Eric's history, but hearing it in the context of the reproductive story lent it new meaning.

Narrative therapy, first developed by White and Epston (1990), focuses on the idea that patients can review their current self-narration and heal by telling new stories about themselves (Hutto & Gallagher, 2017). For patients struggling with fertility and pregnancy losses, it is often only after

---

[1] All case examples in this chapter have been modified to disguise the patients' identities.

a reproductive trauma has occurred that their story is fully recognized and appreciated. What is important is that the story needs to be told and needs to be heard. Narrative therapy in this context is a natural way for couples to focus on what might have been and coauthor a new story of healing (Romney et al., 2021).

Because each member of the dyad, regardless of gender identity, has their own unique story, knowing how the other feels about creating a family—or not—is essential. In couples therapy, the reproductive story can serve as a catalyst to promote deeper empathy with one's partner. Telling their story to each other forces patients to make conscious what may have been tucked deep inside their psyches for many years. Couples may learn that they no longer have the same reproductive goals—or that the goals have changed as they plunge deeper into treatment and ongoing losses. The emotional and financial toll is enormous, and what should have united them—creating a family—may now be driving a wedge between them.

The strain on the relationship can be significant, eating up resources of time and money. The quest to have a child may become so all-consuming that it overshadows all aspects of communication, daily tasks, social life, and sexual intimacy (Brigance et al., 2021; Soleimani et al., 2015). Communication between partners often gets distorted by ongoing grief and stress. For example, one member of the dyad—"A"—may express more outward symptoms of depression, while the other—"B"—may feel the need to suppress any negative emotions, stay positive, and act like a coach or cheerleader. The danger of this dynamic is that A may feel that B is uncaring and out of touch, causing B to feel resentful, ineffective, and/or helpless.

One commonly held misconception is that females are responsible for all reproductive problems. When statistics are examined, however, the data reveal that males and females share the diagnosis of infertility equally, with about one third of cases attributed to male factors, one third to female factors, and the remaining third to both members of the dyad, with about 20% of these cases unexplained (American Society for Reproductive Medicine [ASRM], 2017). If one person has been diagnosed as having "the problem," they may feel damaged or guilty and may fear their partner will blame them. They may even worry that their partner will leave them in pursuit of someone with whom they can have a family.

Self-blame and/or blame of each other can be enormously destructive to the relationship. For example, a man with diabetes, which affected his sperm, offered to leave his marriage because he blamed himself for their reproductive difficulties (C. H. Shapiro, 2009). One study found that women who blamed their partner had more symptoms of depression and anger, while men who blamed their partner reported lower relationship satisfaction (Péloquin et al., 2018). Not surprisingly, blaming each other causes increased hostility and frustration, which is clearly not conducive to intimacy and support.

Although the task of doing therapy with reproductive patients may seem daunting, a starting point can be recognizing each other's story and each other's pain. Encouraging couples to talk through their personal shattered narratives can open their eyes to their own hurt and each other's. Thus, the reproductive story can be a place to launch empathy and facilitate connection. The case of Anita and Eric illustrates how relationships can erode with reproductive crises and how sharing their personal narratives can solidify the relationship and ultimately deepen empathy for each other, which can reunite them in working together on future goals.

Anita and Eric: Sharing Narratives to Build Mutual Support

Anita felt that Eric had obstructed their desire to have children by putting it off until he finished his degree and established his career. She was furious with him at this delay and put the blame for their infertility squarely on his shoulders: "We've been together for 10 years, and I've tried to be patient. I have been patient! But last year, I put my foot down. Either we were going to start trying, or this relationship was not going to make it!"

I knew there had to be more for Eric than wanting to make sure his career was on sound footing before becoming a parent. Exploring Eric's family history revealed the trauma of his parents' reproductive story—the death in infancy of a baby boy and the impact their trauma had on his life: "There was kind of an altar for him. His ashes are in a box on the mantle—they are there still—and there are pictures of this little baby in every room. My mother lights a candle every year in his honor. I was always a part of this ritual, having to say a prayer, but as a kid, I really had no idea what it was all about. All I knew was that he could do no wrong. If I misbehaved, my mother would say things like, 'I bet your brother wouldn't have done that.' As an adult, I can understand how awful this must have been for them, but his presence was and is still in that house."

I gently asked him how he thought his parents' reproductive trauma had affected his ambivalence about becoming a parent. Although Anita knew this history, it was important for both of them to understand it in the context of their reproductive trauma. Eric thoughtfully and sadly responded by saying, "I guess I've been afraid that we would lose a baby too. I am scared of that. And I wouldn't want to put this kind of burden on another child. Now that I say it out loud. . . . I never realized just how much this has been affecting me."

Anita was tearful as she took his hand: "I always thought about this as something in your parents' past—not in yours. I had no idea that it filled you with such fear." She reflected on her behavior: "I must have reminded you of your mother, pushing you to do things and blaming you. I'm so sorry." As we talked more about the impact this was having on their life, it was important to plant the idea of a new chapter for them. "Just because this is part of your past doesn't mean that it has to have the same impact moving forward. In fact, bringing this into your awareness, what do you think you might do differently as parents?" That question united them in discussing their future reproductive story. They left that day determined to continue therapy and work on it together.

Lydia: Narrative of a Single Parent by Choice

Lydia, a medical technician raised in a traditional nuclear family, was clear about her options: "I'm 38 years old, and I can't wait around any longer. I'm not interested in just having a fling and getting pregnant. It's not that I don't want a partner, but it has to be the right person for me."

Lydia started therapy to address the possibility of becoming a single mother by choice. She and I began working together by discussing her original reproductive story and how that narrative changed over time: "I didn't start out thinking I would go down this path when I was in my 20s. I thought I would find a partner and have a family, like everyone else. But that just didn't happen. I've really struggled with this; I've been in several relationships, but something always felt wrong. Let's put it this way: I'm not single by choice. I've come to realize that I would either have to forego parenthood altogether or do it by myself."

Lydia's story is typical of those who are contemplating becoming a single parent by choice. They are usually motivated because of their age and biological clock. Other life events can create single parenthood, such as separation, divorce, or the death of a partner. These configurations are very different because they do not begin with solo parenthood as its basis. These parents tend to struggle more; not only are they suddenly raising children on their own but they also have to cope with the loss of the relationship.

Lydia was in the process of rewriting her story. The narrative that had been so deeply rooted in her past was undergoing a significant upheaval. She understood that there would be challenges to being a single parent and wanted to make sure she was prepared for this transition. Unlike those who become single parents due to traumatic events, single parents by choice plan and consider how they will manage this enormous undertaking (Jadva, Badger, et al., 2009; Van Gasse & Mortelmans, 2020).

Three of the main topics we discussed were (a) routes for becoming pregnant, (b) how to talk about her decision with her family, and (c) how to manage parenthood as a single mother. Lydia was clear that she wanted to use a nonidentified sperm donor rather than find a willing friend (see Chapter 6 for a discussion of options). More problematic for her was addressing her parents, who were conservative Christians. I asked her what she thought their reproductive narrative as would-be grandparents might be. Would they be disapproving, or might they be delighted? Framing it in this light, Lydia thought it might take them a while to digest but that, ultimately, they would be thrilled. This was yet another way to use narrative therapy, reflecting not only on her story but on her parents' stories as well. It also freed her to imagine their support for her and her baby after birth: "I know they would just dote on my baby—no matter how that child came to be. I would definitely need to use childcare, and I have an amazing network of friends who would be there for me, but knowing that I would be able to call on my parents and have their approval takes a big weight off my shoulders." Lydia was beginning to see her choice as more of a reality than a dream.

A Psychodynamic Perspective

The dynamics in one's family of origin, the time in history, and cultural expectations all play a role in the development of one's reproductive story. The following two case examples illustrate how using a psychodynamic approach can provide clients with insight and create change.

Jake: Intersection of History and Culture

Jake sounded agitated when he called: "I'm having panic attacks. Do you think it might be related to my wife having miscarriages? She just had another. My parents keep hounding me for details. When can I get an appointment?" This all came out in a rush; I knew more would emerge when we met.

As with Eric, reflection on one's past and family of origin plays a huge part in the formation of one's narrative. It not only incorporates the early relationships with one's parents but also the time in history and the society in which one lives. For example, the current trend for women in developed nations is to delay childbearing (Matthews & Hamilton, 2009). Women who have achieved higher levels of education tend to have their first child later in life (Matthews & Ventura, 1997). Consciously or not, factors such as birth order and the number of siblings one has can directly influence ideas about a future family. Trauma in the family of origin also impacts one's reproductive story and thoughts of how life should be: "If one has had a past trauma in one's life, the impact of the present traumalike event will be multiplied and will influence one's current reaction" (Watson, 2005, p. 220). Circumstances such as divorce, blended families, the death of a parent or sibling, poverty, or abuse all contribute to the reproductive story and the story of one's life.

Jake's story revealed itself in our first session together. He was clearly upset about his wife's miscarriages. He felt responsible not only for her well-being but for his parents' as well. His maternal grandparents, now deceased, had been Holocaust survivors; his internal narrative was shaped by his family trauma and world history: "All my life, I've been aware of my family story; it's a legacy that has always weighed heavy on me. I mean, it's not that I dwell on it all the time, but it's just there. And I've been struggling with it a lot now that Lisa has had three miscarriages in a row and no explanation as to why." He started to breathe more easily as he went on: "The rational side of me can accept that random events happen in life, but there's another part of me—and I know this is irrational—that somehow wonders if we are being targeted. I've always struggled with the idea that some higher power should be just and fair. I'd like to believe that, but I can't."

Learning about his family of origin gave him a deeper understanding of the meaning of parenthood. He was aware of how this historic tragedy shaped his views on life: "I know the importance of family; I feel responsible to continue the family line. Every time Lisa has had a miscarriage, I know she's devastated, and I feel like I've let everyone down." His story carried the weight of multiple generations of trauma and loss before him. Basic core beliefs of a just and fair world, where control over one's life was possible, were upended by family history and current reproductive losses.

I asked him to tell me more about his parents and referred back to his comment that they had been hounding him. It did not sound like they were supportive in his time of loss. He sighed and began, "My younger brother is a bit of a mess. He's been in and out of rehab for years. My parents have all but disowned him." He went on to talk about how much pressure he felt growing up: "Lots of high expectations for us." I reflected that he must not have wanted to disappoint them. "So true," he replied, "especially since dealing with my brother was always such a strain. He's never going to give my parents the grandchildren they want." We talked about him feeling guilty in relation to numerous sources: survivor's guilt reflected in his family's escape from annihilation and guilt for being the "chosen" son. I commented, "Sounds like there was no room for you to make any mistakes. How do you think this relates to Lisa's miscarriages?" He sighed deeply, "It's starting to make sense. I have felt guilty about that too. I feel like I'm really letting everyone down."

Over time, as we spoke about the dynamics in his family, he became more aware of just how strongly his life was shaped by wanting to please everyone. He recognized how much having a baby meant for him, not just because of his own desire to build a family with Lisa, but also because of his parents' wishes and his feelings of honoring his deceased grandparents. His grief was intensified by generations of trauma and the pressure to ensure that the family line would not stop with him. He gained insight into his parents' anxiety (the "hounding") and was able to reassure them that he and Lisa were seeking the best medical care they could find. His growing insight helped alleviate guilt and grief and allowed him to focus on his relationship with Lisa instead of his parents' needs.

Jessica and Matteo: Family Dynamics

Jessica, 37 years old, and her husband, Matteo, had been through multiple unsuccessful IVFs, producing few embryos. Because of the extensive financial burden the treatment had placed on them, Jessica's parents had offered to help. Her parents were eager to have grandchildren (this would be their first), and because they had the means to do so, there was no hesitation. Matteo was a little concerned because his family was not in a position to help financially, and he did not want them to feel "less than." He also worried that Jessica's parents would feel a kind of ownership of their grandchild because of their gift.

Their situation changed dramatically when, at the last round, their fertility doctor suggested using an egg donor. Much to her surprise, Jessica was relieved: "The odds of getting pregnant will be so much greater using a 25-year-old donor's eggs, and I won't have to shoot myself up with all these hormones again! I can't wait to get started." Matteo was on board, too; it had been a long haul, and he was also ready to get off the IVF treadmill. When they addressed this new development with Jessica's parents, they were surprised to get such a negative reception, especially from Jessica's mother. Jessica said, "It felt like I was getting disowned. She absolutely refused to help finance this. If this baby wasn't going to be genetically related to me, she didn't see the point. I actually think it's because the baby wouldn't be genetically related to her! After all their generosity, I was completely floored. And it made me look at Matteo's worries about indebtedness to them in a new light."

The couple's treatment shifted: It was now not only about their fertility crisis but also included the uncomfortable family dynamics that Jessica had with her mother. Matteo was also deeply hurt and angry, as if he was not worthy of creating a child in this family. As we dug deeper into her past,

Jessica could see a similar pattern with her mother—one that she often had repressed in an effort to keep the family peace. While her past concessions to her mother's narcissistic needs had been tolerable, both Jessica and Matteo were not willing to accept this demand. "Of course, it adds a new level of financial stress on us," said Matteo, "but it also gives us freedom to make our own choices." Jessica added, "This is going to be a new chapter in my relationship with my mother, one that is long overdue." Jessica was finding her footing and sense of independence and recognized this as an area of growth.

A Cognitive Perspective

"We started trying, thinking it would take a few months," Yumi began, "but I got pregnant first try! I've always been healthy—no broken bones, I even have all my wisdom teeth." She was shocked when she had a miscarriage at 10 weeks. Her narrative of being healthy and strong vanished in an instant. Not only did her basic assumption of being in great health crumble but now her reproductive story was also filled with trepidation and fear.

When a patient's reproductive story falls apart, whether due to a perinatal loss, infertility, or, in many cases, both, their fundamental core beliefs (highlighted in Chapter 3) about themselves, their relationships, and the world come crashing down. As we discussed, mental health practitioners need to listen for and understand the depth of the meaning of these losses. Along the same lines, listening for distortions in patients' perceptions of themselves and working to repair their thinking and behavioral responses to these reproductive crises is a natural accompaniment to narrative work.

Stress and trauma can activate negative core beliefs (Wenzel, 2017). Insecurities about oneself and how one fits in can become exacerbated when a pregnancy fails. Old wounds from the past can get triggered, especially those from adolescence, a time rife with self-doubt and desires to be accepted. Struggles with infertility may elicit painful childhood memories of defeat—not getting invited to a party, not making the team, being bullied for being "different." Incidents from formative years can create global self-assessments such as "I'm not good enough" or "I'm a loser." These negative attributes—many of which are inaccurate—are all too familiar and can be rekindled by reproductive trauma. The current trauma can provide "proof" of the unhelpful beliefs about oneself.

Even those who hold positive core beliefs—"I'm strong and healthy," or "I can achieve what I set out to do"—can be thrown into despair when those self-assessments are shaken. For some, the negative assessment is about the future: "I can't be happy unless I have a baby," or "My life is meaningless without children." These beliefs carry such profound meaning—across cultures, socioeconomic levels, and religious beliefs—it becomes clear why one's core sense of self comes into question.

Traditionally, cognitive behavior therapy (CBT) examines patients' negative thoughts and beliefs and helps to reframe and restructure these in a more positive light. It also addresses patients' behavior in promoting change by active involvement in homework outside of the therapeutic hour. CBT has been shown to be effective in reducing infertility stress (Faramarzi et al., 2013), as well as distress from recurrent miscarriage (Nakano et al., 2013). A study that incorporated mindfulness into stress reduction for infertility showed significant positive findings (Fard et al., 2018). *Mindful meditation* has been defined as "the awareness that emerges through paying attention on purpose, in the present moment, and nonjudgmentally to the unfolding of experience moment by moment" (Kabat-Zinn, 2003, p. 145) and has been incorporated into CBT practices. Rooted in Buddhist philosophy, mindfulness-based stress reduction (MBSR) has been used to help people cope with the emotional distress of infertility (Patel et al., 2020; Wang et al., 2023). The standard MBSR program teaches individuals to use meditation and yoga and is conducted in an 8-week format (Khoury et al., 2015). Patients can also be taught to take "mindful moments" to focus on the here and now as a way to decrease their stress (see Chapter 12 for more detail).

Yet another tenet of contemporary CBT includes the idea of *acceptance*— that is, helping patients see their value despite the trauma that has occurred. It is a recognition that their life encompasses more than having a baby. Wenzel (2017) stressed that all these therapeutic techniques need to be incorporated and nurtured by the therapeutic relationship to be most effective.

The Cognitive Impacts of Stress

In the previous chapter, we focused on the grief process as representing a large portion of the therapeutic work clinicians do. Stress reduction is another important component of our work in helping patients through these crises. Simply put, we want patients to feel better, and using cognitive reframing techniques as well as mindfulness has proven useful. Stress is a complicated human emotion stemming from external stimuli. It is a reaction to feeling pressured, frightened, or out of control and goes away once the situation is resolved. According to the National Institute of Mental Health (2022), stress can negatively affect one's mind and body, with symptoms such as worry, headaches, high blood pressure, or insomnia. Anxiety, however, is an internal reaction to stress, with an unrelenting and persistent feeling of dread.

A survey of five different fertility clinics found that 56.5% of women and 32.1% of men scored significantly for depression, and 75.9% of women and 60.6% of men scored significantly for anxiety (Pasch et al., 2016). The proclivity toward depression and anxiety caused by infertility and pregnancy loss has been well-documented in the literature (see Bhat & Byatt, 2016; Galst, 2018; Rooney & Domar, 2018, for reviews). While the evidence is clear that reproductive trauma causes stress, is the opposite true? Can stress cause infertility or pregnancy loss? If this was found to be true and stress could be reduced or eliminated, it follows that there could be an increase in pregnancy rates. However, the question of whether stress causes reproductive issues has produced mixed results.

Early explanations of reproductive trauma were based on the psychogenic theory, suggesting that a woman's unconscious conflicts with becoming a mother were the root of the problem. Advances in the understanding of medicine and a woman's reproductive system have largely debunked this theory, yet many patients continue to believe that their psychological state affects their ability to get pregnant and stay pregnant (Negris et al., 2021). A review of the research on whether stress causes infertility has shown equivocal results (Galst, 2018). While there is some evidence that stress can affect hormones and disrupt ovulation, a direct cause-and-effect relationship is not evident. Stress has also been associated with lower semen levels and decreased libido. It has been reported to impact people's desire to continue fertility treatments and contribute to overall self-care (Bhat & Byatt, 2016). While stress may affect reproduction to some degree, we know that women under intensely stressful conditions (e.g., famine, war, rape) have conceived and carried pregnancies to term.

It is also unclear whether stress reduction increases pregnancy success. Some research has suggested that mind–body groups that incorporate relaxation, CBT, exercise, and nutrition not only decreased stress but also increased pregnancy rates (Domar et al., 2000). Likewise, a study of infertile Japanese women found a higher pregnancy rate in those who had attended structured group interventions, which included psychoeducation, problem solving, relaxation training, guided imagery, and support (Hosaka et al., 2002). However, meta-analyses found that while psychosocial interventions effectively reduced negative affect, pregnancy rates were unlikely to increase because of psychological treatment (Boivin, 2003; de Liz & Strauss, 2005).

The last thing we want for patients is for them to blame themselves for causing their reproductive crisis. The belief that if they could just relax and think positively was in their control and would help with conception adds more stress rather than eliminates it. If a patient enters psychotherapy or a mind–body treatment with the idea that it will improve their chances of having a baby, it is logical to think their distress will increase if it does not happen: "Assuming that there exists a negative impact of stress on reproductive outcome, but without clear evidence, has the potential *to blame the victim and add additional guilt and frustration* [emphasis added] to an already burdened population" (Galst, 2018, p. 7). The self-blame that accompanies such thinking is destructive and can promote a downward spiral of negative affect. Patients need to be reminded that "conception is not a skill" and that having a baby is a complex, biochemical process that can get derailed at any point.

Yumi: Cognitive Reframing for Posttraumatic Stressors

We return now to Yumi, whose firm belief in herself as healthy and strong was shattered by a miscarriage. This case illustrates how processing her reproductive story, understanding what happens when core beliefs are destroyed, and using CBT can combine for effective treatment.

"I Googled it," she began. "Stress can cause miscarriages! I didn't realize just how much stress I was dealing with. Work was insane—my supervisor was out on medical leave, and I was getting more work dumped on me; my husband was thinking of switching jobs; his parents were coming for a visit; and we started talking about moving because we were going to have a baby! I've always powered through tough situations, but I think it all was having an effect on my baby." Here was how she framed her life: Do not let anything bring you down or get in the way; set your mind to it, and you'll get through. She was applying this sense of self to her reproductive story as well.

I recognized that some of her core beliefs had been challenged by this miscarriage. What I gleaned from our early conversations was that her confidence had been shaken, and she was trying to make sense of what happened—all this ran counter to her basic beliefs in herself and the world. The fact that she had gotten pregnant "on the first try" reinforced her sense of health and invincibility—only to have that come crashing down around her. She was trying to regain control by finding evidence that miscarriages are caused by stress. She thought, "If l can just get rid of the stressors, I'll be able to have a baby." Her goal for treatment was to learn how to better control and manage stress.

Sensing there were more thoughts and feelings tangled up inside her, I asked her how else she felt responsible for this pregnancy's demise, noting that it is not uncommon for women to blame themselves for their loss, even if it is not valid. This seemed to strike a chord, and she broke down in tears: "I think Rick is treating me differently now. Like I've let him down. He seems to be tiptoeing around me—I think he's blaming me for all this." "What do you imagine you did to cause this?" I asked. My hunch was whatever she thought he was blaming her for could be translated into her blaming herself. "Well, I just never slowed down, I guess. I mean, the doctor said I could keep exercising. That usually is a great way for me to control stress. I think Rick believes I did too much." I gently challenged her thinking, suggesting that Rick's "tiptoeing" might be interpreted a different way. I wanted to open up different possible meanings for his behavior to reframe her negative thoughts. "I guess maybe he's just worried about me. I guess I haven't really bounced back." It was important for her to have permission to grieve and to label it as grief.

"It's only been a month since your loss," I assured her. "I don't know anyone who can bounce back after such a short time. You and Rick are still both grieving the loss of this pregnancy, the loss of your dreams for the future. Also, the way you think about yourself. You said you usually power through tough situations, but maybe this one is different." We talked more about her relationship with Rick and the need to talk about their loss. This was new territory for them to work on together.

In ongoing sessions, we focused on tuning in to her feelings and not jumping to conclusions about what others might be thinking. I suggested that she keep a journal; together, she and I could try to disentangle her irrational thoughts from her overwhelming negative emotions. I also suggested she try to breathe and slow down racing thoughts whenever she felt defective or less than. She agreed that "buying time" by slowing down helped her see situations from multiple perspectives. "I was waiting in line at the pharmacy the other day. The woman in front of me was pregnant, of course," she rolled her eyes. "I just knew she was going to turn around and ask me if I had kids. I feel like I'm a magnet, just attracting these questions." She smiled and continued, "At first, I could feel the rage inside me. Of course, it triggered me. And then, I took a deep breath and tried to understand it from a different perspective. You would have been so proud! I knew it didn't really matter how I answered her and that it wasn't her fault; she was just trying to be friendly. So, I said, as cheerfully as I could, 'Not yet, but working on it!' and that was that." Yumi's ability to restructure her thoughts and emotions was growing, and with it, she felt more in control.

After a few months, when she and her husband were ready to start trying again, she crumbled with anxiety, knowing there was a possibility that she could have another miscarriage. What if it was not stress that was the cause of her previous loss? What if there was something else wrong with her? It was important to normalize her worry—most people who have had a pregnancy loss live in fear of another one. I let her know that for all the people I had worked with, subsequent pregnancies were always filled with anxiety. Because breathing techniques had been so helpful to her, I suggested she continue to do them when these anxious feelings arose. "We will get through this together," I consoled. "It's unfortunate you have to relive your loss in order to try again, but there's really no way around it. Reducing your stress is not going to guarantee a perfect pregnancy, but hopefully, it will help you feel better in the process." She smiled, "I guess I don't have to power through this. In fact, I know I can't power through. I also know I'm not alone; Rick is on board, and now I've got you too!" Recognizing that there were likely to be bumps in the road ahead and that we could not predict the end of her reproductive story, she was ready to forge ahead.

SUMMARY: THE END OF THE STORY

The beauty of the reproductive story as a tool in therapy is for patients to know that there is a beginning, middle, and end to the story, regardless of their sexual orientation or the clinician's theoretical orientation. As we have seen, patients enter therapy in the middle of their crisis, with their reproductive stories deeply rooted in their pasts. Childhood conflicts, roles in their family of origin, concepts of themselves as adults, and the complications in their intimate relationships all contribute to the present trauma. Bringing their stories to light allows them to envision different ways they may unfold. It opens up feelings of control by considering options for the ending of their reproductive story that they may have been unable to imagine before. Like-wise, it has the potential to generate a sense of well-being that is attainable once again. Patients come to accept that their reproductive trauma has changed them forever but also that there are ways in which they have grown and matured through the process.

6

WHO IS THE PATIENT?

Third-Party Reproduction and Adoption

Blood makes you related; love makes you family.

—Unknown

Donors (of gametes or embryos), surrogates, and birth parents who relinquish children for adoption play a huge part in helping individuals and couples achieve parenthood. This chapter focuses on the various roles of reproductive counselors: Not only do we help people who hope to become parents manage a host of emotions but we also evaluate and educate third-party participants. Do they wholly understand the significance of the role they play? Are they capable of carrying through with their commitment? Can they give full informed consent? At the same time, we are tasked with making sure the recipients of third-party reproduction—the parents to be—are fully aware of the psychological, moral, and cultural issues that can occur by creating a family this way. In addition, birth parents go through their own grief and loss; we may be called on to counsel them through feelings about their decision.

https://doi.org/10.1037/0000400-006
Reproductive Trauma: Psychotherapy With Clients Experiencing Infertility and Pregnancy Loss, Second Edition, by J. Jaffe

This chapter focuses on how to do these assessments and why we do them, what is important to address, and how we educate third-party donors to have a complete understanding of this undertaking. Likewise, the recipients, the intended parents, of third-party reproduction—while not being assessed—benefit from receiving counseling. The decisions that intended parents need to make are numerous: Should they do this at all, and if they do, should they use a directed or known donor? Is it better to use a nonidentified donor?[1] Should they pursue adoption or embryo donation? Critical in educating recipients is the issue of disclosure to the child. Intended parents can find clarification as they express all these concerns with a reproductive mental health practitioner.

It can be helpful to view all participants in third-party reproduction—the donors, surrogates, birth parents, and recipients—through the lens of the reproductive story. Understanding that everyone involved has a personal story can humanize the process. We know that heterosexual couples, now recipients, did not think their story would turn out this way; sensitivity to the shift in their story and how they can rewrite it can help them through this process. While single parents by choice and LGBTQ+ parents may understand the necessity of using a donor, how to choose one can raise emotional questions. Those who are doing the giving—of their gametes (donors), their body (surrogates), or their child (birth parents)—may need support as well in thinking through legal, ethical, and social hurdles. It is important to consider the emotional and psychological meaning behind their contribution, and as such, they, too, are our patients.

WHO IS EVALUATED AND WHY?

This section addresses the needs of the various participants in third-party reproduction and the role the reproductive mental health practitioner plays in counseling and evaluating them. The decision to use a donor and the decision to donate should not be taken lightly. It is vital for all parties to fully understand the short- and long-term ramifications of the donation process.

---

[1] The term "nonidentified donor" has replaced "anonymous donor" with the understanding that anonymity is becoming less possible, especially due to the increased use of DNA testing (Practice Committee of ASRM and the Practice Committee of SART, 2021).

The Recipients

When a heterosexual couple comes to the point in their fertility treatment when they need to use donor gametes—whether ovum, sperm, or embryo—they are faced with complex emotional decisions. They must contend with the loss of a biological connection to their offspring to become parents and build their family. Their reproductive story has come to a crossroads, with varying paths in front of them. For some, this is a bridge they cannot cross, but for those who do, it is essential that they know what is involved, what they can expect, and what is still within their control. This is why a consultation with a reproductive mental health professional can be helpful.

Some questions that recipient couples and individuals think about—be they heterosexual, same-sex, or other—are practical; some are more spiritual or ethical:

- What are the advantages and disadvantages of using a known, directed donor versus a nonidentified donor?
- If a donor is known, will that relationship change, and if so, how?
- If the donor is unknown, on what basis is the choice made?
- Is it ethical to create a child when there are children to be adopted?
- Is using a donor tampering with nature?
- Does it go against cultural or religious norms?
- Will the partner not genetically connected to the child be able to attach?
- What will other people think?
- Should one disclose the biological origins to the child? How and when should they be told?

Although recipients are not mandated to meet for consultation, it is strongly advised—on the basis of this list of questions—that they do. Recipients may be hesitant and anxious about meeting with a mental health professional; some fear that a counselor will act as a "gatekeeper" and decide whether they are fit to become parents. At the outset, it can be helpful for the counselor to define their role, reassuring the intended parent(s) that the primary purpose of the consultation is psychoeducational (Sachs & Toll, 2015). The mental health professional can act as a guide in bringing up issues that may have a psychological impact on the recipients in the present and the future. The following sections will provide some answers to the questions posed earlier.

The Choice: Nonidentified (Anonymous) Versus Directed (Known) Gamete Donors

Once the decision has been made to use donor gametes, the question arises as to how to choose one and whether to use a known person (e.g., a family member or friend) or a nonidentified donor (a candidate from a sperm or oocyte bank). Same-sex and single parents who know they must use donors also face the decision of whether to use an identified or nonidentified donor. It can help clients think of this as a kind of decision tree; it also allows providers to see what questions arise and how they can be addressed because there are advantages and disadvantages in either case.

If the recipients decide to use an unidentified or anonymous donor, the next branch of the decision tree is: How do they choose? In some countries, the doctor or clinic selects the donor for the recipients based on matching physical characteristics (Thorn, 2006). In other countries, including the United States, an essentially free market exists; people can find donors through their doctor, donor banks, agencies, or even on the Internet. It is strongly advised that recipients make sure the source of a match is legitimate and safe. Those specializing in matching recipients with donors give varying degrees of information about the donor: medical history, family background, academic interests, hobbies, and why they have decided to donate their gametes. In addition, baby photos and/or adult photos of the donor may be made available. For many, picking someone whose physical characteristics and interests match the partner whose gametes are not being used is central to their decision (Sachs & Toll, 2015). Other factors that inform the decision of recipients include health (mental and physical), race, education level, and hobbies (Sachs & Burns, 2006). Many hours can be spent poring over the options; clinical experience suggests that a general resemblance is usually desired. Many hope that the child will blend into the family, with physical differences not readily apparent. In addition, some recipients may want a "proven" donor—someone who has either successfully donated before or is already a parent. It can be exceptionally traumatic not to have a successful outcome because of problems with the donor's eggs or sperm.

In the past, donor anonymity was thought to be the best practice to protect donor-conceived children. There was fear that these children would feel different, that their parents would feel estranged, and that the donor would somehow be involved in the family (Golombok et al., 2013; Shanley, 2002). Much of what we know about how secrecy affects children comes from the literature on closed adoptions. Again, it was thought that anonymity was in the best interest of the child. Research on adoption, however, has shown that children benefit from knowing about their biological connections (Golombok et al., 2013). Similarly, for donor-conceived children, there has been a growing awareness of the child's needs and rights to know their genetic origins. While the responsibility of disclosure to the child rests on the recipients, keeping this information from them may become impossible, given the rapid growth of genetic testing (Harper et al., 2016). An unintended discovery might even take place in a high school biology class, where a cheek swab could reveal genetic origins.

If recipients choose to use a directed or known donor, what are their reasons? A study of predominantly lesbian women who searched for sperm donors online found it was important to meet him and learn more about him before donation. It gave them the opportunity to vet the donor for suitability and characteristics such as kindness, openness, and reliability (Jadva et al., 2018). These are some reasons recipients turn to family or friends; recipients may feel more secure because they can trust the donor. In addition, questions about the donor's medical, social, and educational history would not be a mystery (Baetens et al., 2000). The costs involved should also be noted, with the possibility of fewer financial barriers to treatment with a known donor.

One of the biggest benefits of using gametes from a family member, either oocyte or sperm, is that it allows the recipient to retain some genetic link to the child. Because there may be a physical resemblance between the donor and recipient, the connection may feel even stronger. There is also the possibility of a special bond developing between the donor and the child (Mindes & Covington, 2015). However, other concerns about the ongoing relationship between donor, recipient, and child may arise. A study looking at father-to-son sperm donation found several reasons for this choice: maintenance of a genetic link, strong emotional bond between the father and son, and the father's age (too old to be confused as the "father"; too old to have a negative relationship with daughter-in-law in the future). There were considerable disadvantages to this situation as well: The father's age came into play again because of possible medical concerns regarding chromosomal abnormalities, but the perils involving emotional and ethical issues were even more of a concern (Nikolettos et al., 2003). Other studies considered the relationship between recipients and known oocyte donors: While their bonds may deepen, they also were not without emotional risks. Some donors expressed concern about seeing the donor offspring (Purewal & van den Akker, 2009). Boundaries may feel blurred: Will the donor feel entitled to make decisions about parenting? Will questions about resemblance create awkward moments for parents and donor alike? How will disclosure to the child be handled? What happens if a falling-out occurs? If the donation does not result in a pregnancy, how will that affect their bond?

The Ethics Committee of the American Society for Reproductive Medicine (ASRM; 2017) has given guidelines for intrafamilial gamete donations. These arrangements are generally acceptable, except when a consanguineous relationship occurs, as in a sister donating gametes to her brother's wife. Although not technically incestuous, other arrangements can give the impression that they are and should be thoroughly examined. An example would be a brother donating his sperm to his sister, who is using an egg donor. While these preparations are made with consenting adults, the children from these arrangements may suffer unintended consequences (Ethics Committee of ASRM, 2017). These are important issues for the recipient, donor, and therapist to consider because the impact on the family relationships and the offspring can have long-lasting effects.

Embryo Donation

In undergoing in vitro fertilization (IVF), more embryos are often produced than can be transferred in any one cycle. These excess embryos are usually frozen and stored for use by the couple to produce a sibling child at some later point. It is estimated that as of 2013, nearly 2 million embryos were being stored in the United States (Christianson et al., 2020). That staggering figure is indicative of parents deciding that their family is complete; what then to do with these stored embryos? The possibilities that currently exist are to discard them (let them thaw), donate them for scientific research, transfer them when the possibility of pregnancy is not likely, or donate them to another couple. For some couples, the idea that embryos would be discarded or used for scientific research is unacceptable, akin to abortion. There has been a growing movement, especially among some religious groups, that encourages embryo donation (ED) to other couples who are struggling with infertility. Those receiving donated embryos can experience pregnancy and childbirth and have control over the prenatal environment. In this sense, ED can be a good solution for both sets of parents—the donors and the recipients.

Although ED is a viable possibility in reproductive medicine, it is prohibited in some countries and is used less frequently than other family-building options (Goedeke et al., 2015). Perhaps this is because it involves significant psychological, legal, and ethical considerations for both the donors and the recipients. ASRM recommends psychoeducational counseling for all parties involved (Practice Committee of the American Society for Reproductive Medicine and the Practice Committee for the Society for Assisted Reproductive Technology, 2021). It is essential that both the donating and recipient couples understand that a full sibling will exist, although raised in a different household. It is important for all participants to consider the impact on the children involved. In addition, it is important to discuss if, how, and when to disclose, with the knowledge that, like children created with gamete donation, anonymity may not exist. The following are some questions that families should consider and be counseled on:

- Will the two sets of parents attempt distance and secrecy, or will they consider an open relationship and allow the siblings to meet?
- How might it feel to meet the baby born by the recipients?
- Might the donor family find fault with the recipient family in how they are parenting?
- Might the recipient family feel judged by the genetic parents, worried that the donor children will think their "real" parents are the donor couple?
- How will the issue of consanguinity as a future possibility between the siblings be addressed?

There has been little research on the development of families created through ED. One study compared ED with IVF and adoptive families and questioned whether an absence of genetic ties would influence parents' feelings of attachment (MacCallum et al., 2007). Their findings suggest that genetics played no role in the parents' investment in their child. Whether there was a biological link or not, these parents, who went to great lengths to have children, were highly invested in parenthood. They also found no evidence to support the idea that pregnancy (with ED or IVF) resulted in a better parent–child bond than adoption. The physical prenatal bond was not essential to positive parental attachment (MacCallum et al., 2007). This supports the idea that attachment to the desired child starts much earlier than pregnancy; it begins with the development of the early reproductive story. The bond is psychological rather than physical, an important distinction in helping couples make complex family planning decisions. It should be noted that donation in this study was anonymous; the children were still quite young, and the recipients were hesitant to disclose ED.

In contrast, a study from New Zealand analyzed the experience of ED from both the donor's perspective and the recipient's (Goedeke et al., 2015). In New Zealand, counseling for embryo donors and recipients is mandatory and requires both separate and joint sessions for all involved. Like open adoption, the needs of both families are addressed in these joint counseling sessions, thus eliminating the issue of anonymity and perhaps some of the difficult and awkward feelings that can arise between the families. It was found that the genetic link was regarded highly by both donors and recipients: That tie connected the two families in immutable ways. There was agreement that the offspring had rights to the information about their genetics for medical needs and establishing their sense of identity. The researchers also noted that the donors, knowing that they had no legal rights to the child, still felt a connection and moral responsibility for that child. Donors and recipients perceived each other as extended families, with contact being flexible, ranging from social media contact to spending family gatherings together (Goedeke et al., 2015). While still in its early stages, perhaps this model of joint counseling for the two involved families will serve ED and the resulting offspring in positive ways in the future.

So far, we have discussed ED in terms of surplus embryos created through IVF. A relatively new and divisive phenomenon is the creation of embryos specifically for donation purposes. These are not excess embryos that were a product of IVF; rather, they are made expressly to create embryos for recipients. The first of its kind, a Texas company (The Abraham Center of Life) offered batches of embryos for sale (Dickenson, 2008). Not surprisingly, this brought up many controversial ethical questions. Although this center expressly called it such, is this really embryo donation? Is it ethical to purchase an embryo according to certain characteristics (e.g., height, hair color, athleticism, IQ)? Human embryo banks, where made-to-order embryos are for sale, smack of eugenics and treat embryos as a commodity (Dickenson, 2008). (It should be noted that this center closed the same year it opened, but others have since opened). However, is this different from selecting a donor that matches one's partner's features? Some have argued that creating embryos in this manner is no different than buying sperm or eggs (Cohen & Adashi, 2013). More questions arise: Should more "desirable" embryos cost more? Will batches of ready-made embryos be split between prospective parents to save on costs? What happens to any surplus embryos?

While all these questions are vital to consider, the most important is, as always: What is the impact on the children? How will it affect them? Will they learn of their biological roots, or will these donors remain anonymous? Will they know their family medical history? Is there a danger of children from the same batch raised in different families meeting as adults and reproducing themselves? Because the creation and sale of embryos is not future science fiction but is happening now, standards of care need to be set in motion to protect these families and their offspring (Klitzman & Sauer, 2015).

DISCLOSURE: TO OTHER ADULTS AND THE OFFSPRING

Disclosure in all third-party arrangements is often the most anxiety provoking to the recipients. Issues regarding disclosure are twofold: telling one's adult cohort and telling one's child(ren). The questions this can raise—who to tell, when to tell, what should be told, how much should be shared, and whether to disclose at all—are topics that should be discussed in consultation with a reproductive mental health care provider. While decisions may change over time, opening this up for discussion with the recipients at the onset can ease some of their anxiety.

Some couples may feel embarrassed about the need to use a donor, whether egg or sperm, not wanting their fertility issues to become public knowledge. Anecdotally, some couples have reported that they have told no one but have actually disclosed to at least one person—such as a friend because they needed help with a shot or a mother because they always tell her everything—without realizing that what they thought was told in confidence may inadvertently get leaked. What happens if the donor is a family member? How does that impact disclosure? What happens at a family gathering if someone slips and spills the beans? How do couples manage their feelings when a friend, who was supposedly not in the know, randomly asks about what it is like to choose a donor? There are times when recipients feel as if they are being judged for not adopting; others worry about being questioned about the "real" mother or father. Recipients may doubt their parental identity as it is; to have others question it can feel devastating. These are some of the concerns that haunt recipient parents and make them debate what is best. Feelings can range from being extremely open about the experience to wanting to protect their partner from any challenging questions to wanting to keep procreation choices entirely private. One partner may feel different than the other, bringing up even more struggles in this process.

Regardless of how partners decide about opening up to others, the key issue parents face is disclosure to their offspring. Here again, many questions arise: Should this be kept a secret? If not, how do you tell a child, when do you tell them, will they feel confused or "different," and will they fantasize about their "real" parent? Does a child have the right to know their biological origins? What is the potential harm to the child should they find out inadvertently? It is interesting to note that whichever side of the argument parents fall on, their motivation is the same: They are trying to act in what they believe is in the best interest of the child. Parents' desire to protect their child from the possibility of insensitive comments is often what motivates them to keep conception details secret, whereas disclosing parents are more concerned that a secret of this sort would disrupt their family dynamics of trust (Nachtigall, 2005, as cited in Orenstein, 2007).

Charlotte and Will: To Tell or Not to Tell?

Charlotte and Will's 4-year-old son, Ben, looked just like his two older siblings—same curly dark hair, dimples, and smiles.[2] Except Ben's siblings lived in another state, and, at present, even though they all got together once or twice a year, they had no idea that they were biologically related. The donor's family was close friends with Will's parents, and the match was made for embryo donation. Charlotte and Will came to therapy to discuss their uneasiness with the situation; they were struggling with whether to tell Ben. After all, the families did live far apart, but if they were to tell him, how should they do it?

Much of what we know about disclosure to children about their genetic roots comes from the literature on adoption and the effects of keeping secrets within a family. In the past, adoptive parents were advised not to tell their children their origins. It was thought that secrecy and maintaining the myth of a "normal" family was in the child's best interest. However, research into "closed" adoptions provided insight into how ineffective and potentially harmful this practice was. For example, a study of over 800 adopted individuals described ongoing issues regarding secrecy, lies, and a sense of betrayal regarding their adoption. These feelings manifested even more when adopted individuals had children of their own (Kenny et al., 2012). With "open" adoption, the adoptive and birth families share identifying information and can have varied amounts of contact before and after the adoption. The prevailing consensus is for open adoptions and that adopted children should be told about their adoption as soon as possible.

McGee et al. (2001) argued that many of the issues raised by adoption parallel gamete donation. Like closed adoption, it had been thought that the children conceived through gamete donation would be better off believing in the integrity of their family; not knowing would allow them to blend in. Past research on sperm donation indicated that most parents did not plan to disclose their use of donor gametes (Klock et al., 1994). A study on women who received oocyte gametes found that fundamental beliefs and values influenced their decision. While all were concerned about the child's welfare, their worries varied from those who believed it was the child's right to know to those who wanted to protect the child from stigma, citing there was no compelling reason to tell them (Hershberger et al., 2007).

Some argue that parents' rights should prevail and that it is a matter of free choice whether they disclose (Patrizio et al., 2001). More recently,

---

[2] All case examples in this chapter have been modified to disguise the patients' identities.

however, disclosure to offspring, whether conception was through donor gamete or embryo, has been strongly encouraged (Ethics Committee of ASRM, 2018a). In fact, in many countries,[3] legislation has been enacted to remove donor anonymity completely (Benward, 2015). Once more, the best interest of the child takes precedence. In the United States, while the decision ultimately rests on the parents, ASRM strongly encourages disclosure to donor-conceived persons and considers counseling essential for both the donors and recipients. It also urges clinics, agencies, and donor banks to cooperate in allowing the donor-conceived person to learn about their conception (Ethics Committee of ASRM, 2018a).

Reasons in favor of disclosure are as follows: Knowing one's origins and birth story is important to the child's identity. "Identity is developed in part by the stories that one hears about one's biography, who one takes to be kin, how this kinship is formed and, at a fundamental level, who one believes to be one's parents" (Frith et al., 2018, pp. 189). Disclosure allows for open and honest communication and avoids family secrets, which can become toxic. Children are incredibly perceptive when they sense a secret; they may not know exactly what it is, but they can tell that something is amiss. By openly discussing a child's origins, research has found that the relationship between parent and child can be strengthened (Ethics Committee of ASRM, 2018a; Freeman, 2015). As discussed, the revolution in genetic testing and the possibility of offspring discovering a different family story than they had originally thought could potentially be devastating. The rise of genetic testing may put an end to any kind of donor anonymity (Harper et al., 2016). There is also support for disclosure so that offspring can have accurate medical information for themselves and future generations. Likewise, the risk of consanguinity can be minimized if genetic roots are understood.

Considerations against disclosure are also important to address. Remember that the reason for nondisclosure is also based on what parents feel is in the best interest of their child. They worry that the child would feel different if their birth story differs from the "norm." Parents naturally want to protect children from any psychological turmoil. There is concern that the child would not think of their mother or father as their "real" parent, creating confusion and disruption in the family. Parents may also worry that their child will want to find out more information about their donor and seek them out. Parents using donor gametes may struggle with shame regarding

---

[3] To date, the following countries require identifying information to be available: Switzerland, the United Kingdom, Austria, Norway, the Netherlands, Sweden, Finland, New Zealand, and several states in Australia (Benward, 2015; Ethics Committee of ASRM, 2013b).

their infertility. They certainly have a right to privacy; disclosing why they needed to use a donor can bring up myriad issues of grief and loss. In this vein, they may want to protect their partner from the judgment of others. Finally, there may be cultural or religious tenets that they are breaking to create their family. Rather than risk the disapproval of other family members, or worse, if there is a chance that family members would reject the child, keeping the genetic origin of their child a secret may seem like the best action to take (Benward, 2015; Ethics Committee of ASRM, 2018a; Patrizio et al., 2001).

Table 6.1 summarizes reasons for and against disclosure. It was helpful to review this with Charlotte and Will. My personal bias—the necessity to fully disclose to a child about their genetic origins—had to remain out of the discussion; it was ultimately up to them to parent as they thought best. However, it was important to add to the conversation that this had to be a shared decision between them and the donating family. Considering the bond between the two families and their ongoing visits, it seemed inevitable that if one set of parents disclosed, the other had to as well.

When, How, and What to Tell?

If parents do decide to disclose, they must be well prepared; it can be an emotional and anxiety-provoking task, potentially raising issues of grief and loss around their fertility. Mental health professionals trained and sensitive to all the concerns of using a donor, whether gamete or embryo, can provide emotional support, grief work, psychoeducation, and guidance through this uncharted territory. ASRM guidelines state, "counseling and informed consent about disclosure and information sharing are essential for donors and

TABLE 6.1. Reasons for and Against Disclosure to Children

Reasons for disclosure	Reasons against disclosure
• Formation of child's identity	• May be disruptive to the child
• Trust within the family, avoidance of secrets	• Desire to have a "normal" family
	• Desire to keep infertility private
• Positive effect on parent–child relationship	• Protection of partner; concerns child will reject the nongenetic parent
• Avoidance of accidental disclosure—through someone "spilling the beans" or through genetic testing	• Cultural reasons (e.g., gamete donation not accepted)
• Protection against inadvertent consanguinity	
• Acquire an accurate medical history	

recipients" (Ethics Committee of ASRM, 2018a, p. 601). Counseling ideally takes place before the use of donor gametes or embryos so that the recipients can effectively manage this challenge.

One of the questions frequently asked by parents is, "When is the right time to tell my child?" The consensus appears to be that earlier disclosure is better; incorporating this into the child's story of their birth allows the child to take in the information and feel as if it is something they have always known. While a preverbal child will not be able to comprehend the information, it gets absorbed into their identity over time. It can be helpful to have parents practice talking about it while their donor-conceived child is still in utero, normalizing it and learning to manage their emotions. As the child develops and is able to ask questions, their parents will likely have told the story on multiple occasions and can feel secure in answering their child's curiosity. This type of disclosure has been categorized as the "seed-planting strategy" (Mac Dougall et al., 2007). Research on how parents feel about early disclosure has been predominately positive: "It will be easier to discuss their conception as they get older because it's already out in the open" (Rumball & Adair, 1999, p. 1396). Children in this category responded mostly with interest and inquisitiveness, and as most children do, wanting to hear their birth story again and again.

Some parents want to disclose when it feels like the "right time" or when the child is "old enough to understand." These parents believe there is an optimal time for their child to have the cognitive skills to understand the biology of reproduction (Mac Dougall et al., 2007). This can prove problematic as parents may never find the right time and postpone disclosure because of their anxieties (Benward, 2015). A survey of adults who were conceived via donor sperm described what it was like for them to find out about their story. Those who were told early on were described as having an "always known" narrative. Others, however, found out accidentally when they were older, some because of health issues, some through overhearing conversations (Frith et al., 2018). Teenagers in the midst of an already challenging time of identity development were shaken. Traditionally, the question "Who am I?" arises in adolescence. With donor-conceived children, another layer of self-questioning can be amplified by wondering about genetic origins (Benward, 2015). Those who were adolescents or adults when they discovered their genetic origins felt lied to and betrayed and questioned what other deceptions had taken place in their lives and families (Frith et al., 2018).

Reproductive mental health professionals are in a unique position to help parents through disclosure decisions. We can advise them on what the research has shown and help them work through their grief, loss, and fears.

We can also suggest ways of how to talk to their offspring. It is often a stumbling block, and parents wonder, "How do we talk about this? What do we say? How much or how little should be shared?" As with any conversation with a child, the language used needs to be age appropriate. For very young children, telling a story about how grownups sometimes need help to have a baby can be a good start. Some refer to gametes as "seeds" in their initial explanations to their child. Young children often begin the conversation by asking, "Where do babies come from?" This can be a great opening for parents to explain how their child came to be. Research has suggested some of the themes of these stories: wanting a baby and not being able to have one, needing seeds from another person, or needing special doctors to help (Rumball & Adair, 1999). Another way to approach the subject is through picture books that address third-party reproduction. This can make it easier for the child to understand and for parents to be guided in approaching the subject. Clinicians might want to have a selection of these books on hand to share with parents in their initial consultation. If parents know about these resources beforehand, it can ease their minds about how to approach talking with their child. Some parents even create personalized books, adding how the parents fell in love, pictures of the embryo, or sonograms in which their child is the main character. Benward (2015) recommended leaving these books accessible to the child so they can read them whenever they like.

Charlotte and Will gravitated to the idea of "needing a seed." They decided to plant some beans with their child Ben as a family project and talked about how plants grow: "We told him how much care it takes and what plants need—water, sun, soil. He loved it. And then we said that babies need lots of love to make them grow too. We told him that he was a seed once and that we got a special 'Ben' seed from our friends."

Parents also need to understand that this is hardly a one-time conversation. As children grow, their understanding and questions will change. The story will be repeated and expanded over time; details can be added as the child's comprehension grows. Rumball and Adair (1999) found that a gradual disclosure, based on the child's understanding, had little impact on the child; it was seen as a nonevent. This may not be the case when children are told in their latency or adolescent years. A longitudinal study found that children's psychological well-being and family relationships were better if they were told about their biological roots before age 7 (Ilioi et al., 2017).

What is the best way for parents to broach this topic with older children? Parents who chose to find the "right time" relied on the child's ability to understand the biological processes involved. Some parents talked about the different parts needed to make a baby and that either mom's or dad's "part" did not work. They also talked about having to reach out to a special person or doctor for help. In addition, parents wanted to convey how much their child was wanted and loved. The goal of disclosure in this manner "normalized the use of donor gametes, minimized the importance of the actual donor, and protected the legitimacy of the parents in their social role as the 'real' parents" (Mac Dougall et al., 2007, p. 530). If parents are clear about what a "real" parent is (the people who raise, nurture, and love a child) as distinguished from a genetic connection, they can convey that message to their child, reduce their own anxiety, and help their child through this transition.

Unfortunately, anxiety can build the longer parents put off this task. Donor-conceived adolescents often sense something is not quite right even though they cannot name it. Research on children who were told later in life (teenagers and young adults) found that they had more negative feelings than those who knew at a young age. Anger, trust issues, and feelings of betrayal were common themes expressed by this group when they found out about their conception (Frith et al., 2018; Jadva, Freeman, et al., 2009). If parents seek out the support of a mental health professional, we can advise them on strategies to guide them through this process. With an older adolescent or adult, it is not the biological understanding of donor conception that is the focus; rather, it is the relationship with the parents that is of concern. Whenever possible, it is best if both parents are able to disclose together; it can also be helpful to jointly practice beforehand what to say and how to handle the response. Parents should be understanding about the initial shock and anger that their offspring are likely to feel. Rather than get defensive, it can help if parents recognize how hard this must be for their offspring to hear. Parents can also express their own struggles and why they waited so long to talk about this (Benward, 2015). As in all these disclosures between parents and their offspring, it is not a one-time discussion. Adolescents and adults will no doubt need to process this, may want more information about their donor, and may question if siblings or half-siblings exist. Now that they are in on the "secret," they may wonder who else in the family knows—do they also need to keep a secret from other family members? How this affects their reproductive story and their ideas about parenting is important to consider. These are clearly complicated psychological dynamics; reproductive mental health clinicians will be faced with these issues as more and more families are created with donor eggs, sperm, or embryos.

COUNSELING DONORS, SURROGATES, AND BIRTH PARENTS

Thus far, the discussion has focused on the function of counselors in working with intended parents. These consultations are psychoeducational and focus on matters such as the recipient's grief and loss, disclosure issues, parenting concerns, possible half-siblings, contact with the donor, and challenges of anonymity. A referral should be given if more in-depth counseling is necessary when, for example, a client is struggling with grief. Another role that reproductive mental health professionals play is in assessing gamete donors, whether sperm, oocyte, or embryo. Here, our function is not only psychoeducational but also includes a psychological evaluation assessing the donors' appropriateness to donate. We are called on to assess and support donors and surrogates through this family-building opportunity. Likewise, we work with adoptive parents and birth parents in what can be an emotionally complex decision to relinquish a child for adoption. This section focuses on what motivates the "givers" in third-party reproduction, why psychological counseling is so important, and what role psychological testing plays.

Donors (Oocytes, Sperm, and Embryos)

Aside from all the medical requirements that must be met in the evaluation of a gamete or embryo donor, guidelines also strongly recommend psychological assessments consisting of clinical interviews and, where appropriate, objective, standardized psychological testing (Practice Committee of ASRM and the Practice Committee of the Society for Assisted Reproductive Technology [SART], 2021). While these guidelines encourage psychological testing "where appropriate," one could argue that it is appropriate for all donors. Donation of one's gametes is not a trivial consideration for the donors, recipients, or children-to-be. Having as much information as possible about a prospective donor is of utmost importance; using a donor is a major life decision that affects all parties involved.

It is essential that donors, directed or nonidentified, be able to give full informed consent for the use of their gametes. When we work with donors, they are our patients, and our role is twofold. The first role is to provide them with psychoeducation, answer questions they may have, and bring up matters they may not have considered. In essence, we need to prepare them mentally and emotionally for their present circumstances, as well as what it may mean to them in the future. Discussing issues with donors is not meant to dissuade them but to provide them with a comprehensive understanding. Presenting as full a picture as possible ensures informed consent.

Our second role, through a clinical interview and testing, is to rule out behavioral or mental health disorders, which would disqualify prospective donors. It can feel uncomfortable to inform a donor that they are not suitable, but it can also provide them with opportunities to get help and address any social or psychological issues they may have.

In our psychoeducational role of counseling the donor, the mental health practitioner can provide information about the donation process and explore the possibility that there might be long-term emotional consequences of gamete donation (Ethics Committee of ASRM, 2009). For example, it may feel very different to a woman in her early 20s to have a genetic offspring "out there" than it might feel later in her life. Feelings may arise as donors create families of their own; they may become aware of the implications for their own children (i.e., potential half-siblings; Braverman, 2015). Should donors disclose their donation history to an intimate partner or their children, and if so, how? How might they feel if the donor-conceived child seeks them out? They should understand that anonymity likely will be impossible with the rise of DNA testing. The donors themselves may be interested in learning about who the recipients are and the outcomes of their donation (Ethics Committee of ASRM, 2009).

For directed gamete donation, the implications of the multiple overlapping relationships must be addressed. In a sister-to-sister donation, for example, the genetic "mother" is also the child's aunt; cousins will be genetic half-siblings. How all participants (donor and recipient) manage these complicated dynamics and what they anticipate it will look like in the future are essential topics for reproductive mental health counselors to discuss. In the case of known donors, three clinical interviews are recommended: one with the recipient and partner, one with the donor and partner (if one exists), and finally, a group meeting with all parties involved. Mindes and Covington (2015) provided a list of several topics and questions that should be addressed in these sessions, including evidence of coercion, dynamics among all involved (current and past), future impact on all parties, future involvement of the donor in the child's life, implications for the broader family or social network, expectations of treatment or how to cope if treatment fails, and disclosure to the donor-conceived child as well as to other children in the recipient's or donor's family.

As stated, mental health providers also serve as appraisers and gatekeepers should psychological issues be revealed in the clinical interview or testing of gamete donors. The clinical interview includes taking a thorough family history and assessing mental health disorders, relationship issues, current life stressors, coping skills, financial and emotional stability, and any history of abuse, substance use, or legal problems. It should also include explorations into their motivation: What factors made them decide to donate? Research has suggested, especially with known donor situations, that feelings for the intended parents and not wanting to see them in pain motivated donors (Purewal & van den Akker, 2009; Yee et al., 2007, 2011). In a Swedish study of anonymous oocyte and sperm donors, it was found that the motivation for donating gametes was primarily driven by the wish to help infertile couples. Even when monetary compensation was provided, altruism was the most salient motivating factor (Svanberg et al., 2012). Similarly, in Belgium, the majority of sperm donors cited altruistic reasons, with only about a third motivated by financial compensation (Thijssen et al., 2017). Although altruism and compensation are generally cited as primary motivators, secondary motives include a desire to pass on their genes and answer questions about their own fertility (Josephs & Van den Broeck, 2015; Van den Broeck et al., 2013). While motivation should not exclude people from donating, it can provide insight into their candidness and character.

Psychological testing using a standardized assessment instrument, such as the Minnesota Multiphasic Personality Inventory (Hathaway & McKinley, 1940) or the Personality Assessment Inventory (Morey, 1991), is used to screen for mental and behavioral disorders. Testing can confirm clinical impressions but can also reveal underlying psychological issues. While our role is not to act as a gatekeeper for intended parents (unless severe pathology is exposed), we are in this role with donors. Potential donors may be excluded if they or family members have a history of significant psychiatric disorders, they engage in high-risk sexual or drug activities, they are under excessive distress, or they are in an unstable relationship. Any "rejected" donor should be made aware of concerning factors and given referrals for ongoing counseling.

Thus far, the focus has been on the role of reproductive mental health professionals in consulting with and assessing oocyte and sperm donors. Couples who have created embryos through IVF (now considered the donor) have the option to donate them to another individual or couple (the recipient). For mental health clinicians, the recipients, as well as the donors of these embryos, are our clients, and just as with gamete donors, psychoeducational consultation is strongly recommended (Practice Committee of ASRM and the Practice Committee of SART, 2021). The issues to be addressed in embryo donation are even more complex because full genetic siblings will be raised in another family.

Do the donors have the right to choose the potential recipients? In *conditional embryo donation*, some donors indicate that there should be age requirements for the recipient; others express concern about alcohol and drug use, education level, financial security, and sexual orientation (Frith & Blyth, 2013; Wånggren et al., 2013). Conditional embryo donation implies that there will be an open and nonanonymous relationship between the two families. It has been argued that this "relational" model better meets the needs of the children born from this arrangement, allowing them information about the donor family (Frith & Blyth, 2013). As with the open adoption model, the degree of "openness" varies according to the needs of the families involved.

Consultation with a mental health practitioner who is trained in understanding these complex dynamics is essential for both the donor and recipient families. Guidelines for a psychoeducational consultation, as put forth by ASRM and SART, urge separate consultation sessions for the donors and the recipients and a joint session with all parties involved (Practice Committee of ASRM and the Practice Committee of SART, 2021). The joint session gives each family an opportunity to discuss their expectations: what contact they may have in the future, how they will handle communication with each other, their thoughts about disclosure, and their fears and worries. In this context, it can be helpful to discuss the reproductive stories of all involved and how—together—they are writing a new one. Because this is a relatively nascent way to build a family, remind them that it would be normal if circumstances arose that posed questions; it can be helpful to encourage them to seek out the guidance of a mental health professional for support at those times.

Surrogates: Evaluation, Support, and Controversies

As with gamete and embryo donors, reproductive mental health counselors advise, evaluate, and support surrogate carriers, as well as the intended parents. The commitment made by a surrogate, who vows to carry and care for a pregnancy and give birth to a child whom she will not parent, is physically and psychologically challenging. She will be engaged with the intended parents for months, and the trust between both parties is enormous. The intended parents must rely on the surrogate to take good care of herself, eat well, get enough rest, not smoke or use drugs or alcohol, and show up for her prenatal care. It also requires trust that the surrogate, who must have previously given birth and is parenting her own child, will part with the infant without conflict. However, the surrogate needs to trust that the intended parents will support her and her family throughout the pregnancy and not interfere with her right to make decisions about her body.

Traditional surrogacy (TS), in which a woman carries a child for an infertile woman by using her own eggs, has been reported as far back as the beginning of recorded history. It can be thought of as the earliest form of fertility treatment (S. N. Covington & Patrizio, 2013). Since the development of IVF, traditional surrogacy has been largely replaced by the use of a gestational carrier (GC), whereby the gametes are either from the intended mother or an egg donor. TS can be problematic because the woman may be more likely to bond with the child created with her own gametes while still in utero. In addition, after birth, the child may resemble her or her other children, increasing attachment. The concern with TS is that the surrogate will not want to surrender the child; as such, TS is far less common and less accepted today than GC arrangements (Strasser, 2015).

Cultural beliefs and laws about surrogacy vary around the world. Some countries allow it within their borders but have banned any "cross-border reproductive services." India, for example, passed a law forbidding foreigners from applying for surrogacy in India. The law addressed complaints about the exploitation of Indian women, many of whom had poor living conditions and dealt with agencies that failed to pay them (Saran & Padubidri, 2020). In Cambodia, where international surrogacy had been legal, there are now government restrictions. In a case involving a Cambodian surrogate, a Chinese intended father, and a Russian egg donor, the surrogate was forced to raise the child or risk going to jail. The intended father, who is gay, was sentenced for human trafficking and sentenced to 15 years in prison (Beech, 2022). Other countries restrict surrogacy to heterosexual couples; others allow it only if it is altruistic (i.e., there is no financial compensation to the surrogate). Although these restrictions are not present in the United States, surrogacy is not treated equally throughout the country; the rights of the surrogate, the offspring, and the intended parents can differ from state to state (Lahl et al., 2022). Some states ban surrogacies altogether, some only allow altruistic surrogacy, while others permit commercial GC arrangements (Simpson & Hanafin, 2015).

Surrogacy raises long-standing controversies: First, should it be allowed at all, or does it violate traditional family mores and structures? Does payment to a surrogate equate to the commodification of a woman's body? What are the surrogate's rights in terms of making choices for herself? What if an abortion is deemed necessary? This is an intensely emotional process for the surrogate as well as for the intended parents, and conflict can arise between the parties involved. Because of this, it is recommended that the intended parents and the GC have legal counsel and partake in psychological consultation and testing (Practice Committee of ASRM and Practice Committee of SART, 2017).

As with known donors, an initial group consultation with the GC, her partner, and the intended parents is advised. Mental health professionals can address questions and concerns in this group setting and set the stage for ongoing dialog. It can be helpful to suggest additional group sessions throughout the pregnancy and postpartum period. This allows for conflicts, if any, to be aired and resolved, creating a solid basis for teamwork.

In terms of the reproductive story, surrogacy is a new and distinct chapter for all participants to grapple with. As with other third-party interventions, intended parents are challenged by the loss of control over the prenatal period. Anxiety can be particularly high; it is important for them not to be overly intrusive and understand the autonomy of the GC. It is equally important for the intended parents not to be absent. Sometimes, in their effort not to be overbearing, the intended parents give the GC too much space, creating abandonment feelings for the GC and making her question the parents' commitment. Open communication between the GC and the intended parents can make for a better outcome for all. The following vignettes typify what intended parents and surrogates may feel:

> **Intended Parents:** We were matched with a surrogate—and we're so excited but also anxious as hell! We get to meet her next week. What should we ask her? We want to know why she decided to do this, of course. And we want to know if she will be okay using our doctor. I guess we just want to get to know her, but it feels so intense to trust a stranger with our baby. This feels crazy!

> **Surrogate:** My friend is doing this now for a couple, and I got intrigued; it's such an amazing thing to be able to do. Of course, I'm nervous about meeting them—what if they don't like me? I know they must have gone through so much to get to the point of needing me. What's it going to be like for them? And what's it going to be like for me? I loved being pregnant with my daughter. Yes, I know there's money involved, but mostly, I'm thinking about how I am going to change this couple's life for the better. I'm excited for this adventure, but I have to admit, it also feels a little crazy!

There are a number of important issues for a GC to consider before she makes a commitment; these can be addressed in consultation with the mental health practitioner's evaluation. The GC and her partner should be prepared for the possibility of medical risks and complications that can occur in any pregnancy (i.e., miscarriage, ectopic pregnancy, bed rest, gestational diabetes, disability, or death), the medications she will likely take for the IVF process, and the possibility that IVF may not work. Because maternal vulnerability is disproportionately higher in the Black community than the White community, a GC who is a woman of color should be made aware of the statistics (Valerio et al., 2023). GCs also need to be aware of prenatal diagnostic testing, some of which can put the pregnancy at higher risk for miscarriage and which she may not have done during her own pregnancy. A study comparing surrogate pregnancies with nonsurrogate pregnancies found that surrogate pregnancies were more often labeled as high risk and were more likely to result in C-section deliveries (Lahl et al., 2022). The surrogate and her partner should also be prepared for how this pregnancy might affect their relationship, the possibility of sexual abstinence, the effect on their child(ren), and how it could impact her employment (Practice Committee of ASRM and the Practice Committee of SART, 2017).

Part of the dialog between GC and intended parents should address the birth itself. Is there a preference for a specific doctor or hospital? What are the hospital's policies? Who will be present? Who will hold the baby first? These and other postpartum issues can be addressed in the psychological consult. As stated, the intended parents often worry about what it will be like for the surrogate to relinquish the baby after birth. While the surrogate is legally required to do so, feelings of loss are not surprising. Attachment occurs by caring for this baby in utero. Clinicians should discuss the possibility of postpartum depression or anxiety occurring. For example, some surrogates who agreed to pump and supply breast milk for the newborn found it emotionally challenging when there was no physical baby present (Lahl et al., 2022).

This is a long journey for surrogates and intended parents to embark on. How it ends is equally important as how they were matched or found each other. Research has shown that surrogates benefit from some ongoing contact with the family she has helped to create; GCs need to feel validated for their enormous gift. Showing respect and appreciation to the GC can minimize any feelings of exploitation (Simpson & Hanafin, 2015). It is also recommended that the surrogate's children get to meet the parents and the new baby for a sense of closure. These two families share an undeniably unique bond, and research has shown the long-term impact of surrogacy to be generally positive. Some surrogates have some difficulty shortly after the birth, but this tends to lessen with time (Jadva et al., 2003). In fact, in a 10-year longitudinal study, it was found that surrogates felt good about the experience, had their expectations met or exceeded by the intended parents, and had positive feelings about the child (Jadva et al., 2015). These results were confirmed in a meta-analysis of research articles: It was found that the well-being of the children born via surrogacy was comparable to IVF or naturally conceived children, and the psychological well-being of the surrogate's children was also found to be good (Söderström-Anttila et al., 2016). It appears that one of the primary factors in creating a positive surrogacy experience for all parties involved is communication; even if contact is infrequent, the key to success seems to be the open and respectful relationships they maintain.

Birth Parents and Adoptive Parents

There is a significant difference between relinquishing a child via surrogacy and adoption. In surrogacy, the decision to surrender the child to the intended parents is made before pregnancy; the surrogate is intentional in this decision, and arrangements with the intended parents happen before any medical intervention takes place. In adoption, however, it is only after a woman conceives that birth parents face an emotionally and psychologically difficult choice. Birth parents must contend with myriad decisions in this process; their needs for psychological support are clear. This section focuses on the decision-making process for intended parents, as well as helping birth parents cope with their decision, grief, and loss.

Many same-sex couples and single people choose to adopt instead of using donor gametes; although they may have fertility issues, most do not. For most heterosexual couples, the decision to adopt is a result of the long and arduous process of fertility treatments and failures. Some view adoption as a last resort, a kind of "backup" plan when all else has failed (Daniluk & Hurtig-Mitchell, 2003). The well-meaning but simplistic advice given to those struggling with fertility issues—"Why don't you just adopt?"—ignores the logistic and emotional hurdles of the adoption process (Malavé, 2015). The transition in one's reproductive story from the wish to become pregnant and have a biological child to the wish to parent a nonbiological child is a huge shift. The reconfiguration of the family to include a nonbiological child is not easy and may have multigenerational implications because grandparents and other relatives may need to shift their views as well. Infertility can create a narcissistic wound that should be healed and mended as much as possible before adoption. The goal is for parents who adopt to actively choose adoption rather than passively resign themselves to it. Reproductive mental health practitioners can help by having clients recognize the multiple losses they have endured and the significant losses of the birth parents as well (Cudmore, 2005).

This triad of adoptive parents, birth parents, and adoptee creates a complex family structure that is outside the mainstream ideals of rearing one's own biological child and having just one set of parents (Malavé, 2015). For the adoptive parents, the birth parents can seem like a constant threat looming over them. Many feel insecure and anxious that they will not be chosen by a birth parent. The vulnerability they feel in putting their future parental status in the hands of a birth parent or an agency can feel demeaning and judgmental. There are also fears that the birth parents will change their minds when the baby is born. There are worries that the child will eventually reject them as not being their "real" parents and want to seek out their idealized birth parents in the future. Reproductive counselors can help adoptive parents understand "the reality that the birth parents are, in fact, psychologically present in the adoptive family system" (Malavé, 2015, p. 205). The fear of a future loss is understandable in the context of so much uncertainty and loss in dealing with infertility. Normalizing their fears and, at the same time, having adoptive parents find empathy for the birth parents' loss can create a greater understanding of their child's needs and mitigate their own feelings of self-doubt and insecurity. The following vignettes illustrate what adoptive and birth parents typically feel:

> **Adoptive Parents:** This was harder than we thought it would be. Creating a brochure about ourselves—actually having to sell ourselves—felt so artificial and humiliating. We had to be all smiles when what we've gone through has been anything but. But it worked, and we were chosen. And now we have an incredible little bundle; it actually feels right!

> **Birth Mother:** I love my two kids, but honestly, it's a struggle. I mean, I'm a single mom, and there was no way I would be able to manage an infant. I've got to work! I knew this was the right thing to do for this baby, as hard as it was for me to say goodbye to her. What made me pick this couple? I don't know . . . they seemed solid and seemed like they really loved each other. That was what sold me. And they want to keep in touch—let me know how she's doing and all. It's hard, but I know she'll be ok.

Birth parents also have reproductive stories that, when originally imagined, most likely did not include the idea of relinquishing a child. While adoptive parents may feel indebted to a birth parent, they may also make negative assumptions about a birth parent, usually the birth mother: How could she relinquish a baby? It has been noted that birth parents are the least studied members of the adoption triad but certainly not the least affected by it (Baden & Wiley, 2007). Closed or "confidential" adoptions, which were the norm for much of the 20th century, were thought to protect the birth parent's privacy and lessen the stigmatization of illegitimacy (Ge et al., 2008). Homes for unwed mothers were available to "protect" teenage or unwed women and allow them to proceed with their pregnancy and adoption in secret, in essence, to "erase" the pregnancy. The image of a young, White, unwed mother as the typical birth mother is far from accurate, and yet these are the women who were most often whisked away to these facilities. Many were forced to surrender their babies to not bring shame to the family and were given the message that they would forget that any of it happened (Adams, 2017). On the contrary, it was found that women who were coerced into relinquishment had higher levels of grief, guilt, and shame that persisted (De Simone, 1996).

With the U.S. Supreme Court decision of *Roe v. Wade* in 1973, granting the right to an abortion, women had more choices regarding an unwanted pregnancy. Research has shown that abortion legalization was related to a decline in adoptions (Bitler & Zavodny, 2002). As of this writing, however, with the Dobbs decision (2022) overruling *Roe v. Wade* and the federal right to abortion, more women will likely be put into the position of relinquishing their children. Although some women get pregnant accidentally and do not want to parent, many women who choose to relinquish already have children of their own and know what it takes to raise a child, financially and emotionally. It is estimated that 40% of birth mothers have children other than the one they are relinquishing (Smith, 2006). Their motivation to relinquish is for the sake of the child and the family they already have.

Mental health professionals may be called on to help with adoption decisions for the birth mother or, in some cases, the birth parents. Birth mothers report feelings of loss and isolation, even in the case of open adoptions. Birth mothers, often the center of adoptive parents' attention as their pregnancy progresses, may feel discarded and abandoned by the adoptive parents once the baby is born. It is important to remember that postdelivery, birth mothers go through a postpartum period; the normal hormonal and physical changes that their body goes through, including lactation, can feel uncomfortable and disruptive. They report difficulty getting back to "normal" (Baden & Wiley, 2007).

The early post-relinquishment period (broadly defined as the first 2 years) can also be a time of significant distress, dominated by feelings of grief. A study that examined the post-relinquishment feelings of women found that 75% rated their emotional health as very poor, poor, or neutral (Brodzinsky & Smith, 2014). Some accounts have described birth mothers' lifelong struggles with relinquishment, including symptoms of depression and anxiety. Although the child was relinquished, they remain "psychologically present" (Fravel et al., 2000). Part of what birth mothers grapple with is the feeling that they are carrying a secret: They feel they are unlovable and unworthy and that they would be scorned if their secret were to be disclosed. Many have reported difficulties in intimate relationships and attachment issues with subsequent children. Especially with closed adoptions, they often worry about their child: Are they alive and safe? Open adoption, however, seems to mitigate some of these negative feelings. Knowing that their child was doing well and having some involvement in the life of the adoptive family brought a sense of peace and comfort (Krahn & Sullivan, 2015).

Baden and Wiley (2007) list several factors in the effective psychological treatment of birth mothers, including not minimizing the effect of this loss, expressing all the accompanying feelings (e.g., anger, guilt, self-blame), understanding that fantasies of reunion are to be expected, normalizing the need to fill the hole left by relinquishment, and avoiding the numbing experiences of alcohol or drugs. Reproductive counselors and birth parents need to recognize that these feelings can emerge at any point. Triggers such as birthdays and holidays can be painful reminders because birth parents may reflect on their decision. While the pain of relinquishment may never fully be extinguished, having adequate support and some kind of ongoing involvement with the child and the adoptive family has helped birth mothers cope better and be more satisfied with the adoption process (Ge et al., 2008).

The focus here is on relinquishing a child in a planned adoption, usually at birth; it does not address the dynamics that take place when a child is taken away due to adverse conditions in the home. Nonetheless, the most underrepresented person in the adoption triad, both in the clinical and research literature, is the birth father. For obvious reasons, he is less involved in the pregnancy and may be less involved in any adoption decisions as well. Although he is often ignored, it does not mean he is unaffected. All men have reproductive stories, and birth fathers should not be excluded. In the case of unintended teenage pregnancies, these young men's reproductive stories are most likely completely disrupted; they have been "faced [with] the challenge to become adults and parents at the same time" (Clapton & Clifton, 2016, p. 157). As noted by Condon et al. (2013), fathers' attachment can stem from a bond "which is activated in fantasy before the baby is even born" (p. 25).

Birth fathers have been reported to have feelings of pride, along with a profound sense of grief, loss, anger, guilt, and powerlessness over decisions about adoption; some even felt suicidal. Feeling excluded from the decision making, invisible, and disenfranchised, birth fathers' experiences, especially in closed adoption circumstances, are emotionally distressing. They also have to contend with feeling stigmatized and judged (Cornefert, 2021). The long-lasting effects can be seen in struggles with subsequent relationships with partners and children (Clapton & Clifton, 2016). The "psychological presence," as Fravel et al. (2000) described for birth mothers, exists for birth fathers as well, with persistent feelings of shame and inadequacy and wondering about the child (Clapton & Clifton, 2016; Clapton, 2019). Cornefert (2021) suggested looking at the experience through an ambiguous loss lens, where there is a lack of closure, leaving birth parents continuously seeking resolution. Just as it is for women, relinquishment is a lifelong process, and the feelings men have parallel those of women.

Even in open adoption situations, birth fathers are often not consulted. It is with surprise when they are and joy when they are able to have ongoing contact with their child (Cornefert, 2021). In a study of birth fathers (although the sample size was small), it was found that there was a positive impact not only on their lives but also on the lives of the child and adoptive parents. Birth fathers saw themselves as part of the "village" raising the child (Clutter, 2020). This result was corroborated in a larger study: With contact and openness, birth fathers reported greater satisfaction with the adoption process and higher adjustment levels (Ge et al., 2008). In the past, adoptive parents were amenable to a level of openness with the birth mother but not the birth father (Sachdev, 1991), but times have changed. It is important for mental health clinicians and all other practitioners in the adoption process to think of the birth father as an active participant.

SUMMARY

Everyone involved in creating a family brings with them a host of feelings. As reproductive mental health practitioners, we are privileged to witness the care and thoughtfulness of all involved—from intended parents, donors, and birth parents. Our care and thoughtfulness can make the process easier: We provide support, relieve anxieties, and deepen the understanding of each other's reproductive stories as families are created and grow.

7 ADJUNCTS TO REPRODUCTIVE PSYCHOTHERAPY

Life itself seeks fulfillment as plants seek sunlight.

—B. K. S. Iyengar

Many reproductive patients will pursue additional treatment options aside from traditional psychotherapy in their quest to decrease negative psychological symptoms, access support, and explore every avenue that may offer success. Services outside of traditional psychotherapy can feel like lifesavers— for example, being able to reach other people on the Internet day or night for support can buoy clients in despair. Adjuncts can include online support, in-person or virtual peer support groups, eye-movement desensitization and reprocessing (EMDR), Chinese medicine, yoga, and/or changes in lifestyle to promote well-being.

There may be downsides to these adjunctive therapies, and in this chapter, the plusses and minuses will be explored. The last thing we want for patients is to get misinformation or be retraumatized, so encouraging them to take care before pursuing alternative treatments is essential.

https://doi.org/10.1037/0000400-007
Reproductive Trauma: Psychotherapy With Clients Experiencing Infertility and Pregnancy Loss, Second Edition, by J. Jaffe

SUPPORT GROUPS

Group interventions have a long history of helping patients through all types of medical or psychological conditions. A simple Internet search can provide patients with information on groups specific to infertility or pregnancy loss, as well as groups addressing adoption or the use of a donor or surrogate. Groups may be gender specific, structured for couples, led by a peer who has had a similar experience, or led by a professional and may meet in person or virtually. Research has suggested that group counseling is one of the most effective interventions to normalize infertility trauma (Boivin, 2003). In general, groups can provide a sense of belonging, validation, normalization of emotions, and education (S. N. Covington, 2006; S. N. Covington & Adamson, 2015). Reproductive patients often feel their world is shrinking because they no longer "fit" with friends who are pregnant or have young children. As discussed, the psychological framework of patients may have moved into parenthood, but their lack of a child keeps them feeling disconnected from other parents. In addition, they may feel disengaged from those who do not have children because their interests or focus has shifted. Because one of the most difficult aspects of reproductive trauma is isolation, group interventions can provide some of the social interactions that patients crave. Finding others "in the same boat" is reassuring and can provide hope, support, catharsis, and education.

Perhaps the best-known emotion-focused support group for infertility in the United States is RESOLVE: The National Infertility Association. Barbara Eck, a nurse undergoing her own infertility, founded RESOLVE. At its inception, the goals were to help couples work through the anger and grief of infertility and decrease their sense of isolation. Educating the public about infertility as a legitimate medical issue was also an early objective (Menning, 1976). Since that time, RESOLVE has evolved and grown; it now provides support groups around the United States and promotes political advocacy on the state and federal levels for health care coverage, research, and education.

Aside from in-person and virtual support groups, online support can fulfill patients' needs for technical and medical information, emotional guidance, and encouragement. Having the freedom to shed a tear in the privacy and comfort of one's home can bring relief. Online communities may use bulletin boards, chat rooms, or private messaging, allowing users to post and reply to messages from all over the world; participants can "lurk" or actively engage. The support is not unlike traditional support groups in content, and many people prefer seeking help online rather than in face-to-face groups because of the anonymity it provides (allowing individuals to pose questions or discuss issues without embarrassment). Clients also appreciate the ability to unload at any time of day or night and feel a sense of control in deciding when to participate or not (Malik & Coulson, 2008). The privacy of online support benefits those who would not be open to in-person therapy or support for cultural reasons. Another reason for the popularity of online support is that some patients may not live in a location where a "live" support group is available. Likewise, circumstances like COVID-19, where in-person contact was avoided, have made online resources even more valuable.

Online support groups specifically for pregnancy loss benefit patients in similar ways. A survey of online pregnancy loss users found that they felt supported and less isolated and appreciated its convenience, ease of access, and anonymity (Gold et al., 2012). Another plus is that there is a greater possibility for men to join who are less inclined to attend in-person groups (O'Leary & Thorwick, 2006). Other research found that it provided a virtual meeting place to share grief and discuss issues such as the attachment to their child during the duration of the pregnancy—even if for a short time—and the continuation of this bond even after the loss. Common topics include the enormous sadness they all shared; the dread of holidays, birthdays, and due dates; the anxiety of a subsequent pregnancy and fear of another loss; advice in dealing with the grief that the siblings of the unborn child are experiencing; and the use of meaningful rituals and symbols (Capitulo, 2004).

Although many find support groups helpful, they may not be right for everyone. Some patients are, by nature, private and not comfortable sharing their personal lives with a group. Others can become overwhelmed by the intensity of pain that can permeate these groups as members process their personal experiences. If a patient is at a particularly vulnerable time, they may find it difficult to read or hear the stories of other members. One study found that over half the subjects who participated in online support for infertility described disadvantages, including reading about other people's negative experiences, reading about others' pregnancies, getting inaccurate information, and finding it addictive (Malik & Coulson, 2010). There is also the risk of trolls (someone who causes disruption), fakers (someone who pretends to have experienced perinatal loss), or someone who is suicidal attending the group, which can be potentially harmful and frightening to those seeking help (Carlson et al., 2012; Hammond, 2015). In addition, some may become obsessed with their online community, which thereby interferes with their daily life and real-world interactions (Malik & Coulson, 2008). Clinical observation suggests that the sheer amount of time patients spend searching for information and support can cause them to lose sight of time and perspective. While information can provide relief, it can also increase anxiety and further questions and doubts.

One of the most emotionally challenging events that can occur in a group happens when one of its members becomes pregnant. Although this is the goal of group participants, feelings of joy and jealousy are likely to collide and set up a divide between the haves and the have-nots. What can make this situation more manageable is if it is addressed directly within the safety of the group. The group can serve as a way to discuss what is so painfully present on a daily basis and learn ways to manage, cope, and be better prepared when it occurs in the real world (S. N. Covington, 2006).

EYE-MOVEMENT DESENSITIZATION AND REPROCESSING

EMDR is a recommended treatment for posttraumatic stress disorder. By reprocessing traumatic memories and adverse life occurrences, EMDR allows for the constructive resolution of emotional distress (F. Shapiro, 2002). Unfortunately, research on EMDR and its use with pregnancy loss or infertility patients is sparse. There has been some research on the effectiveness of EMDR on women who have had traumatic births (Chiorino et al., 2020; Pašalić & Hasanović, 2018). One case study of a 36-year-old woman who had suffered two ectopic pregnancies and three failed in vitro fertilization (IVF) procedures showed promise. On completion of her EMDR protocol, psychosomatic symptoms (headaches, stomachaches, insomnia, shortness of breath) disappeared, and she was able to consider another IVF or adoption (Vučina & Oakley, 2018). Anecdotally, colleagues trained to practice EMDR have also reported positive results in treating the emotional trauma of reproductive patients. This is yet another area that warrants further studies.

COMPLEMENTARY AND ALTERNATIVE MEDICINES

Alternative medicine has been in use for many conditions for a long time. Complementary and alternative medicines (CAM), defined as those practices not considered part of conventional Western medicine, include the use of herbs and acupuncture, diet regimens and dietary supplements, and yoga, among others (Wieland et al., 2011). Many reproductive patients turn to these "natural" remedies to try to enhance fertility, wanting to try everything in their quest to have a baby. A study in the United States found that wealthier couples who had not yet achieved pregnancy and those who had a fundamental belief in its effectiveness were more likely to use CAM (Smith et al., 2010), and women were more likely to use CAM than men (Facchinetti et al., 2012). While some patients have had success with alternative medicine, the research to date is limited and offers mixed conclusions. In fact, the use of CAM may have deleterious effects, interfere with implantation and early pregnancy (Boivin & Schmidt, 2009), and possibly cause preterm birth (Facchinetti et al., 2012).

Perhaps the most frequently used alternative remedy is traditional Chinese medicine (TCM). Although it has been used to enhance human reproduction for centuries, there are limited controlled scientific studies that prove its effectiveness. TCM relies on a combination of medicinal herbs and acupuncture to restore the balance of life energy or *qi*, defined as "the most indispensable energy that makes up the vitality of the body and maintains life activities" (Huang & Chen, 2008, p. 212). According to TCM, if qi is blocked, disease will set in; the body must return to a healthy equilibrium to heal. TCM is appealing; it gives patients a greater sense of control over their reproductive health, especially if they are dissatisfied with traditional Western medicine (Rayner et al., 2009).

Acupuncture is believed to increase blood flow to the uterus and ovaries, thus producing favorable uterine conditions for conception (Westergaard et al., 2006). Early studies found that acupuncture improved IVF pregnancy rates; however, subsequent studies have shown contradictory results. In a meta-analysis conducted to assess the role of acupuncture, no evidence of improved live birth or pregnancy rates was found (Cheong et al., 2013). A study comparing acupuncture with a combination of acupuncture and medicinal herbs (whole-systems TCM or WS-TCM) found that using WS-TCM was associated with greater odds of live birth (Hullender Rubin et al., 2015). The use of medicinal herbs, conversely, has come into question as they may actually do harm (Facchinetti et al., 2012). It should also be noted that despite recommendations from their physician not to take herbs, some patients did so anyway (Domar et al., 2012).

This is an area that begs for more research. The supposed "natural" aspect of TCM has much allure, along with patients' desires to leave no stone unturned. Because the results of studies on TCM are so varied, clinicians may find themselves in a bind when patients want to use it. Whether or not it enhances fertility, many patients find it helpful in reducing stress and anxiety and providing structure and control.

Diet and Dietary Supplements

Another arena where patients can gain a sense of control is in regulating their diet. A proposed *fertility diet* consisting of eating more seafood, poultry, whole grains, fruits, and vegetables has been associated with better fertility in both men and women (Aoun et al., 2021; Gaskins & Chavarro, 2018). A meta-analysis reviewing 104 studies summarized the effects of diet and dietary supplements. For men, a high intake of dairy products and trans fats may have a negative impact, while taking supplements such as vitamin B12, vitamin D, zinc, and folic acid may positively affect sperm. As with men, high dairy and trans-fat consumption may also negatively impact fertility for women. Supplements for women indicated that vitamin D may be beneficial for disorders such as polycystic ovarian syndrome, insulin resistance, or low anti-Mullerian hormone levels, while folic acid and zinc may decrease the risks of ovulatory infertility (see Aoun et al., 2021, for a full review). Chavarro et al. (2007, 2008) examined women's dietary habits over an 8-year period and found that using multivitamins, particularly folic acid, at least three times per week was associated with a lower risk of ovulatory infertility. Not only is folic acid essential for proper cell division and recommended for the prevention of neural tube defects in developing fetuses but there is also evidence that it is related to lower frequency of infertility, lower instances of pregnancy loss, and higher success in infertility treatment (Gaskins & Chavarro, 2018).

There is a popular notion that being on a gluten-free diet will enhance fertility. A quick online search reveals scores of gluten-free success stories, but the scientific literature is not as promising. It is true that women who have been diagnosed with celiac disease and go on a gluten-free diet do have better outcomes (Krawczyk et al., 2022). Celiac is an autoimmune disease with complications such as recurrent pregnancy loss or unexplained infertility (Farzaneh & Khalili, 2019). The question then arises: If a woman has recurrent losses or unexplained infertility, does she have celiac? A meta-analysis of 20 studies, which used a strict definition of celiac disease, found that it is not more common in women with infertility than in the general population (Glimberg et al., 2021). For those who do not have celiac, eliminating gluten does not increase positive results when using assisted reproductive technologies and could, in fact, do more harm than good by generating deficiencies in the diet (Krawczyk et al., 2022). Once again, the hope for a simple solution—especially for unexplained infertility—is appealing, even if not scientifically proven.

It is important that patients recognize that dietary changes do not guarantee success. Consultation with their physician and/or a nutritionist should be encouraged, and the disappointments and psychological frustrations need to be addressed as part of their psychotherapy. As they might with any intervention, patients can become obsessed with food, often depriving themselves to an extreme in a perhaps misguided effort to enhance their fertility. Diets can be seductive, especially to those who feel compelled to try everything as part of being thorough. With so much feeling out of control, strict adherence to a diet may be a way of taking charge of what is happening.

Yoga

As discussed, a belief held by many is that stress and tension can cause infertility and pregnancy loss. There is no doubt that relaxation techniques and exercise, such as yoga, are beneficial to one's health, but whether it improves treatment outcomes for reproductive patients remains controversial (S. N. Covington & Adamson, 2015; Ota et al., 2021). Meta-analysis studies have produced mixed results, as it has with mind–body interventions. While the effects of yoga on anxiety, depression, and quality of life for women undergoing fertility treatment yielded a decrease in overall psychological distress (Dumbala et al., 2020), there is limited evidence that it improves fertility outcomes (Darbandi et al., 2018). Ota et al. (2021) explored the endocrine functions of women with infertility who practiced Hatha yoga compared with a control group. The findings indicated that although yoga may affect hormonal changes, there were no differences in pregnancy outcomes between the two groups.

SUMMARY

The search for therapeutic interventions by and for reproductive patients is vast and complex. Reproductive patients are a vulnerable group; in the vast industry that reproductive medicine has become, patients may fall prey to unproven theories. Both clinicians and patients need to distinguish between programs that claim to increase pregnancy rates and those that claim to increase coping skills. Because so much of patients' reproductive stories feel out of control, it makes sense that they grab onto cures that may not be supported by much evidence. It provides them with a sense of empowerment and control. Many alternative and adjunct medical protocols may be psychologically appealing but do not necessarily increase conception rates or live births. More rigorous, scientifically based studies are necessary to know which treatments are most effective, and patients need to guard against false assertions.

Some people believe that positive thinking will promote positive results. Patients often blame themselves when a pregnancy or IVF cycle fails, citing they were not relaxed enough or had negative thoughts. The self-blame that accompanies such thinking is destructive and can promote a downward spiral of negative affect. Our job is to remind clients that having a baby is a complicated biological process—even if it is "natural"—and that it is not controlled by one's thoughts, positive or negative. Patients need to be repeatedly reminded that conception is not a skill. Giving patients permission to tell their stories and express their anxious or negative thoughts provides relief. That which is unspeakable gains in intensity, so verbalizing thoughts and feelings makes them more manageable. If anything, suppressing or internalizing negative thoughts can cause physical stress and tension. It is especially important to remind patients that overwhelming feelings are normal and inevitable, given the magnitude of their reproductive traumas and losses.

8 FROM REPRODUCTIVE TRAUMA TO GROWTH

Healing and Change

We must be willing to let go of the life we have planned so as to accept the life that is waiting for us.

–Joseph Campbell

Posttraumatic growth (PTG), terminology coined by Tedeschi and Calhoun (1995), refers to the potential for positive change following a major catastrophic life event. This concept is as old as time—out of hardship can come growth; we learn and develop from the obstacles we encounter in life. While Tedeschi and Calhoun have made it clear that trauma is not necessary for growth and that experiencing trauma is not anything anyone should have to go through to grow, they make the case that "those who are forced to struggle with [traumatic events] can experience highly meaningful personal changes" (Tedeschi et al., 2015, p. 514).

The idea that one's life narrative can be rewritten posttrauma fits with the concept of rewriting one's reproductive story. As is addressed later, Tedeschi and Calhoun identified a variety of ways changes in the narrative

https://doi.org/10.1037/0000400-008
Reproductive Trauma: Psychotherapy With Clients Experiencing Infertility and Pregnancy Loss, Second Edition, by J. Jaffe

can be realized: a greater appreciation for life, more meaningful relationships, a greater openness to new possibilities, a sense of personal strength, and an enhanced recognition of spiritual or existential development (Peterson et al., 2008; Ramos & Leal, 2013; Tedeschi & Calhoun, 1995, 2004; Tedeschi et al., 2015). This chapter explores the concept of PTG in general and how it specifically applies to reproductive trauma.

DISRUPTION IN THE ASSUMPTIVE WORLD

Daily life is filled with tasks and schedules: getting kids to school on time, picking them up and taking them to their extracurricular activities, making dinner, and performing the bedtime routine, not to mention taking care of our own work and household needs. We come to expect and assume the patterns of our lives, not just from day to day but also through the course of our entire lives. Developmental psychology teaches us that there are specific times in life to anticipate growth and change. Erikson's (1963) developmental model (eight stages from infancy through old age) posits that certain tasks need to be mastered within each stage to transition successfully to the next phase of life. Some challenges evolve along the way: Inner forces (instinct, temperament, personality) and outer forces (family, community, culture, history) are constantly at play in achieving a sense of self-regulation, equilibrium, and growth (Batra, 2013).

A traumatic event can occur at any time or phase of development that can completely derail one's progress. The assumptive state, the solid ground on which one bases one's life, is thrown into disarray and chaos, leading to an abrupt disintegration of one's foundation. Indeed, the story that has been constructed from early childhood is suddenly deconstructed. The reconstruction of one's narrative may provide the richest experience (Neimeyer, 2004). Applying this to the concept of the reproductive story is simple and straightforward: The story that was established and evolved since childhood becomes deconstructed with a negative reproductive event. Reconstructing the reproductive story—by grieving the story that was and creating new possibilities—is the task of therapy.

As assumptions become reestablished, the struggle with one's new reality posttrauma can determine the extent of PTG (Cann et al., 2010). It has been noted that it is not the traumatic event itself but the struggle that occurs in the aftermath of the event that leads to PTG (Tedeschi et al., 2015). In the process of rebuilding a new assumptive world, individuals can reexamine many aspects of their lives, which can then lead to new possibilities. As Tedeschi and Calhoun noted, "Posttraumatic growth is not simply a return to baseline—it is an experience of improvement that for some persons is deeply profound" (Tedeschi & Calhoun, 2004, p. 4).

HOW DOES GROWTH OCCUR?

Tedeschi and Calhoun (2004) noted that a narrative surrounding the trauma develops: There exists the time before and after the trauma, with the traumatic event as the turning point. The schemas that were destroyed provided understanding and meaningfulness in the world before the trauma and need to be reevaluated and reassessed. "A goal was possible then, but not now. A philosophy or belief may have seemed true then, but not now" (Tedeschi & Calhoun, 2004, p. 10). It is the time after the crisis when a cognitive rebuilding of shattered assumptions can occur. Growth is facilitated as a result of the struggle to make sense of the trauma and its aftermath.

Part of reconstructing one's world includes two types of rumination: intrusive and deliberate. *Intrusive rumination* can occur without a person wanting it; thoughts and/or images occur automatically (Triplett et al., 2012). This can cause a great deal of distress in the form of flashbacks and reliving the trauma. People need to cope with their overwhelming emotions and grief to address the traumatic experience more deliberately. *Deliberate rumination,* however, is the process of intentionally thinking about the traumatic event to try to understand what happened and what it means for one's future (Ramos & Leal, 2013; Tedeschi & Calhoun, 2004; Tedeschi et al., 2015; Triplett et al., 2012). Research has suggested that this is a key factor in developing PTG. "The degree to which the person is engaged cognitively by the crisis appears to be a central element in the process of posttraumatic growth" (Tedeschi & Calhoun, 2004, p. 12).

The rebuilding of a new assumptive world posttrauma is aided by deliberate self-disclosure with select people in supportive and safe environments. Being able to share one's story with a therapist or a trusted friend or family member over time is a way to begin making sense of the unimaginable. Although most mental health professionals do so automatically, it bears stressing how important listening is when clients have been traumatized. They may need to tell their story repeatedly; clinicians should listen without offering solutions to the problem (Tedeschi et al., 2015). Deep questions about the meaning of life may emerge, and incorporating the trauma into a new set of core beliefs can lead to newfound meaning in life. Clinicians can also point out and label when they observe aspects of PTG in a client, thus reinforcing the positive process.

HOW IS CHANGE REALIZED?

The Posttraumatic Growth Inventory (PTGI) was developed to measure possible areas of growth. Although other assessments have been constructed to measure PTG (Ramos & Leal, 2013), the PTGI is the most widely used measure and reflects five distinct domains of growth, which are described next (Tedeschi & Calhoun, 1996; Tedeschi et al., 2015; Ramos & Leal, 2013).

Personal Strength

Out of adversity, individuals can recognize their ability to rise to the occasion and deal with future struggles and challenges. The feeling of "I can do this" can fill people with strength and purpose. There can be a sense of mastery over their posttrauma vulnerability, with an increase in their capability to move forward.

Relationships With Others

It is often only in the aftermath of a crisis that people discover who they can count on. These life events may bring out the best and worst in others. While some relationships may lead to great disappointment when anticipated support is lacking, other relationships may grow stronger. Trauma survivors who disclose personal information may feel an increased sense of vulnerability, which may also lead to greater intimacy and higher emotional connections with others. Likewise, PTG can be seen as fostering a greater sense of compassion for others, especially those who have also experienced a similar trauma.

Greater Appreciation of Life

Priorities have been reported as changing posttrauma. Specifically, greater attention to the smaller things in life, which may have been considered insignificant before, was noted by Tedeschi and Calhoun (2004). Daily pleasures may be valued as more important than previously judged; there is a sense of not taking things for granted. In essence, being more mindful may be a natural consequence in one's life because a change in priorities can take place posttrauma.

Spiritual Development

Experiencing a trauma often raises existential questions in people, especially related to the meaning of life. Depending on an individual's initial belief system and cultural values, changes or development of a new belief system will vary. For some, faith in a higher religious entity will increase, while for others, it may be challenged. The common thread is questioning one's beliefs: "Why has the trauma occurred? What is the point of my life? Why should I go on?" Although answers may not be found, through the questioning and struggle posttrauma, individuals have reported a deeper awareness of life and have found it more satisfying and meaningful.

New Possibilities

Posttraumatic reflections and questioning of one's life can lead individuals to pursue new interests or change the emphasis on what is important to them. Past assumptions or core beliefs may be revised, opening up novel options. While growth can take many different avenues and does not necessarily have to correlate with the traumatic event, many trauma survivors dedicate their lives posttrauma to rectifying the wrongs they experienced. Survivors of gun violence may fight for gun reform, and survivors of a disease may lobby for more research to be done. A couple who suffered a perinatal loss after several weeks of their child struggling to survive in the neonatal intensive care unit (NICU) made memory boxes for other parents with similar outcomes. These are all examples of PTG and how the trauma can facilitate new opportunities for personal development.

One point needs to be stressed: PTG does not necessarily decrease levels of distress or increase levels of contentment. As Tedeschi et al. (2015) wrote, "Posttraumatic growth may lead to a more fulfilling and meaningful life, but it seems not to be the same as simply being carefree, being happy, or feeling good" (p. 505). Growth from the trauma and distress from it may coexist; negative feelings may persist for years, if not for a lifetime. Those emotions can propel people to make positive changes in their daily lives and long-term goals. There is no "cure" for the traumatic event, but using it in one's new reality of life can bring richness and satisfaction in ways otherwise not thought possible.

REPRODUCTIVE TRAUMA AND POSTTRAUMATIC GROWTH

Much of what has been studied has focused on the negative impacts of infertility and pregnancy loss. There is no doubt that the aftermath of a failed pregnancy or a failed pregnancy attempt can be seen as traumatic. In the past few decades, however, researchers have turned their attention to the potential for positive gains from these physical, psychological, and emotional struggles. What kinds of growth might reproductive patients experience? What factors are important in fostering this growth? How can we, as clinicians, promote growth while at the same time recognize the ongoing importance of grief and mourning, the ongoing continued bonds with the real or imagined child? Reproductive trauma leaves an indelible mark on individuals and couples. While the past cannot be erased or whitewashed and should not be, living with the trauma and moving forward with one's life is essential.

Before exploring the empirical research on reproductive trauma and PTG can begin, it is necessary to address differences, if any, among the psychological consequences of infertility, early pregnancy losses, and stillbirth. Some researchers suggest that attachment to an unborn child is stronger according to the progression of a pregnancy. In other words, the longer the gestation, the greater the attachment and grief response. Some have postulated a hierarchy of sadness: The earlier the loss, the less impact it will have (Goldbach et al., 1991). Other research, however, has reported that gestational age is not a factor in bonding. It may be that the commitment to the pregnancy and its meaning predicts the intensity of grief and loss (Lovell, 2001). This is in keeping with the model of the reproductive story, which postulates that the parent–child bond and attachment exists much earlier than a pregnancy, even before conception. This model also incorporates those struggling with infertility—the *psychological parents*—as having just as profound a loss. Health care practitioners should not downplay patients' reactions—regardless of when the loss occurred (Krosch & Shakespeare-Finch, 2017).

The research on PTG and reproductive trauma has focused on dividing and comparing these various markers of loss. For the sake of seeing if PTG exists in this population and, if so, what aspects of it are salient, some studies have looked at infertility only (Ayaltu & Bayraktar, 2017; Paul et al., 2010; Yu et al., 2014; Zhang et al., 2021), while others have addressed PTG in patients suffering pregnancy loss (Krosch & Shakespeare-Finch, 2017; Ryninks et al., 2022; Winograd, 2017) and parental bereavement (Waugh et al., 2018). Consistent among all the findings is that posttraumatic growth was identified regardless of the type of loss suffered and across a variety of cultures and ethnicities.

Several factors have been noted for PTG to occur: cognitive processing, social support, and self-disclosure. The research mentioned previously for PTG and reproductive trauma also cites all these elements. Tedeschi and Calhoun (1996) described the need for deliberate rumination. Cognitive engagement in the aftermath of the trauma provides a means of reassessing one's previously held assumptions and a way to reconstruct a new belief system. One study comparing stillbirth and miscarriage found that women who had a stillbirth had a greater need to talk and ruminate, greater challenges to their assumptive beliefs, more severe posttraumatic stress disorder, and thus greater PTG than those who had an early miscarriage. They also noted that women who had a miscarriage felt they did not talk enough about their loss, perhaps due to the shame surrounding it or that others did not know about the pregnancy (Ryninks et al., 2022). However, it is important not to minimize the grief following a miscarriage or the potential for PTG. As Krosch and Shakespeare-Finch (2017) noted, the disruption in core beliefs predicts perinatal grief, symptoms of posttraumatic stress, and PTG. A cognitive shift is necessary when the previous assumptive world comes crashing down. "Put simply, when sense cannot be made, trauma persists; when sense can be made, it is through reorganization of schema that often leads to personal change" (Krosch & Shakespeare-Finch, 2017, p. 426). Working through the disruption of core beliefs and rebuilding schemas, not the traumatic event itself, leads to PTG (Tedeschi et al., 2015).

Another key element found throughout the literature and across cultures is the power of social support and PTG. Increased emotional support led to strengthened ties in marital relationships when dealing with infertility, especially when active coping or solution-based strategies were employed (Ayaltu & Bayraktar, 2017; L. Schmidt et al., 2005; Yu et al., 2014; Zhang et al., 2021). A study addressing infertility in Chinese women noted the importance of support from the whole family in helping women cope with infertility and promoting PTG (Yu et al., 2014). Perceived social support from family also had a positive effect on PTG in a study of Turkish infertility patients (Ayaltu & Bayraktar, 2017). Social support can also take the form of peer or professionally led groups, where patients' isolation can be reduced and coping skills and information can be shared. It has been suggested that self-disclosure about the trauma and loss in these settings can promote closeness, strengthen relationships, and promote PTG (Tedeschi & Calhoun, 1995, 2004).

Many studies found that the amount of time since the trauma occurred was another significant factor in the development of PTG. The cognitive work involved in rebuilding core beliefs does not happen instantaneously but takes time (Krosch & Shakespeare-Finch, 2017). In an overview of the literature on bereaved parents, Waugh et al. (2018) noted that time since death was significantly correlated with PTG, with mothers whose children died more recently reporting less growth. It may be a life-long process to make meaning and sense out of reproductive trauma, regardless of the specifics of the event itself.

WAYS TO FACILITATE GROWTH

- "Let's put things in perspective. There are still things that annoy me—like the dishwasher broke last week—but it just doesn't get to me like it used to. It's a hassle, but that's all it is."

- "When I hear people complain about trivial things, I think, 'You don't have a clue!'"

- "My sister has always been my rock, but I treasure her more now than ever. If I ever took her for granted before, I sure don't now."

- "When I'm out in the supermarket, I stop and wonder about all these other people. What's their story? Being wrapped up in our own lives, we can forget that other people struggle as well."

- "Now, when I see a pregnant woman, I take nothing for granted. In the past, I might have said, 'Is this your first one?' Now, I don't make assumptions like that. And I would hate to put her in that horrible, awkward place of having to explain herself to a complete stranger—or lie about the baby she lost."

- "I finally decided to put myself out there on social media. I was sick of hearing things like, 'You just need to relax.' So, I wrote a blog on what is okay and what is not okay to say to someone who has infertility. The responses were amazing—with lots of people saying, 'I never thought about that. Thank you.'"

This is what we hear from patients as they find meaning again in their lives. Many have a renewed appreciation for the people in their lives and a growing compassion for others. Time and again, they describe themselves as trying not to take things for granted and having more kindness and tolerance toward others. There seems to be an overwhelming desire to give back and help others, especially through circumstances they have experienced. Having a different perspective, brought about by the reproductive trauma they experienced, opens up avenues to pursue that they previously would never have considered. One patient decided to volunteer at a NICU; another became an active member of a support group and continued in an advisory capacity long after her loss was resolved. You, the reader, may have turned to practice in this specialty area out of your own reproductive trauma. An investigation of mental health professionals and nurses in the field found that 52% had a history of infertility. About 70% of those surveyed opted to focus on reproductive medicine after receiving their diagnosis (S. N. Covington & Marosek, 1999). Another study of psychologists found that 42% of participants entered the field of reproductive psychology because of their own experience (Marrero, 2013).

Of course, having personal experience is not a prerequisite to work in this area, and by no means is it sufficient knowledge to work in this field, but using the trauma to help others through it can be viewed through the lens of PTG.

It is essential to be attuned to patients' changing schemas and their revised life and reproductive narratives. Tedeschi et al. (2015) discussed the clinician's role as an *expert companion*. They stated, "We view ourselves as *facilitators* rather than creators of growth, and *companions* who offer some *expertise* in nurturing naturally occurring processes of healing and growth" (Tedeschi et al., 2015, p. 510). As facilitators, they stressed the importance of listening without trying to solve the problem; to be an engaged listener affects both the patient and clinician: "Being open to the possibility of being changed oneself, as a result of listening to the story of the trauma and its aftermath, communicates the highest degree of respect for clients, and encourages them to see the value in their own experience" (Tedeschi et al., 2015, p. 511).

Clinicians need to listen for these areas of growth in patients. An off-handed remark about a broken dishwasher could easily get overlooked in a meeting with a client; however, our ability to tune in to the possibility that this is PTG is an important element of care—a changing attitude toward life's abundant hassles, a new way of managing them and putting them in perspective is growth. As facilitators, clinicians should take note and label the changes patients have made as positive. Timing is also a critical factor; too early on in treatment posttrauma is not a good time to address PTG. Clients need to process the trauma, which may mean repeating their story over and over before being ready to address changes that may arise from it. They may not believe that anything good could ever come from their trauma, but over time, with emphasis on their cognitive struggle to make sense of the event rather than the actual event, clinicians' active listening can register change (Tedeschi et al., 2015).

In working with reproductive patients, focusing on how they might rewrite their reproductive story may open up the possibility of PTG. Being able to imagine a future self—with or without children—can promote a new life narrative, incorporating what they have learned from the trauma. One patient who had to terminate her pregnancy because of risks to her life was able to recognize a willingness to consider other ways to become a parent, something she would never have considered before. Another patient, after years of infertility and conflicts about whether to pursue more reproductive treatment, made the decision to remain child free. The excitement of new possibilities did not erase her grief. Understanding that her goal of becoming a parent was no longer attainable made it possible for her to see that new goals and new dreams were feasible. In reassessing her life narrative, she decided to return to school to explore other possibilities and dreams.

POSTPARTUM ADJUSTMENT AND GROWTH

For many clients, the achievement of parenthood—through a successful pregnancy or adoption—fosters PTG (Paul et al., 2010). While remnants of trauma may remain, having a baby can promote growth after reproductive trauma. Studies that looked at the attributes of parenting and the emotional well-being of children born using assisted reproductive technologies found that the quality of parenting was superior to that of naturally conceived children (Golombok et al., 1995, 2006). Similarly, parents through surrogacy were shown to have better adaptation and psychological well-being than natural-conception parents (Golombok et al., 2004). A conclusion one could draw from these studies is that the parent–child relationship may be strengthened because of the great lengths patients took to become parents. They truly do not take it for granted and thus have a greater appreciation for parenthood and their children and evidenced a strong measure of growth in the greater appreciation of life. This kind of growth after reproductive trauma affects not only the parents but also their children.

While much growth and healing can occur, it can be quite startling to patients and their friends and family when anxiety and depression continue after the birth of a child. Pregnancies are often fraught with anxiety and fear of failure. Patients, having experienced so many losses, may be convinced that another loss is inevitable. As one patient described it, "I am constantly worried. Every time I go to the bathroom, I do this mental dance, preparing to see blood from a miscarriage. It's like I can't bear to risk being taken by surprise if I do miscarry, so I am constantly on guard for it." Once a baby is born, patients may be shocked and feel guilty if they experience adverse postpartum reactions, especially after negative reproductive events. Having worked so hard and waited so long to finally have a baby, these new parents feel they do not have the right to complain. Social expectations that they should be happy may cause them to censor negative emotions (Olshansky & Sereika, 2005). The idealization of themselves as perfect parents with a perfect child makes any expression of negativity seem ungrateful (Garner, 1985).

Clinicians working with clients postpartum can be instrumental in normalizing and treating the phenomenon. The idealized view of a new baby—adorable, content, and happy—often differs from the reality of sleeplessness, difficulty feeding, colic, and isolation. Postpartum reactions can also be viewed as reproductive traumas; the reproductive story has gone awry, whether conception was natural or assisted by technology. The transition to parenthood is a huge adjustment for all new parents, whether or not there is a postpartum diagnosis; it is a time associated with many stressors and pressures. Many disorders get lumped into the category of postpartum adjustment: baby blues, postpartum depression and anxiety, and postpartum psychosis. Each category should be differentiated for proper diagnosis and treatment.

Baby blues is a relatively mild reaction occurring within the first few days after birth. It may include tearfulness, fatigue, anxiety, and irritability and usually resolves after 10 days postpartum (Beck, 2006). Although the symptoms are not acute, it is estimated that 60% to 80% of women experience postpartum blues (Vieira, 2002). *Postpartum mood and anxiety disorders* (PMAD), including anxiety and depression, include symptoms of obsessive thinking, anxiety attacks, unrealistic worry about the baby, or suicidal thoughts (Beck, 2006). The most serious of this group of disorders is *postpartum psychosis*. Although episodes of postpartum psychosis often make the news, the incidence is, in fact, rare. Only about 1% of new mothers develop a psychotic reaction (Vieira, 2002). Symptoms include delusions, hallucinations, emotional lability, and agitation; these women are likely to be dangerous to themselves and/or their babies (Beck, 2006).

While a thorough investigation into postpartum reactions and treatment is beyond the scope of this book, it is important for counselors to consider that patients who have had reproductive trauma, be it pregnancy loss or infertility, can suffer trauma after a baby is born as well. Referrals for a psychiatric assessment must be considered because PMADs respond well to medication. Cognitive behavior therapy is also effective (Davoudian & Covington, 2022). Asking questions about a patient's daily activities, social interactions, and eating and sleeping patterns can offer clues into how they are functioning. One new mother confessed that she slept under the baby's crib because she was so anxious. Another described feeling as if her brain was turning to mush: "I don't have anyone to talk to. There is just so much crying I have patience for. I know it's not rational, but there are times of the day when I hate my baby, hate myself, hate my life." The assumptions and beliefs about themselves as parents and about their babies can be reframed and normalized. After so much has been invested in creating a family, the pressure to fulfill expectations about their newborn and themselves may feel even more impossible to achieve.

SUMMARY

The end of this chapter of the reproductive story, whether it includes a baby or not, can be a time of great reflection and growth. Often, changes are not immediate but happen after some time has passed. Working as expert companions and listening for when and where posttraumatic growth occurs, we can help clients gain insight and facilitate a new narrative for the future.

PART **II** THE PROVIDER'S VIEWPOINT

9 WHAT PATIENTS WANT TO KNOW ABOUT REPRODUCTIVE MENTAL HEALTH PROVIDERS

The problem with self-disclosure has been, and remains, whether the disclosure is done for the therapist's benefit, the client's, or both.

—Maroda, *Psychotherapist Revealed*

Thus far, our attention has been on the needs of the clients with whom we work. We have addressed the traumas they have experienced and their profound grief and loss and focused on various ways to apply the reproductive story in treatment. Here, in Part II, we shift the emphasis from clients' needs to our own. This chapter and the following ones explore the complexities of our relationships with clients. The focus is on our role not only as a provider but also as a real person sitting across from a client. The impact of doing this type of work is explored. Where we are in our own reproductive story—and how that can change the treatment we provide—is an area that is rarely addressed. How we answer questions, what we might share about ourselves, how we share it, and when and why we reveal parts of ourselves can be key to the success or failure of a therapeutic relationship.

https://doi.org/10.1037/0000400-009
Reproductive Trauma: Psychotherapy With Clients Experiencing Infertility and Pregnancy Loss, Second Edition, by J. Jaffe

Clients reach out to reproductive mental health providers in the middle of their reproductive trauma; they are struggling to make sense of the world and their lives. We are ready to help with all our therapeutic skills lined up, our listening caps on, and our empathy dial set to high. It can be disconcerting when a client asks a question about us right off the bat. After all, in our quest to learn about a patient, the questions usually come from us. Patients may, however, want to know things about us. It makes sense that they would want some information as they bare their souls; naturally, they need to be able to trust us. They may ask about our training, how long we have been in practice, or where we went to school, which may be straightforward to answer. They may also ask us how we got into this specialized field. How do you answer that one? Often, there is a question behind the question: "Are you going to get me and understand what I'm going through?"

The elephant-in-the-room question is, "Do you have kids?" What does it mean for clients if their therapist has children or not? These kinds of personal questions posed to clinicians can push beyond the conventional boundary of therapist privacy and anonymity (Leibowitz, 2009). In an unscientific survey, I once asked for a raise of hands from a group of therapists at an American Society for Reproductive Medicine meeting: "How many of you have been asked if you have children?" Not surprisingly, nearly the entire room put their hands up. This question is often asked in the field of reproductive psychology.

WHO WE ARE TO CLIENTS

Every client who enters a therapeutic relationship is unique and likely has an image—correct or not—of who a mental health professional is and what they do. Whether we are providing ongoing psychotherapy or psychological assessments, clients may have preconceived notions and assumptions about us before we even meet (Weiner, 1975). Perhaps they think of us as a fountain of wisdom or fear us as somehow having X-ray vision into their deepest secrets and shame. Do we represent their mother or father? Do they want to gain our approval? Or perhaps they see us as a friend who offers advice. How they address us can indicate a hierarchy of sorts—do they call us by our first name or address us more formally? I have received many phone calls from clients seeking therapy, as we all have. I am sometimes referred to as Dr. Jaffe, while at other times, the message starts with "Hey, Janet." The ways we are addressed can indicate very different ideas about how patients view us before we have even scheduled a first appointment.

What patients expect from therapy and their relationship with their therapist can be observed in initial sessions but changes over time. With reproductive patients, their crisis needs to be addressed, first and foremost, with empathy and support. There have been times in my clinical experience when I have felt as if I was just a neutral presence in the room, where a patient's feelings could be discharged like air being released from a balloon. On several occasions, after working with someone for weeks, they may come into session asking if a painting or some other object they noticed for the first time is new. That is a signal that a shift has occurred; I am beginning to be seen as a real person, not just an anonymous receptacle for their grief and pain. This is when more attention to coping strategies, family history, relationship issues, and a deeper understanding of the meaning of their losses can be addressed.

Being genuine with patients is essential. The basis of the therapeutic alliance is truthfulness—emanating from the patient as well as the therapist. While readers of this volume are undoubtedly skilled clinicians, it can be helpful to think back to basics: "Being genuine does *not* mean that a therapist must express every feeling he has and disclose all of his personal concerns" (Weiner, 1975, p. 27). It does mean that whatever we choose to disclose comes from a sincere and real place. It also means that while we are focused and conscious of the patient's needs, we are also reflecting on our own. What about the patient's story arouses angst in us? Do we feel overwhelmed, and if so, why? As discussed further later, patients' reproductive stories can be painful to hear. This work is not for the faint of heart, especially if the therapist has had experiences similar to the client's.

ANONYMITY IN THE DIGITAL AGE

In reviewing an old textbook on psychotherapy, I laughed out loud at how much has changed since it was written. The text discussed the possibility that a patient could find out where their therapist lived by looking them up in the telephone book (Weiner, 1975). Does anyone still have a telephone book? Now, anyone with access to the Internet can find out a lot more about us than where we live. Wu and Sonne (2021) noted that patients can discover details about the therapist's education and training but also information about their social relationships and/or political views. Research has found that nearly 70% of clients searched for and found personal information about their provider, but only about a quarter of those told their therapist (Kolmes & Taube, 2016). As therapists, we are not immune to this desire for knowledge; we may look up information online about clients as well. In a survey of a wide range of mental health professionals, nearly half of the participants intentionally sought out information on the Internet about current clients (without the client's awareness or consent), while 28% accidentally discovered information (Kolmes & Taube, 2014).

The whole nature of therapist self-disclosure has been transformed because of the Internet (Zur & Donner, 2009). Therapist self-disclosure has historically been a controversial topic, made even more so by the ease of clicking on a mouse. Clients may access public records for free, and for a small fee, many sites provide other information as well (L. Taylor et al., 2010). Once again, technology is moving faster than our ability to process the changes. Social media sites such as Facebook and LinkedIn, professional websites, and Listservs all provide information that clients may be able to access. There are sites to help people find a therapist where therapists are encouraged to introduce themselves and provide their background. In today's ubiquitous rating system of "likes" and "stars," therapists may be reviewed online and have no idea of their ranking. It is disconcerting that information about us is available to clients without our knowledge or consent. As therapists, we do not necessarily have control over what is posted about us and have no idea what clients may read about us (Zur, 2015). Aside from the information we intentionally choose to have online, therapists may inadvertently disclose material, and once it is online, it is forever there. As Zur and Donner (2009) stated, everything therapists post online can be read by clients.

An interesting study surveyed 695 psychologists and psychology graduate students about their use of social networking websites (L. Taylor et al., 2010). The researchers noted that on many websites, anyone listed as a "friend" could also post on someone's page. This should be of great concern to therapists because someone other than the page owner could post photographs, private information, embarrassing stories, and so on. Some participants in the study found pictures of their clients on web pages of their family or friends, with no prior knowledge of these connections. Others reported being matched on dating sites with current or former patients. The researchers also noted that clients could send a "friend request" to their therapist, putting the clinician in a potential bind. How might the client feel if the request is rejected? However, accepting it could lead to a potential boundary violation and exposure of the therapist's personal information. Discussing these real-life interactions with clients is grist for the mill and may actually strengthen the therapeutic alliance. The clinician is in a position to model openness to discuss issues and resolve conflicts.

THERAPIST SELF-DISCLOSURE: THE BASICS

The nature of the therapeutic relationship is unusual. It is an intimate, warm, and personal connection between two people, but the focus is completely unequal and one sided. We expect clients to reveal as much as possible about themselves while we reveal little. The focus is on them as we do our best to help. Given the level of intimacy, it may feel like a friendship of the deepest level, but therapy is a professional relationship that concentrates on the patient's needs, not the therapist's (Knox & Hill, 2016). Thus, when therapists share anything about themselves, the balance in the relationship may shift in new directions.

Therapist self-disclosure can be defined as anything about the therapist made known to the client that is personal rather than professional (Zur, 2015). Broadly speaking, it can be "anything that is revealed about a therapist verbally, nonverbally, on purpose, by accident, wittingly, or unwittingly, inclusive of information discovered about them from another source" (Bloomgarden & Mennuti, 2009, p. 8). Intentional and personal sharing of information is what most therapists identify as self-disclosure (Zur, 2009), but patients can learn a great deal about us by observing our race, ethnicity, gender, age, accent, and office furnishings; how we dress; jewelry we may wear; and even our perfume or aftershave (J. E. Barnett, 2011; Peterson, 2002; Stricker, 2003; Zur, 2015). With the growth of telemedicine and therapists working outside the traditional office space, patients may even get a glimpse into the therapist's home. They may hear a dog bark or a baby cry or see family photographs or other identifying information. We can also accidentally run into patients at the grocery store, a school function, a place of worship, or another public place. This is more likely to happen in small and rural communities where, by virtue of the setting, our personal lives are more transparent (Zur, 2009). One therapist described an awkward dinner party with a client sitting across the table from her (she was able to leave early gracefully).

What therapists should avoid is disclosure of a personal nature that is not in the service of the client or the therapeutic relationship. Burdening a client with one's relationship issues or other hardships is never appropriate. It can create a role reversal in which the client finds themself in the role of taking care of the therapist (Zur, 2015). There are times, however, when disclosures of this sort are unavoidable. If the therapist has a medical condition that requires taking time off, being honest with patients is probably the most beneficial. As discussed later, pregnant therapists have no choice but to reveal this personal side of their lives.

To fully understand the special needs of reproductive patients, it is helpful to review how different theoretical orientations view therapist self-disclosure with clients in general. Traditional psychoanalytic theorists regard self-disclosure as a detriment to the therapeutic process because it shifts the focus from the patient to the therapist. The belief is that by introducing "real" elements of the therapist, the patient's fantasies about their therapist will be distorted. More recent psychoanalytic-psychodynamic thinking posits that strict neutrality is not only impossible to maintain but also that revealing an authentic self may enhance the therapeutic experience (Bloomgarden & Mennuti, 2009; Knox & Hill, 2003).

This contrasts with other theoretical positions that consider self-disclosure by the therapist to be an integral part of therapy. Humanistic therapists, for example, feel that self-disclosure promotes genuineness in the therapist–client relationship (Rogers, 1951) and, as a result, helps clients to be more candid and disclose more of themselves. The therapist's openness validates and normalizes the client's plight, helps reduce the power differential, and acknowledges that all human beings suffer (Ziv-Beiman, 2013). Similarly, feminist therapists promote self-disclosure to equalize power in the therapeutic dyad. They also share opinions regarding political and social issues so patients can give full informed consent; part of the philosophy is to transmit feminist values (Mahalik et al., 2000; Peterson, 2002; Ziv-Beiman, 2013). Cognitive behavior therapists view self-disclosure as a way to challenge irrational thinking by providing feedback, normalizing problems, and modeling corrective behavior (Goldfried et al., 2003). In relational-cultural therapy, the therapeutic connection is the key to healing (Jordan, 2000). It values diversity and explores the intersection of social and cultural identities, emphasizing the overlap of personal issues with sociopolitical and socioeconomic considerations (Frey, 2013). As such, a therapist's authentic reaction to the client's suffering validates the client's experience and allows for a shared healing process to take place (Comstock, 2009). Disclosure may also happen more frequently with certain clinical groups. Those seeking care for drug and alcohol addiction, for example, often seek out providers who are in recovery themselves. Likewise, LGBTQ+ clients may feel better understood, feel they can process feelings of marginality, and feel more accepted if their therapist is part of the community (J. E. Barnett, 2011; Patton, 2009; Zur, 2009).

What, When, Why, and How Much Should Therapists Self-Disclose?

Regardless of our theoretical orientation, we need to keep several questions in mind: Is it important for the patient to have this information? How will the information affect them? Will it be helpful or harmful? What is our motivation to disclose? Is it truly to benefit the patient, or does it derive from our own needs? What should or should not be said? The question of utmost importance is: Is this disclosure in the patient's best interest? The American Psychological Association (APA) has several guidelines relating to self-disclosure, including the *Ethical Principles of Psychologists and Code of Conduct* (hereafter referred to as the APA Ethics Code; APA, 2017), as do the National Association of Social Workers (2021) and the American Counseling Association (2014). APA Ethical Principle A states, "Psychologists strive to benefit those with whom they work and take care to do no harm" (APA, 2017, p. 3).

A good rule of thumb for all mental health practitioners, regardless of how they were trained, is to practice *nonmaleficence* (avoid doing harm to the patient) and *beneficence* (do what is helpful for the patient). This code of conduct is echoed in APA Ethical Standards 3.04 (Avoiding Harm) and 3.08 (Exploitative Relationships; APA, 2017). These standards recognize the potential power differential in the therapist–client relationship. Although the APA Ethics Code does not specifically discuss self-disclosure, "concerns about client exploitation often are raised in relations to therapist self-disclosure" (Peterson, 2002, p. 22). If therapists are disclosing for their own needs, disclosure clearly should not be part of the therapy and can be considered unethical. Each case should be uniquely assessed using sound clinical and thoughtful judgment. What should not be disclosed are therapists' current stressors, personal fantasies, finances, or sexual or relationship issues (L. Taylor et al., 2010).

Under what circumstances should a therapist disclose, and what information is appropriate when working with the psychotherapy population in general, and as is discussed in the next section, with reproductive patients in particular? As stated, self-disclosure should serve the client and the therapy (Knox & Hill, 2003). How a client perceives a disclosure is "dependent on the context and the place in time in the evolution of the therapeutic relationship" (Cornell, 2007, p. 54). If the therapeutic alliance is robust and positive, the chances are that the disclosure will be received in a constructive manner. Myers and Hayes (2006) found that when the therapeutic relationship was sound, therapists received higher ratings if they made disclosures (compared with no disclosures), but if the alliance was weak, disclosures were perceived negatively. Levitt et al. (2016) found that disclosures that humanized the therapist and those that conveyed a similarity between therapist and client were related to better clinical outcomes. These may be "aside" comments, perhaps about a movie they both saw, a recent holiday, or other aspects of life outside therapy. Similarly, a study of 185 therapist disclosure events found that disclosures of feelings and insights were rated higher than disclosures of facts (Pinto-Coelho et al., 2016).

Self-disclosure also depends on the client's traits. Some clients with poor boundaries or reality testing might find therapist disclosure unsettling. Peterson (2002) discussed the danger of disclosure to patients who might want to take care of the therapist, feeling burdened by what has been revealed. Caution should be taken, especially if a particular client might be inclined to take on the characteristics of the therapist. Other times, disclosure may be contraindicated if the client is self-absorbed and cannot see the therapist as a person in their own right. At one point, I moved office locations, and while I did not think of it as a self-disclosure, a patient decided that he could not continue treatment in the new office because it was "too upscale." My effort to process this change with him and his feelings that he did not deserve a new office were not successful, and his treatment was terminated.

Clearly, self-disclosures are nuanced and variable. Therapists should be aware of and attuned to the patient's history and needs, but the length of time a client is in treatment and the strength of the therapeutic alliance are also important factors to be considered in self-disclosure. Depending on the nature of the therapy, too much disclosure too early on in treatment, before a strong and safe attachment to the therapist is established, may be less effective. Gibson (2012) described the changing nature of disclosure from the beginning to the end of therapy. In the beginning, what gets disclosed may be more informational and biographical, but as treatment continues, the therapist might share more emotional or immediate experiences with the client. These may be used in the service of the therapy; what is relevant to the patient can strengthen the relationship and facilitate a strong alliance. Toward the end of treatment, clients may want to know more about the "real" person (Gelso, 2011). Self-disclosures around termination may be effective in making the therapist more human (Knox & Hill, 2003). Gelso (2011) described the ending of the therapeutic relationship: "Indelibly left are their humanness and their human experience of the ending of their relationship" (p. 100).

Knox and Hill (2003) identified seven different types of therapist self-disclosure:

- *facts*: disclosing one's credentials and professional experience
- *feelings*: describing one's feelings in situations comparable to what the patient is describing
- *insight*: sharing perceptions of one's life as similar to the patient's
- *strategy*: discussing how the therapist would handle a similar circumstance

- *reassurance or support*: normalizing the patient's feelings by revealing one's own
- *challenge*: divulging personal experience that is the same as the patient's
- *immediacy*: relating the patient's behavior with others to analogous behaviors the patient displays with the therapist

Clinicians may choose to disclose to model behavior or emotional expression, normalize clients' reactions, provide empathy and reassurance, and increase the sense of similarity between the therapist and client (Peterson, 2002). As discussed later, these can be helpful justifications for self-disclosure when working with reproductive patients.

If we are to disclose to clients, how much or how little should be expressed? One study found that increases in therapist self-disclosure decreased patients' symptoms; patients also reported liking their therapist more (Barrett & Berman, 2001). Psychologist Judith Ruskay Rabinor, discussing self-disclosures in her practice, described them as turning points, not only for her patients but also for herself (Rabinor, 2009). Irvin Yalom stated,

> If therapist disclosure were to be graded on a continuum, I am certain I would be placed on the high end. Yet I have never had the experience of disclosing too much. On the contrary, I have always facilitated therapy when I have shared some facet of myself. (Yalom, as cited in Rabinor, 2009, p. 55)

The ability that disclosures can have in facilitating treatment can be powerful. Too much self-disclosure, however, can be overwhelming. Patients may feel confused or burdened by too much information, feeling distracted from their therapeutic needs. The last thing they need is to worry about us or, in a role reversal, feel like they have to take care of us. However, too little disclosure can also pose problems. There is a risk that nondisclosing therapists will be viewed as cold, rigid, uncaring, and aloof. The danger is a disruption to the therapeutic alliance and, potentially, the termination of therapy. The bottom line is that disclosure can be an effective treatment tool, but it should be used judiciously and only when it can promote therapeutic goals (Barrett & Berman, 2001; Hill & Knox, 2001; Knox & Hill, 2003; Peterson, 2002; Stricker, 2003; Zur, 2009). Table 9.1 lists some of the benefits and risks of self-disclosure in the therapy setting.

Self-Disclosure With Reproductive Patients

With pregnancy and children at the forefront of their attention, it is not unusual for patients with reproductive concerns to wonder about their therapist's parental status. As noted, probably the most frequently asked question is, "Do you have any children?" Or they may ask in a less direct manner,

TABLE 9.1. Benefits and Risks of Therapist Self-Disclosure

Benefits of therapist self-disclosure	Risks of therapist self-disclosure
Builds therapeutic alliance	Focus is on therapist and not client
Models self-expression	May feel burdensome to client
Increases trust	Client may feel need to take care of therapist
Decreases sense of isolation	May create a role reversal
Normalizes and validates	May interfere with client's needs
Decreases power differential	Does not promote therapeutic goal
Increases client self-disclosure	May feel unsafe
Promotes viewing therapist as human	Negatively changes feelings about therapist

"Why do you specialize in this area?" For therapists not working with reproductive patients, these questions may seem innocent and innocuous; it may feel equivalent to a patient asking where the therapist went to school. For patients coping with reproductive trauma and loss, however, these questions are invariably emotionally loaded. Reproductive patients are vulnerable, grief stricken, and traumatized and may suffer deep narcissistic wounds. Therefore, questions about their therapist's reproductive circumstances can mean many different things. They may wonder if their therapist is a friend or foe; in other words, did the therapist have difficulty conceiving too, or did they sail through it all? They may wonder, "Will you understand?" Or are you like other well-intentioned but misguided people who offer advice and are insensitive to the enormity of their loss? If you hesitate in your response, will that make the patient feel even more damaged? If you do not disclose, will the patient feel unworthy, as if you look down on them or do not trust them? If you do disclose, what does it mean to the patient? It goes without saying that just because a client asks for personal information, we are not obligated to share it, but either way, there may be consequences. So many thoughts are swirling around, deliberating on the best response to give to that particular client, all in a manner of seconds.

As we know, not all therapists who work in the field of reproductive psychology have had their own reproductive trauma. Likewise, therapists will be at various stages in their lives regarding reproduction, ranging from some not ready to have children to some actively trying to others being well past reproductive age. The approach to how one answers the elephant-in-the-room question "Do you have kids?" will depend on several factors: where you are in your own reproductive story (discussed in the next chapter), whether you have children, whether you have experienced a reproductive crisis, what you think it will mean to your client, and how comfortable you are in sharing this kind of information. In general, returning the attention to the client is essential after delivering any self-disclosure. The implicit message is that the focus is on the client, not the therapist (Knox & Hill, 2003).

Using the seven disclosure categories that Knox and Hill (2003) proposed, we can walk through a range of disclosures about having children or not, being in treatment for infertility, and suffering through losses and how clients might respond to what the therapist may say. "Clearly, these different types of disclosures are used at different times and can have different impacts on the therapy process" (Knox & Hill, 2003, p. 530). Obviously, not every scenario will be possible to predict, but for therapists, being prepared is far better than being caught off guard and stumbling through a difficult therapeutic moment, which can be important to the client and their growth.

Disclosures of Facts

Disclosures of facts take place when therapy is just beginning. Perhaps a new client would like to know your training or where you are from. In reading the literature on these types of disclosures, time and again, one's parental status is included in these kinds of "facts." Perhaps it is a nonissue with the general psychotherapy patient, but it is at the crux of the therapeutic matter with reproductive patients. What is most salient is what it means to the patient. Often, it can be helpful to ask just that. Sometimes saying, "I am happy to answer your question, but what would it mean to you if I did have children or didn't?" The facts then become fodder for a deeper conversation. The stage is set for how seriously you take the patient's concerns. In turning the question back onto the patient's needs and back to the issues of the therapy, it is less about your answer and more about your ability to listen for their pain.

Disclosures of Feelings

Disclosure of feelings has to do with the feelings the therapist and patient may share. A common theme for reproductive patients is the uncertainty of what may happen and the lack of control that permeates a wide variety of circumstances: "Will I produce enough eggs? Will I miscarry again? Will my baby survive the night in the neonatal intensive care unit?" Disclosure in this circumstance has less to do with the therapist sharing their specific experience and more to do with sharing their feelings. Being able to sum up what a patient is feeling is a way of building rapport and acknowledging an understanding of their feelings—for example, "As I hear you talking about your story, so much of it feels frightening because so much of it is out of your control. You don't know how this is going to turn out."

Disclosures of Insight

Disclosures of insight are more deeply rooted in how you, the therapist, might be affected by a similar situation. For example, one patient struggling with fertility issues described how upset she got when a friend asked her if she ever thought about adoption: "I know she was trying to be supportive, but it just made me so angry. Like I never had heard of adoption before." The therapist responded, "I've been in situations like that myself, where a friend just doesn't understand. I have even found it difficult to continue certain friendships," to which the patient replied, "Yes! Exactly! And then I start to feel like a bad friend! I need to stop worrying about other people and take care of me." Because this was a theme for her in therapy, it was a step forward for this patient not to take responsibility for everything, especially her reproductive difficulties.

Disclosures of Strategy

When patients are going "down the rabbit hole," as they often do during a reproductive trauma, it can be helpful for therapists to help untangle their negative thinking and emotional stasis. In helping them get "unstuck" and find equilibrium, disclosing what we might do and how we might handle the situation can be valuable. It is almost as if we become the patient's executive function at that moment by sharing how we would approach the problem. One patient, who had a history of sexual abuse, was told by her male doctor that he was going to get her pregnant. He was likely trying to convey encouragement, but the way it was said was triggering for her. Once again, she felt trapped in a situation by a male and could not see a clear way out. Knowing there were other female doctors in the same practice, the therapist suggested she transfer her care. As carefully as possible, he said, "If I were in your position, I might consider switching doctors. You don't have to keep seeing this doctor just because you started out with him." The patient was not sure: "Do you think I can do that? They won't be angry with me?" The therapist reassured her that it happens all the time. There was a wave of relief in the room. Giving her permission by disclosing a viable exit strategy enabled her to move forward.

Another example of a strategy disclosure can be seen in a patient who was obsessed with doing research. This is a common occurrence with reproductive clients, who often mobilize their lack of control over their reproductive lives into the search for the perfect doctor, acupuncturist, nutritionist, or psychotherapist. Understandably, they do not want to leave any stone unturned and may go through cycle after cycle, trying different treatments to maintain a sense of hope. After establishing a good rapport with one such client, the therapist suggested a strategy that might ease some of the pressure the client was putting on themself: "Of course, you want to do everything right. Sometimes, in these kinds of situations, it helps me to think of what's good enough instead of what's perfect. I know 'good enough' doesn't sound, well, good enough, but when I've tried to make things perfect, it has created more stress and anxiety for me than it relieves." Not only did this intervention establish a strategy for reducing the patient's anxiety it also humanized the normal and expected response to the desire to find control.

Disclosures of Reassurance and Support

We probably make disclosures of reassurance and support without even realizing it. If a woman starts treatment after a miscarriage and has been told by well-meaning people to move on from it, she may be depressed and worried that she cannot manage her feelings. A reassuring response might be, "Of course, you feel down. You just lost your baby. I would feel the same way. This is not something that you can just easily move on from. You are grieving." Not only does this disclosure ("I would feel the same way") let her know that it is normal to grieve a pregnancy loss but it also lets her know that it is something that should not be minimized.

Disclosures of Challenge

While other self-disclosures may reveal something about the therapist's feelings or ways of handling a particularly challenging situation, disclosures of challenge reveal more about the therapist's experiences, specifically about their reproductive challenges as they relate to the client's. If both the client and therapist have struggled with infertility, the therapist might reveal her own trauma: "I have also gone through years of trying to have a baby. I know for myself how much stress this can cause. Your feelings are normal; I felt this way too." A benefit from this type of disclosure is that patients may feel that their therapist trusts them and that therapists are real human beings with their own issues; a disclosure of this sort helps patients not feel alone, thus enhancing the therapeutic alliance (Barnett, 2011; Knox & Hill, 2003). Talking about one's hardships, however, is not without risk. It may feel like too much of a burden on the patient to know personal information about their therapist.

It also makes a difference where therapists are in their reproductive stories. As discussed in the next chapter, if the therapist discloses about ongoing struggles, they might inappropriately be using the therapy for their own needs and not be effective in helping their client. As Knox and Hill (2003) recommended, if possible, "therapists [should] limit their disclosures to those issues with which they no longer struggle" (p. 538).

Disclosures of Immediacy

Disclosures of immediacy refer to interactions that happen within the therapy relationship itself. They are in-the-moment responses from the therapist about something occurring within therapy, and in this sense, they are somewhat different from the other types of disclosure previously discussed. They focus on the therapist's reaction to the immediacy of the moment rather than on other types of reflections the therapist might share.

For example, consider an infertility patient who has come to the end of the possibility of using her own gametes to have a child. She and her therapist have focused on this loss and the grief it entails but also on other possibilities of creating a family, including using an egg donor or adoption. The patient had discussed using a donor with her partner; both felt it was not the right choice. They did not want one parent to have a genetic connection with a child and not the other.

It seemed logical to the therapist, although not a given, that they might consider adoption. When this was broached in therapy, the patient stopped making eye contact, looked at the clock, and went silent, all reactions not characteristic of the patient. The therapist disclosed her observation and noted the changes in the patient: "What just happened?" This led to an opportunity to discuss some underlying issues the patient had kept hidden from the therapist. The patient then revealed that she had relinquished a child for adoption as a teenager and had never really processed all the feelings surrounding that event. She felt forced into the decision by her parents and could not disentangle her guilt about it from feelings about infertility. Not only was she afraid to discuss it with her therapist but she had also not told her husband. How could they possibly consider adoption when all this was swirling inside her and causing great angst? It became clear that the therapy had taken a shift with the therapist's perception, disclosing it, and addressing the underlying issues from the past.

Naomi and Alex: Taking a Risk With Disclosure in Treatment

In this section, we discuss a hypothetical case and how you, the therapist, might respond to a client's questions about you. As a reminder, there is no right way to approach each unique client and their needs. As discussed, factors regarding disclosure can depend on the strength of the therapeutic alliance (Hanson, 2005; Myers & Hayes, 2006), patient characteristics and personality (Peterson, 2002), and stage of treatment (Barnett, 2011; Gelso, 2011). Other factors that must be considered are your needs, your training, your theoretical perspective, where you are in your life, and whether there are personal crises you are contending with—in particular your own reproductive trauma (Bloomgarden & Mennuti, 2009; Knox & Hill; 2003; Mahalik et al., 2000; Patton, 2009; Peterson, 2002; Ziv-Beiman, 2013). As reported, disclosure is riskier if the therapist's issues have not been resolved (Knox & Hill, 2003).

A new patient, Naomi, calls to set up an appointment.[1] She has been referred from her fertility clinic to help her and her partner, Alex, process decisions in the next steps of their treatment. Whether you are a provider embedded in the clinic or private practice, a disclosure about you as a professional who works with reproductive patients has already been established. She lets you know that she and Alex are not on the same page, which has made moving forward impossible.

Naomi is 38 years old, and Alex is 40. Both are professionals and doing well in their careers. When taking a history of their fertility struggles, you are conscious of where they sit in the consulting room, who does most of the talking, and how they interact. They unsuccessfully tried two rounds of intrauterine insemination and are trying to decide whether to move on to in vitro fertilization, as recommended by their doctor. Naomi is ready to jump in, but Alex is more hesitant. He is cynical about the clinic and wonders how much of their recommendation is about improving his and Naomi's chances and how much is about "lining their pockets." As part of your intake, you explore their relationship, how they met, how long they have been together, and how they have coped with other tough decisions. About 5 to 10 minutes before the end of the session, you ask if there is anything else they would like to let you know in this first meeting or if there are any questions for you. Alex wants to be reassured that therapy will be covered by insurance; Naomi asks, "Do you have kids?"

The most critical concern is how your response will facilitate this couple's needs and the therapy. How will it be received? Because this is the first session, and you are just getting to know them, you may not be sure what to do. You certainly do not want to be dismissive, nor do you want to overwhelm them with information about yourself. One factor in this decision-making equation is Naomi and Alex; the other factor that needs just as much consideration is you. How you respond may depend on where you are in your reproductive story (see Chapter 10). If, for example, you do have children and are past trying to build a family, you may feel more at ease with revealing your parental status. In this case, you may say, "Yes, I do have children, but I,

---

[1] The case of Naomi and Alex has been modified to disguise the patients' identities and protect confidentiality.

too, struggled to have them." At the other end of the spectrum, if you are in the midst of fertility treatment yourself, you might say, "No, I don't have children yet, but I'm hoping to," or you might feel comfortable revealing more: "No I don't have children, and I'm going through my own struggles with it." Note that all these answers are succinct without providing great detail about your experience. However you answer, the next question should come from you, directed back to them: "How does this make you feel?"

Yet another approach to answering this direct question is to say, "I am happy to answer you, but I'd like to explore this with you a bit more first." Sometimes, it helps to have a better understanding of why this particular question is being posed before you decide to answer it. The patient's fantasies can then be used to gain a deeper sense of their pain and needs. After a discussion of this sort, you may ask the client if they still want to know the answer, giving them a sense of control. Whether you delve into their ideas about you first and then answer or answer directly and then uncover their feelings, the point is that your answer leads to further investigation about them and their feelings.

This is key: No matter what your response is, moving the focus away from you and returning it to the patient is critical. Asking Naomi and Alex how your disclosure to them feels is a perfect way to bring it back to their therapy and issues. Knox and Hill (2003) noted that the therapist should "follow their revelation with the implicit message that the proper focus of the therapeutic work is on the client, not the therapist" (p. 536).

Let us consider what your disclosure to Naomi and Alex might mean to them:

- You are approachable and want to know more about them. You are open to discussing any feelings they may have.

- You are a real human with genuine emotions and have a positive regard for them. You are building a relationship of trust.

- Perhaps you have created a space where they feel less alone and feel safe.

- You may be serving as a role model. By disclosing something about yourself and then investigating their feelings about it, you have set the stage for their comfort in disclosing more about themselves.

- You are normalizing and validating that fertility treatment is fraught with painful emotional and psychological distress, which often comes out as conflicts in the couple.

At the end of the first session with Naomi and Alex, you may let them know that the decision to continue therapy with you is up to them. In some ways, this, too, is a disclosure: We serve as *expert companions* in this process (Tedeschi et al., 2015) in our effort to promote healing and growth (see Chapter 8). Our role is to be a facilitator, not a decision maker. In giving Naomi and Alex control over their treatment, you are communicating that you respect and value their input and are happy to be part of their team.

SUMMARY

Gone are the days when a mental health practitioner is "like a mirror," as Freud suggested, only reflecting what the patient reveals (S. Freud, 1912/2000, p. 18). There is more information about us through our professional and/or personal online presence than we may realize. What remains true is that patients are curious about who we are as people. While this is the case for any psychotherapy client, it may be particularly true for reproductive patients. Being aware of the risks and benefits of therapist self-disclosure is necessary; when used judiciously, thoughtfully, and with great care, self-disclosure can be an effective tool in helping clients work through the trauma of infertility and pregnancy loss and rebuild their lives.

10 THE THERAPIST'S REPRODUCTIVE STORY

The doctor is effective only when he himself is affected. Only the wounded
physician heals.

—C. G. Jung, *Memories, Dreams, and Reflections*

Clients enter therapy or pursue third-party consultations while they are in
the middle of a personal reproductive story that is not going as they thought
it would. It is a time of great upheaval; not only are they grieving the loss of
a real or imagined baby but they may also be feeling bad about themselves
and their relationships with their partner, family, and/or friends and may be
struggling with how to make the future meaningful.

What is often not spoken about is that we—as mental health professionals
and human beings—have reproductive stories as well. Our stories have an
impact on the clinical work we do. We not only call on our professional
training as we treat clients but we also use our personal reflections and life
experiences to add to the therapeutic work. Being aware of our conflicts and
wounds—especially if they include reproductive trauma—allows us to use

https://doi.org/10.1037/0000400-010
Reproductive Trauma: Psychotherapy With Clients Experiencing Infertility and
Pregnancy Loss, Second Edition, by J. Jaffe

them constructively in the service of our clients. This chapter focuses on the psychological narrative of the mental health professional and the powerful effect our story can have on the work we do.

THE WOUNDED HEALER

The concept of the wounded healer can be traced back to Greek mythology. In the myth, Chiron, known as the wise centaur, was famous for healing the sick and teaching healing arts to others. As the story goes, a stray arrow shot by Heracles wounded Chiron. Despite being wounded, he continued to heal the sick and injured. Even with all his wisdom, however, Chiron was not able to heal himself and was in excruciating pain, but being immortal, he could not die. In the end, Chiron exchanged his immortality to free Prometheus. (Prometheus was also in agonizing pain. As a punishment for stealing fire from the gods to give to humans, Prometheus was bound to a rock where an eagle pecked out his liver every day, only to have it grow back, with the cycle repeating again and again). Chiron gave his life to healing others, and even in death, he sacrificed himself to save another (Burton, 2021; Daneault, 2008; D'Aulaire & D'Aulaire, 1962).

Jung (1951) referenced the wounded healer as an archetype, drawing from the myth of Chiron and applying it to psychology. Jung believed that wounded healers could develop insight from their experiences and use it to help others. It has also been suggested that understanding one's wounds is an "*essential component* of compassion and healing" (P. Martin, 2011, p. 13). It is the ability to draw on our suffering—which no one is immune to—and use it in the service of helping and healing that can strengthen empathic connections with patients. As described by Zerubavel and Wright (2012):

> Importantly, being wounded in itself does not produce the potential to heal; rather, healing potential is generated through the process of recovery. Thus, the more healers can understand their own wounds and journey of recovery, the better position they are in to guide others through such a process, while recognizing that each person's journey is unique. (p. 482)

In other words, just because therapists have been wounded does not make them experts. This is a critically important point because we do not want to assume that our personal experience is similar to that of the client we are treating. The process of understanding and managing the wound is what matters; the therapist's self-reflection and growth prevent interference with the patient's therapy and the therapeutic relationship.

How much our wounds have healed is yet another significant issue. If the counselor's wounds are not mended—or mended enough—the client's needs may get sidelined (Gelso & Hayes, 2007). As discussed in Chapter 9, self-disclosure is much riskier if the therapist is in the midst of unresolved issues (Knox & Hill, 2003). Even if no disclosures are made, our unhealed psychological injuries can interfere with our role as healers. Indeed, if the wound is fresh, the therapist may lose objectivity; they may view their clients' needs from their self-centered vantage point.

Psychotherapists and counselors frequently choose this profession because of their own suffering; painful childhood experiences have often been cited as the motivation to enter the field of psychology (Barnett, 2007). Research suggests a link between one's history of trauma and the desire to specialize in trauma care (Weingarten, 2010). As noted, many reproductive mental health practitioners who have had their own reproductive crises choose to specialize in treating clients who are struggling to create a family (S. N. Covington & Marosek, 1999; Marrero, 2013). We may identify with patients' feelings of loss, trauma, grief, or disenfranchisement. As long as we can use what we have learned from our experiences in the service of the client, we are doing a good job.

One thing is important to note here: Even if our wounds are healed—or mostly healed—they may get reactivated in the process of doing therapy with reproductive clients. Hearing their stories may trigger feelings that we need to address. In this sense, we can view healing as an ongoing process for clients as well as ourselves. The importance of caring for our mental health and well-being (see Chapter 12) cannot be stressed enough.

STORIES FROM WOUNDED HEALERS

Talking about our wounds to colleagues, supervisors, students, or the general public may feel risky. What will they think of us? Will they judge the quality of our work and think we are impaired or incompetent? When I was doing research for my dissertation, one participant, a senior psychologist, casually mentioned that he suffered from depression. As a budding psychologist, I remember feeling stunned by his confession. Was that not something unspeakable? Was it really okay to admit to being human? Clearly, it is something that has stuck with me these many years.

As often happens in the mental health profession, we do not share our wounds. We may fear that opening up about our psychological injuries might be interpreted as a deficiency in the work of a mental health practitioner.

The concerns about judgment in the eyes of others may result in secrecy and shame (Zerubavel & Wright, 2012). Despite that, several mental health professionals have bravely written about their own wounds and how their struggles affected their clinical work. As discussed later, some of these writers dealt specifically with reproductive loss and trauma. We can learn a great deal from their example and how they managed the impact of their losses on their clients.

One such writer, the psychoanalyst Lynn Leibowitz (2009), decided to remain child free after trying unsuccessfully for 5 years to have children. The cases she highlighted focused on the ever-present question "Do you have children?" (as discussed in Chapter 9, this volume) and what that might mean to different patients. In her journey from infertility to a child-free life, she noted the changes in herself in doing therapy, the evolution in how she approached disclosure to patients, and the discovery of how her trauma could mean vastly different things to each patient. While going through infertility treatment early in her career, she did not routinely answer these kinds of questions without exploring the patient's fantasies first. One patient, for example, told her that she did not seem like a mother because she was not warm or caring (surprising to Leibowitz and not something she felt about herself). Another patient assumed she was not a parent because she did not look tired or out of shape, an assumption and fantasy that this patient had about what a mother should be.

These encounters were painful for Leibowitz; they were not just about her inability to have children but also about how her patients perceived her. Leibowitz stated, "Revealing personal information is a form of self-disclosure, but the factual disclosure is not as significant as the meaning behind the questions and behind my choice to disclose" (2009, p. 84). By exposing parts of herself, she was able to understand her patients better and use their fantasies about her to dig deeper into their psychological state. This exemplifies how important it is not to assume the inner workings of a patient but to investigate what it means to them.

Another example is of a therapist who made the decision not to disclose to her patient; both were going through a reproductive trauma at the same time. Jo Ellen Patterson (2009) was actively pursuing fertility treatments while working with a couple whose child was disabled: "We were similar ages and all struggling with a major developmental milestone—the transition to parenthood—that had gone awry" (p. 24). Instead of sharing any information about her personal life, Patterson used her experience of grief and loss in working with this couple. She was able to garner more empathy and understanding for them without disclosing anything about her own struggle.

Although the situation for her and the couple were vastly different, the psychological issues—the dissolution of their reproductive stories—were the same.

There are times when the wounds of the therapist are impossible to keep hidden, and disclosure becomes a necessary part of the treatment. Dana Comstock (2009), who had been teaching at a university as well as seeing patients, lost her daughter about halfway through the pregnancy. This medical emergency, followed by a 3-month leave of absence, made it impossible not to disclose the stillbirth. Her experience when returning to work was primarily positive as she discussed her loss with clients as it affected them. She stated, "Those explorations felt really different in the context of my now being a 'touchable' therapist, versus being perceived as 'untouchable' prior to my loss" (p. 262). Although she did not go into details, simply stating that she had lost a baby, she described her woundedness as enabling her to shift to a deeper level with her clients.

For Barbara Gerson (2009), disclosure occurred because she was put on bed rest, followed by the termination of her pregnancy. She described this difficult time and the raw feelings it evoked in some of her clients. Some became overwhelmed with their own grief; others were angered by the loss of their fantasy of her as the omnipotent therapist. As difficult as this was for her, she noted that it elicited some of the most intense therapy as she and her patients confronted these deep-seated feelings together. Similarly, Julie Bindeman (2019) discussed the termination of two of her pregnancies because of medical reasons. She described her return to work after each loss, her raw emotional state, and the impact on her clients, forging deeper connections with them in exploring the patterns of their lives.

When asked to write about my own story, realizing that the written word was a disclosure of great magnitude, I struggled with how to manage it (see Jaffe, 2015). Like many of us, I had been trained to see disclosure as a taboo. However, research and clinical practice have taught me that it is necessary under the right circumstances, and that not revealing one's wounds can be detrimental to the therapeutic relationship. It should be noted that just because I have disclosed to some clients does not mean I disclose to all. I have chosen to disclose to patients when they have asked a direct question, and my answer depends on their particular situation, our therapeutic relationship, and my clinical judgment.

My story consisted of multiple miscarriages, several years of fertility treatments, and unknowns. If and when clients ask, I give a simple response: "I, too, had struggles having children." The focus then turns back to them in exploring how learning about my story made them feel. Patients often want to know how my story turned out; was I able to have children after all? The answer is yes, but this is an essential question to explore with them in depth. I have found that most clients feel comforted knowing I had a "happy ending"; it seems to provide a sense of hope. I also stress that their reproductive story could have any number of endings and that our job together is to help them find resolution, with or without children.

All these therapists, including myself, have used their wounds—whether they disclose them to clients or not—to serve the therapeutic needs of their patients. Each of these practitioners has discussed the importance of assessing the unique psychological needs of a particular patient or couple, the therapeutic alliance and trust that has been established or is being created, and the clinical judgment of the therapist. What may be right for one client may not be right for another. Exposing our wounds is risky and challenging, but doing so with thoughtfulness and care can be a valuable therapeutic tool (Leibowitz, 2009; Patterson, 2009).

Speaking openly about our wounds is much easier if they have healed. A scar may be left behind as a lingering reminder, but it is no longer "raw, open, and vulnerable to infection" (Zerubavel & Wright, 2012, p. 484). Research points out that disclosure is much more precarious if the therapist's issues are still current and not yet resolved (Knox & Hill, 2003). Therapists must do enough of their own healing to be able to assist others with comparable experiences (Anonymous, 2007). Clinicians who have some distance from their reproductive journey are less likely to be vulnerable to boundary violations than those who are currently going through family building.

PREGNANCY AND THERAPY: EFFECTS ON PATIENTS AND THERAPISTS

This section focuses on the impact pregnancy can have on the general clinical population. This is followed by a discussion (in Chapter 11) of the unique challenges a therapist's pregnancy can have when working with clients in the middle of their reproductive stories.

Research has demonstrated that the pregnancy of a therapist can be challenging for all psychotherapy patients, not just reproductive patients; it may interfere with the therapeutic process, signaling shifts in the therapist's availability, attention, and priorities. Some clients will "act out" by becoming more needy for fear of abandonment by their therapist, and others may miss sessions or leave therapy prematurely (Way et al., 2019). Patients may display feelings of jealousy toward the baby; a kind of sibling rivalry between the patient and the therapist's unborn baby may develop. Patients may fear that their therapist will focus more on the baby and less on them (L. Covington

& Jaffe, 2022). However, the bond between the patient and therapist may deepen as the therapist becomes more of a real person. Indeed, the pregnancy can act as a catalyst for the emotional growth of both the patient and the therapist (Dombo & Bass, 2013).

What are some of the changes that the therapist's pregnancy can have on treatment? A meta-analysis surveyed several studies that looked at therapists during their pregnancies and postpartum periods (Way et al., 2019). Four key themes were found that help to illuminate the multiple ways pregnancy can affect the therapist, client, therapeutic relationship, and treatment: identity changes, the necessity for disclosure, therapeutic challenges, and guilt.

Identity Changes

The biological changes of pregnancy can impact the therapist's ability to concentrate. It is hard to think about a patient if the therapist is focused on what is physically happening to her. She may be experiencing nausea, excessive tiredness, heartburn, back pain, or any number of the physical discomforts that come with pregnancy. It is to be expected that her normal state of nurturing a client may now be getting redirected toward herself and her unborn baby.

The identity shift that therapists undergo is not just about the physical changes of pregnancy. A shift also occurs psychologically, especially for first-time parents. Colarusso (1990) suggested that the transition to parenthood is a pivotal point in a person's life. It can be seen as a catalyst in redefining oneself. Indeed, it was found that pregnancy caused therapists to reevaluate their personal and professional identities (F. M. D. Schmidt et al., 2015). This new identity, self as parent, can be of concern for some therapists because they worry they will not be able to maintain their professional and parenthood selves concurrently. Therapists described feeling split into two kinds of caregiving roles—one with patients and the other with their unborn child. A third person had entered the therapy room—the unborn baby—thus dividing the therapist's attention. "The dyadic relatedness turns into a triadic form of interaction as a whole new person, much closer to the therapist, now sits between her and the client, both literally and figuratively" (Sharma, 2020, p. 256). No longer able to maintain a position of neutrality, her private life has been exposed.

Pregnancy Disclosure

The second theme addressed in the research was disclosure (Way et al., 2019). As discussed in the previous chapter, there are times when therapist self-disclosure is unavoidable; pregnancy is clearly one of those times. Telemedicine may make the need for disclosure less pressing because it can potentially be hidden for a longer time, but even then, a therapist's pregnancy must eventually be addressed. For obvious reasons, a pregnant person's changing body necessitates disclosure, but for nonpregnant partners in relationships who may be taking parental leave, giving patients fair warning of an upcoming absence is essential.

Across the board, therapists seem to struggle with the timing of pregnancy disclosure. Some analytic thinking promotes waiting to discuss a pregnancy until the client brings it up. Indeed, the majority of therapists waited until the second and third trimesters. However, as noted by Dombo and Bass (2013), asking a woman if she is pregnant is contrary to social norms. Is the therapist pregnant, or is she putting on weight? What an uncomfortable and anxiety-ridden position for both patient and therapist. It is understandable that a clinician might want to wait until she feels the pregnancy is secure, especially if she has had a history of pregnancy loss, but keeping the news of pregnancy from clients for too long can damage trust and rapport.

Regardless of when the disclosure is made, research suggests it can be anxiety provoking for both the therapist and the patient because it reveals a part of the therapist's personal life. There is no right way to reveal a therapist's pregnancy. Factors such as the stage of treatment, level of mutual trust, patient's diagnosis, and feelings the client has regarding the therapist and vice versa all contribute to a need for a case-by-case evaluation and use of one's clinical judgment.

Therapeutic Challenges

According to Way's et al. (2019) analysis, clinicians' pregnancies brought up new therapeutic challenges, with some negative developments but also many positive ones. Not surprisingly, the pregnancy elicited more personal questions, such as the therapist's marital status, sexual orientation, and whether this was planned or accidental. While this kind of questioning breached the "normal" dimensions of therapist–client boundaries, it also allowed the therapist to become more "real." The increased candor was seen as a benefit to the therapeutic alliance—the therapist was no longer just "a therapist"; the pregnancy added depth to the clinical dyad and the therapy (Gerson, 2009; F. M. D. Schmidt et al., 2015; Wolfe, 2013).

Pregnancy also elicited highly charged, difficult material to process in treatment. Themes of sibling rivalry (between the patient and the unborn child), fear of abandonment, and separation anxiety were cited. Jealousy and feelings of being replaced intensified the work. Therapists felt more vulnerable when patients became angry—whether toward the therapist for shifting her focus or the baby for causing the shift (Way et al., 2019). There can be a tendency for clients to act out their anger by arriving late, missing sessions, or abandoning treatment entirely (F. M. D. Schmidt et al., 2015). One troubling theme occurs when the patient has fantasies of the therapist's pregnancy demise. This intense and disturbing material—for both the therapist and patient—may be so distressing that exploring or confronting it is too painful, and it is often left unexplored (L. Covington & Jaffe, 2022; Gerson, 2009; Way et al., 2019).

Guilt

There are times throughout a pregnancy when physical demands, such as nausea, fetal movements, or brain fog, can distract a therapist while in session. With attention divided, therapists have reported feeling inadequate in their role. An inability to concentrate was viewed by many therapists as indicative of poor performance (Way et al., 2019). Some therapists felt guilty for not being available enough for their patients (Dombo & Bass, 2013), causing them to do more to meet the needs of clients. Way et al. (2019) noted that some therapists prioritize their clients' well-being over their own health, holding sessions despite their physical distress. Guilt was one of the most profound feelings reported, especially in primiparous therapists. It is as if the therapist somehow willfully designed her pregnancy to interfere with her patients' needs. This may become even more highlighted as the therapist prepares for parental leave (F. M. D. Schmidt et al., 2015). The combination of therapists feeling inadequate, vulnerable, and concerned about abandoning clients, in concert with reactions from particularly needy patients, contributed to overwhelming feelings of guilt.

Parental Leave

Guilty feelings can be exacerbated by the therapist's necessary parental leave. Regardless of how much leave a therapist takes, the "fourth trimester" is generally considered to be the first 3 months postpartum. How much time a therapist takes off can be dictated by financial constraints, the needs of the newborn, and personal needs. It is a significantly challenging time, with recovery from the birth, hormonal and physical changes, sleep deprivation, and the trials of caring for a newborn. It can also be a time of emotional disequilibrium as new parents redefine their identities, a time when caring for patients is replaced with caring for a new baby and oneself (L. Covington & Jaffe, 2022).

Patients need to be prepared for their therapist's parental leave; it has been recommended that therapists do not work right up until the end of the pregnancy but rather pick a date to begin their leave, with a contingency plan should the baby come early (Dombo & Bass, 2013). Because due dates are just estimates and difficult to predict, pausing treatment on a tentative date can increase a client's anxiety. Parental leave can elevate patients' feelings of abandonment, separation, anger, and neediness. Having witnessed the pregnancy, they are suddenly excluded from the therapist's life. On the other side, therapist's feelings—that they have abandoned their patients—can be just as intense. Jane Waldman (2003) recounted her maternity leave: "The therapist may have a very difficult time admitting both to herself and the patient that the pregnancy actually might not be the best thing for the patient; that the timing of the pregnancy and maternity leave might be especially bad for a particular individual" (p. 58). Part of the guilt is that the patient might be harmed because of the therapist. While not intentional, therapists may overcompensate by arranging extra interim coverage, continuing to maintain contact, or shortening their leave (Way et al., 2019).

Organizing the leave needs to be thought of as part of the therapy (F. M. D. Schmidt et al., 2015). There are several options, all dependent on what is best for the client. One possibility is to transfer care to another clinician—either temporarily or permanently. Another is for the client to wait for the therapist to return to work or use it as a natural point in the therapy to try termination. It may also be a time when alternative, adjunct therapies could be pursued (Dombo & Bass, 2013). While this can be a stressful time, with many intense feelings arising on both sides, the collaborative work between the therapist and client in making a plan can prove therapeutic and promote growth.

Parental leave may come as a surprise to clients of expectant fathers (gay, straight, or other) or nonpregnant partners in lesbian relationships because they have not witnessed the progression of the pregnancy. Fallon and Brabender (2003) noted that none of the male therapists they interviewed told their patients about expecting a baby during their partner's pregnancy. Clients' reactions to learning the news ran the gamut from feeling hurt and betrayed to feeling closer to the therapist for being more real to being nonplussed. Similarly, in cases of adoption, where parents may have to drop everything at a moment's notice, preparation for parental leave is difficult to predict. Adoption may require a special kind of collaboration with patients; they need to be aware of the tenuousness of the situation ahead of time so they are not left feeling abandoned (Dombo & Bass, 2013).

Return to Work

What happens after parental leave? The baby of the pregnant therapist, once part of the therapeutic triad, is no longer present in the counseling room. This "fifth trimester" presents a new chapter for working parents in general, and especially so in the realm of therapy, for both the patient and the therapist who is now a parent (Brody, 2017; L. Covington & Jaffe, 2022; Waldman, 2003): "The return from the maternity leave is very seldom discussed in the literature, but of a high clinical importance" (F. M. D. Schmidt et al., 2015).

There are several factors to consider in the return to work. From the patient's perspective, there may be questions about the baby. Once again, the issue of therapist self-disclosure is prominent: Are the questions related to the reality of the baby, or do they bring up more clinical matters for the patient (L. Covington & Jaffe, 2022; Waldman, 2003)? What concerns need to be addressed regarding the baby and the therapist's absence? As discussed, jealousy, anger, and/or fears of abandonment can dominate the clinical material. Some patients may regress in a childlike way, becoming more needy and wanting more "parenting" from the therapist. Others may identify with the baby and focus on breaches in their relationships with their parents. A new parent therapist may internalize their guilt at the potential for causing such a breach with their child by returning to work (Waldman, 2003). Still other clients may question the care of the baby now that the therapist is back at work, whether the therapist is seeing patients in person or via telemedicine. If the therapist works from home and sees patients virtually, this curiosity may be intensified, especially if the baby's cries can be heard in the background. These questions may evoke criticism of the therapist, implying that the therapist should be attending to the baby and not working in the long-held traditional view that only the mother can provide care for her infant (Fenster et al., 1986, as cited in Waldman, 2003). The guilt this can instill in the therapist can be overwhelming at times.

Being pulled in two directions at once—caring for their baby and caring for patients—the therapist undoubtedly experiences many emotions and challenges (Waldman, 2003). Waldman noted, "In the two years since I have resumed working, I have sometime felt that I was in the wrong place at the wrong time" (2003, p. 56). What stands out from this statement is that it is not just the immediate return to work that is challenging but it can also continue as the baby grows. Breastfeeding puts an additional strain on the working clinician. Whether one is in a clinic setting or private practice, scheduling time in the day to pump, finding a private place to do so, and making arrangements to store the pump supplies and milk can all create more stress for the therapist. It can also be a reminder that the therapist is not with her baby, again highlighting the split in her caregiving roles (L. Covington & Jaffe, 2022).

From this discussion, it is obvious how much a therapist's pregnancy can affect not only the patient but also the therapist. It can be a time of enormous growth for the therapeutic dyad and each individual in it. Understanding the complexities that pregnancy can have for the general clinical population sets the stage for appreciating the powerful effects it can have on the reproductive client.

SUMMARY

We, as caregivers, are not immune to the punches life delivers. Hardships can come in many different forms; no one gets through life without some personal trauma or loss. It is possible to use our wounds to help us as healers; they give a depth of understanding that otherwise might be missing. It is one thing to learn about loss in our studies and another to experience it ourselves. This is not to say that we must go through a traumatic event to do our work. Likewise, our personal traumas do not immediately make us experts in the field; making assumptions that our experiences are the same as a client's is not only unhelpful but may also lead to a therapeutic disruption. We can grow from our personal experiences and use them in the service of treating patients.

In this chapter, we addressed the crises of pregnancy with the general therapy population. Patients can and do have many different feelings regarding the disclosure of a pregnancy, the disruption in care with parental leave, and the therapist's return to work now as a parent. In the following chapter, we turn our attention to the intensification of reactions when the therapist becomes pregnant while working with reproductive patients.

11 THE PREGNANT THERAPIST AND THE REPRODUCTIVE PATIENT

Therapy is an encounter between two people. This book shows the pain, the beauty, and the power possible when therapist and patient meet each other in unpredictable ways.

—Gerson, 2009, p. xxi

Considering the intensity of a therapist's pregnancy in general—from disclosure to the clinical issues that can emerge to practical matters of parental leave and return to work with the new identity of "parent"—we now turn our attention to the even greater disruption that can occur if both the therapist and client are at the same stage of their reproductive life. If we think of the challenges a pregnancy can stir up with the general therapeutic population as a flood, these disturbances can be likened to a tsunami with reproductive patients.

https://doi.org/10.1037/0000400-011
Reproductive Trauma: Psychotherapy With Clients Experiencing Infertility and Pregnancy Loss, Second Edition, by J. Jaffe

WHAT CHAPTER OF YOUR REPRODUCTIVE STORY ARE YOU IN?

Depending on where you are in your reproductive story—and the chapter a particular patient is in—the dynamics of the therapy will be affected. One possible scenario is that you, the therapist, do not have children and do not plan on any in the near future. Perhaps you are child free by choice, but you might be child free not by choice. How might those wounds impact your relationship with your client struggling with infertility or a pregnancy loss? Are those wounds still fresh? What if you are actively attempting to get pregnant, and your client is doing the same? Imagine what happens to the therapeutic dyad if you get pregnant and your client is still struggling. Do you let them know, and if so, when and how? The happiness you feel about achieving this milestone may be marred by feelings of guilt. You do not want to hurt your client in any way, yet here you are with a secret that must eventually be shared. If the situation is flipped, and the client becomes pregnant before the therapist, what are your feelings? Can you maintain a good working alliance with this client if you are filled with jealousy, struggling with competitive feelings, emotionally upset, or angry?

If the chapter of your reproductive story is similar or close to that of your client, you may be able to empathize a great deal with them. However, you may also be at risk of causing painful psychological injuries to yourself by not having enough distance from what you are personally experiencing. There is also a risk to your client: If you are in a crisis or a challenging life circumstance, there is a possibility that your clinical judgment will be clouded.

One therapist I met—we will call her Dr. K—was not only going through in vitro fertilization at the same time as her patient but they were also going to the same clinic.[1] While Dr. K was fully aware of this situation, her patient, Maya, was not. Dr. K did a lot of juggling to keep her clinic appointment times different from her client's and found herself getting more anxious as time went on. We discussed the agony of keeping a secret of this magnitude to herself and the implications for her mental health, as well as Maya's. Dr. K came to the realization that as scary as it would be to address this situation with Maya, it would be worse not to.

Because they had established a good rapport, Dr. K decided to begin the next session by informing Maya: "I need to talk to you about something that may upset you or make you angry, and I want to make sure that we can talk it through together." They were able to discuss their shared wounds

---

[1] The case of Dr. K and Maya has been modified to disguise the individuals' identities and protect the client's confidentiality.

and the empathy Maya felt from Dr. K. They discussed the possibility of a pregnancy happening for one or the other or both and how that might affect the therapeutic dynamic. Dr. K also offered the names of other therapists if Maya chose to transfer care. In this case, the result was positive; by the end of the session, they had made a pact to be open and honest throughout. Dr. K's "confession" allowed Maya to feel less shame. As Maya described it, "Honestly, I'm sorry you are going through this too, but it makes me feel a little better—I'm not alone. It's helpful that I really have an ally to support me through this." Dr. K made sure the focus remained on Maya's needs and not her own. She let Maya know that she had her own resources for support; by no means did Maya need to worry or take care of her.

Miriam Greenspan, a feminist therapist, openly discussed the loss of her infant son with her clients. She noted, "A sudden dose of reality hit hard and became a part of the therapeutic process" (Greenspan, as cited in Comstock, 2009, p. 263). Greenspan discussed her reproductive trauma as a way to break through her clients' fantasies that she was all-powerful. Rather than deny what had happened, she used it in the treatment process: "It didn't interfere with the work. If they were feeling bad for me or wanted to protect me, they would tell me, and we would work on that" (Greenspan, as cited in Comstock, 2009, p. 264).

When a therapist becomes pregnant, a whole host of issues that may have previously been tucked away can and do get released for both the patient and the therapist. While this is true for the general psychotherapy patient, as discussed in Chapter 10, it is magnified for reproductive clients. Suddenly, the therapist's reproductive story comes face-to-face with the client's. As such, special attention must be paid to clients who are also going through their own reproductive trauma while their therapist is pregnant. The following sections focus on the potential disruption to therapy for reproductive clients caused by the therapist's pregnancy. Issues of disclosure and secretiveness, the guilt the therapist may feel, and the anger, anxiety, and betrayal the patient may experience are all set loose by the pregnancy. Attention to intense transference and/or countertransference feelings within the therapeutic dyad is discussed; a third person (the unborn child) has entered the treatment, creating a therapeutic triad.

RUPTURES IN THE THERAPEUTIC ALLIANCE

The therapeutic alliance is one of the best predictors of treatment outcomes regardless of modality. The alliance is built on the affective bond between the client and therapist and their agreement on the tasks and goals of therapy

(Bordin, 1979, as cited in Safran et al., 2011). A *therapeutic rupture*—defined as "a tension or breakdown in the collaborative relationship between patient and therapist" (Safran et al., 2011, p. 236)—if not addressed, can lead to early termination.

Ruptures in therapy occur all the time. A patient might feel pushed or challenged by an interpretation, and the therapist might make a mistake, be distracted, or say something off-putting. A client could interpret a glance at the clock to mean "I am sick of you" when it really might be that the therapist was so engrossed that they lost track of time. Patients may have negative feelings about their therapist and vice versa, but the literature notes that, in most cases, negative things are left unsaid. Patients may be reluctant to bring up negative feelings about the therapist to maintain the relationship. Therapists reported they often only became aware of a patient's dissatisfaction when the patient prematurely quit (Safran et al., 2001).

When therapeutic disruptions occur, they can be fertile ground for working through issues and can actually improve the therapeutic alliance. It has been suggested that ruptures in the therapist–client relationship can promote growth even more than when there are no ruptures (Eubanks et al., 2018). If that glance at the clock could be addressed, the therapist might be able to explore and dispel the patient's negative self-talk, and the alliance could be strengthened. If negative feelings are resolved, the rift then becomes a "repaired rupture" (McLaughlin et al., 2014). The rupture caused by the announcement of a pregnancy, however, may be more difficult to navigate. While it is possible that repairing this rupture may lead to positive outcomes, some reproductive clients may find it impossible to continue treatment with a pregnant therapist.

TRANSFERENCE AND COUNTERTRANSFERENCE: IT IS NOT JUST FREUDIAN

The work of psychotherapy rests on the reality of the intensely personal relationship between patient and therapist across all theoretical orientations. Despite efforts to remain neutral and objective, it is the nature of therapy that verbal communication occurs against a backdrop of nonverbal cues, the physical setting, personality, and cognitive style of both the patient and the therapist. Because of the intimacy of the therapeutic environment, it is inevitable that patients will have feelings and reactions to their therapist, and vice versa. This occurs both in a real sense, in the development of the therapeutic alliance, and in the unconscious realm through the experience of transference and countertransference.

Transference and countertransference are typically associated with psychoanalytic psychotherapy. In actuality, they occur all the time across all therapeutic modalities and all frameworks of human behavior, especially in situations where the balance of power may be unequal. Think about the relationship between a student and professor, for example: The student may desire the professor's approval and work especially hard (an unconscious transfer of approval-seeking needs from a parent), which may cause the professor to put more demands on that student, prompting them to reach higher goals (perhaps stimulating unconscious feelings of a similar relationship with their parents).

In therapy, patients transfer feelings about important people in their lives (typically their parents) onto the therapist. Patients might see their therapist as all-knowing or perfect, in part because of their own feelings of inadequacy. However, they may project negative feelings onto the therapist, viewing them as cold and withholding (when, in actuality, the therapist is attentively listening), perhaps unconsciously turning the therapist into their unavailable parent or partner.

Countertransference refers to the feelings therapists have toward their clients. It has been defined as the "internal and overt reactions to clients that are rooted in therapists' unresolved intrapsychic conflicts" (Myers & Hayes, 2006, p. 173). As therapists and human beings, we all have our own personalities and life experiences that enter with us into the therapy session. Our feelings get tapped as we sit with clients; using those reactions in the service of the therapy can be extremely valuable. We have all had "favorite" patients, as well as patients that annoy or anger us. It is important not to take these feelings at face value but to explore within oneself why we are triggered positively or negatively by a particular client. Countertransference used as a self-reflective tool to gain insight into the therapy can be effective and beneficial. For therapists who are also undergoing fertility issues, the potential for countertransference reactions is great (Dombo & Flood, 2022). This necessitates deep self-reflection and attunement to our patients and ourselves.

Waldman (2003) wrote about a case that exemplifies transference and countertransference, which occurred during her pregnancy and postpartum. Her client, a 40-year-old man, struggled with his relationship with his needy and, at times, negligent mother, who would spark anger and rage in him. As Waldman stated, "This patient felt envious of my baby at the same time that he identified with the baby" (p. 61). His longing for the maternal care that he was missing was transferred onto Waldman. At the same time, she was aware of strong countertransference feelings in her desire to be his reparative mother: "The shared wish by both members of the therapeutic dyad—that

I would repair [his] faulty mothering—also made it difficult to explore his sorrow and rage at having to share me with the baby" (p. 62). After giving birth, as Waldman cared for her infant, she had a much better understanding of what was missing in the patient's caretaking. The awareness of her counter-transference feelings allowed her to develop deeper empathy and insight into the patient's trauma and loss.

In the case Waldman presented, she was working with a nonreproductive client. Because the literature on pregnant therapists working with repro-ductive clients is virtually nonexistent, we must extrapolate the intensity of potential emotional responses patients will have to the announcement of a pregnancy. As discussed later, the rupture of the alliance, caused by the therapist's pregnancy when a client is also undergoing infertility or reproduc-tive loss, is unlike any other.

THERAPIST PREGNANCY DISCLOSURE AND GUILT

Dr. K and Maya, who were both fertility patients at the same clinic, arranged to keep the dialogue open between them. Neither of them was pregnant yet, and they hoped that they would be able to manage their mutual journey with honesty. This is not always so simple. For reproductive clients, feelings toward their therapist may shift the instant the therapist reveals her preg-nancy. Patients may feel the safety net that therapy had provided suddenly ripped away. Disclosure of a therapist's pregnancy, difficult enough with the general therapy population, is much more unsettling with a reproductive patient. Some fertility counselors may want to hide their pregnancy from fertility patients to protect the client and also buffer themselves against the client's anger or jealousy (Hacham-Lynch, 2014). Both the client and thera-pist may feel thrown off balance (L. Covington & Jaffe, 2022). Unsure of their footing, they both must cope with new therapeutic material; there is likely to be a disruption to the treatment and the therapeutic alliance.

When Should the Therapist Disclose?

When a therapist should disclose is a question that haunts all pregnant therapists, but especially reproductive counselors. For example, it is not uncommon for a therapist not to want to reveal her pregnancy until she feels secure in it; often, that means waiting until the first trimester is over. She may try to hide it with oversized clothes or, if working remotely, may make sure the camera is only exposing her head and neck. Delaying disclosure, however, can create distress. The therapist is holding a secret, and while this can generate angst for the therapist when working with clients in general, the guilt she may feel when working with a reproductive client is likely to be exacerbated. Not wanting to cause harm to her client, she may acutely struggle, knowing that her "good news" may bring anger, hurt, sadness, or jealousy to the person she is trying to help. In other words, the announcement of her pregnancy will cause a therapeutic rupture. Regardless of theoretical orientation, pregnancy disclosure will affect the alliance (Fallon & Brabender, 2003).

Some of the literature on pregnancy disclosure suggests the therapist wait until her client notices her growing belly, putting the onus on the client to bring it up (Uyehara et al., 1995). This can present an awkward situation for clients. As Way et al. (2019) pointed out in their meta-analysis of the literature, many patients were reluctant to articulate their observations of their therapist's pregnancy. It is socially awkward to discuss a woman's weight gain in general, but especially so if that woman is one's therapist (Dombo & Bass, 2013). It is uncomfortable to question a woman about physical changes to her body, and the burden of responsibility in this type of disclosure should be on the therapist and not the client.

Because the therapist's pregnancy has the potential to evoke many psychological issues for clients, leaving enough time to process feelings is essential. This is true not only in the course of the pregnancy but also in the disclosure session itself. Allowing time for discussion of the pregnancy and the impact on the therapy is critical and needs to be thought of as an ongoing topic (L. Covington & Jaffe, 2022). The sensitivity the therapist has to a reproductive patient in revealing her pregnancy can allow for working through the plethora of feelings that will arise.

Reproductive clients often talk about how their friends reveal their pregnancies: "My friend—I thought she was a close friend—announced her baby bump on social media. I am livid. I have shared so much with her about my struggles. She even came with me to one of my doctor's appointments. She could have personally reached out to me—that would have definitely been better than this. I'm not sure I can continue this friendship. I don't exactly know how to handle this." This is a message pregnant therapists can learn from because they, too, struggle to know "how to handle this." Knowing how devastating the news of a pregnancy can be, the therapist may want to delay disclosure for as long as possible, but this is not always the best course of action. Fears of inciting anger, sadness, and psychological pain make this treacherous territory to traverse. As discussed, delaying disclosure can add to feelings of betrayal; holding on to information that directly affects the client can produce anxiety for the therapist and disrupt clinical work. Being aware of the client's presenting problem, the stage of treatment, and the client's history are all factors for the therapist to consider. It has been recommended, in general, that at least 2 to 3 months are necessary for clients to explore their feelings (Dombo & Bass, 2013). For reproductive patients, however, early disclosure may be necessary to give them more time to process their reactions (Way et al., 2019).

Repairing the disruption to the therapeutic alliance and subsequent treatment may be linked to several factors: how the news of the pregnancy is delivered, the length of time in therapy, the particulars of the client's reproductive story and loss, the client's coping, and their personality style. In the case of a long-standing therapy client with a well-established alliance, it may be best for the therapist to openly acknowledge and take responsibility for the potential breach her pregnancy may have on treatment. In the example of Dr. K and Maya, their ability to discuss their shared quest for pregnancy allowed them to process the potential interference to the therapy explicitly.

In another circumstance, if a reproductive patient is relatively new to therapy, it may be wise to address the therapist's pregnancy at the outset or as early as possible. In doing so, the therapist shows her understanding and gives the client the opportunity to choose another provider. This can be tricky because the therapist may not be ready to announce her pregnancy yet. She may feel uncertain that her pregnancy will progress and may not want to reveal such a personal part of herself, especially if she has had infertility or pregnancy losses. Yet another way to handle this is not to take on new clients at all during this time. Depending on circumstances, this may or may not be possible, but not taking on anyone new also circumvents the unavoidable breach that occurs during parental leave.

Disclosure of a pregnancy may also come as a surprise to the therapist when she is not quite prepared. In describing a case where a client directly asked if she was pregnant, the therapist Laura Covington described feeling "caught" (L. Covington & Jaffe, 2022). She had not been ready to disclose her pregnancy to this client or any other but realized she could not lie about it. In a rush of emotions and information, she "confessed" to her client, only to be confronted with a series of other personal questions about the pregnancy. Laura Covington explored her client's feelings. Even though she was feeling anxious and guilty, she used this rupture to focus on her client's needs. As discussed, in any therapist's self-disclosure, it is important to bring the focus back into the therapy and onto the client (Knox & Hill, 2003).

Guilt

The emotions that arise when a therapist reveals her pregnancy to reproductive clients are intense for each of them. From the client's point of view, transference feelings toward the therapist may include anger, feelings of betrayal, disappointment, jealousy, abandonment, and grief. Just like the client who was not sure she could maintain her relationship with a friend who insensitively announced her pregnancy on social media, here is yet another loss the client must bear, another connection that could be lost. Even if the therapeutic relationship is not lost completely, there is no doubt it will change. The pregnancy represents an inescapable dose of reality, with the clinician becoming a real person (Fenster et al., 1986). The therapist's pregnancy creates an emotional gulf—she is now on the other side of the pregnancy fence, leaving her patient behind a closed gate. The client may feel abandoned and, in reality, will be abandoned during maternity leave, even if temporarily. "This is not only transference that needs interpretation; it is a reality, an iatrogenic injury that requires acknowledgement" (Waldman, 2003, p. 58.)

Countertransference feelings that the therapist may have are also powerful. A provider may feel guilty, as if her own needs have come before the client's and have directly caused the client pain. The therapist may also feel exposed, unprofessional, and off-kilter. As discussed in Chapter 10, not only is the therapist coping with the physical challenges of pregnancy but she may also feel a split between her professional and personal identities, being pulled away from caring for patients to caring for herself and her unborn baby. Therapist guilt, especially with infertility or pregnancy loss patients, derives from having something (the pregnancy) that the patient longs for but is struggling to procure. The pregnancy can represent "a physical manifestation of the differences between therapists' and clients' life experiences" (Way et al., 2019, p. 459).

In an attempt to alleviate pregnancy guilt, therapists have been known to go above and beyond what is normal and customary to meet the needs of their clients. They have given in to requests for personal information, conducted sessions when not feeling well, and withstood angry tirades (Way et al., 2019). They may make themselves too available, breaking boundaries that had formerly been set in place. One therapist admitted she felt so guilty that she did not want to charge her patient for the session in which she disclosed her pregnancy (Matozzo, 2000). The guilt of not being available is exponentially heightened when working with reproductive clients. Not only is the therapist feeling contrite about this therapeutic rupture but she may also feel directly responsible for causing the patient harm. The clinician may feel she has broken the basic ethical guidelines of beneficence—doing what is helpful—and nonmaleficence—avoiding doing harm to the patient (American Psychological Association, 2017).

JEALOUSY AND COMPETITION

The issue of jealousy—one of those emotions that we often try to suppress—can hugely factor into the therapeutic disruption. This is especially true when both the therapist and the client are trying to conceive. While the therapist is aware of her patient's fertility issues, it is unlikely that the patient would know of the therapist's attempts at pregnancy. The therapist, with knowledge of the patient's struggles, would be fully aware of the race to pregnancy while the client is in the dark.

In the example of Dr. K and Maya, both patients at the same fertility clinic, Dr. K knew of Maya's status; it was the central reason Maya had entered therapy. Dr. K kept her own fertility issues private, as would be expected, until she realized the countertransference she was experiencing was interfering with the therapy. The situation created a sense of competition for Dr. K. Who was going to win the race? If Maya "won" and became pregnant first, would Dr. K be able to contain her own feelings of loss and celebrate with Maya? If the situation were reversed, with Dr. K achieving pregnancy first, would Maya be able to tolerate it and continue therapy with Dr. K? And when should Dr. K disclose this to Maya? They had agreed on being open about it, but did that mean immediately revealing a positive pregnancy test? Or could Dr. K wait until she felt more sure of herself and the pregnancy?

It would not be surprising if Maya developed negative feelings toward Dr. K (if Dr. K "won" the pregnancy race), perhaps combined with being happy for her. It is a normal emotional reaction to be both happy for someone and jealous at the same time. However, some people can be overcome with jealousy, and although they may not want to admit it, wish ill on that person. Feelings of jealousy may be so intense that the nonpregnant person in the therapeutic dyad secretly wishes for the demise of the pregnancy. In the fantasy, if a miscarriage were to occur, they would be on equal footing again. In their meta-analysis, Way et al. (2019) found the topic of infanticide was largely left unexplored by pregnant therapists. It is reasonable that therapists would feel uncomfortable, distressed, and angry by their patient's insensitivity. Imagine a patient describing her miscarriage to her pregnant therapist. While it is important material to address, the therapist's feelings of vulnerability and anger would be understandable. There may be a subplot to this patient's need to discuss her miscarriage. Instead of directly addressing how upset and angry the therapist's pregnancy made her feel, her aim was to attack the therapist emotionally. Therapists are not immune to these feelings either, as unspeakable as they may be.

The reality is that pregnancy loss can and does occur. If either in the therapeutic dyad had infanticide fantasies, imagine the guilt that would arise and the complications to treatment if a loss occurred. These are deeply repressed emotions and highly dystonic to most individuals. If a pregnancy loss occurs, the necessity of working through it could create another therapeutic disruption. There may literally be a break in treatment to allow time to heal physically from a loss. If the therapist should have a pregnancy loss, it once again establishes her as real and vulnerable. Can patients tolerate this? Do they sublimate their own needs to take care of the therapist? How is it different for the general psychotherapy patient compared with a reproductive client? These are complicated questions that beg for future research. Delving into the relationships of reproductive patients and pregnant therapists, when reproductive stories collide, and how to best address these complex dynamics is an important next step.

THE POSTPARTUM THERAPIST

Returning to work after the birth of a child is yet another challenge for reproductive mental health providers. Not only will patients' concerns and queries regarding her absence need to be addressed but the therapist is also returning as a new mother. Balancing her professional identity with the demands of motherhood is not easy. Sleepless nights, finding time to breastfeed (if she is), and anxiety about caring for this new little person are challenging, especially for first-time parents. The baby, once literally present in the therapy session, is no longer in the room but is a presence nonetheless.

What are some ways the baby's presence is felt? If a reproductive client continues treatment after the therapist's pregnancy and parental leave, they may be curious about the baby. They may inquire about the birth, the baby's gender, or name. They may even ask to see photos; these questions may seem intrusive, and how one responds depends on the established therapeutic relationship. As noted in Chapter 10, clients may also want to know who is caring for the baby while the therapist is working—and the therapist may feel judged about leaving her child in the care of someone else. If the therapist is working remotely from home, a crying baby may be heard in the background. To clients who experienced the pregnancy journey with the therapist, she and the baby are now more "real"; any fantasies or projections are tempered by the reality of the therapist's life.

Questions about the baby may feel like boundary violations. This is self-disclosure on a new level. Keep in mind that when information about the therapist is disclosed, bringing the focus back to the client and therapy is best practice. Curiosity is understandable; reacting rigidly to inquiries could be off-putting. Reflecting on what all this means to the client is essential. Processing this material with a reproductive client can be difficult; emotions are high for both parties. At the same time, for the same reasons, the therapy can be incredibly rich. It may be possible to process deeper psychological territory than ever before.

REPAIRING THERAPEUTIC RUPTURES

In general, it has been recommended that therapists invite clients to explore ruptures in treatment and for the therapist to accept responsibility for them (Eubanks et al., 2018). Acknowledging how the client experiences the rupture is a start to the process of repair. Being open to hearing clients' expressions of disappointment, anger, or betrayal in a nondefensive way can help clients work through—in therapy—many of the feelings they have in dealing with friends, family, and colleagues outside of therapy. Research has suggested, "When therapists are able to respond nondefensively, attend directly to the alliance, adjust their behavior, and address rifts as they occur, the alliance improves" (Safran et al., 2001, p. 408).

With the general population, the disruption caused by the therapist's pregnancy may allow the client to understand their own grief and loss better and work on these issues in therapy. It is far more complicated, though, when working with reproductive clients. If clients are going through a struggle with infertility or pregnancy loss, which may be the reason they entered therapy in the first place, the interference of the therapist's pregnancy may be overwhelming. As previously mentioned, letting reproductive patients know of the therapist's pregnancy as soon as feasible is recommended to process the rupture as best they can. (Way et al., 2019). This kind of therapeutic disruption, however, may be impossible for some reproductive clients to tolerate. Therapists need to be prepared for some patients to seek treatment elsewhere; some may drop out of treatment altogether.

The therapist is in a vulnerable state. She is coping with the upheaval that pregnancy elicits—from a biological, emotional, and psychological standpoint. Developmentally—especially with a first pregnancy—she is experiencing a period of enormous growth (Colarusso, 1990). At the same time, she also must contend with a potentially disruptive self-disclosure, as well as manage the feelings of her clients. The pregnant therapist treating reproductive clients will likely experience anxiety and guilt. She may feel confused and incompetent because there is so little guidance about managing therapists' pregnancies. The emotional tug-of-war between the fertility counselor's joy of being pregnant and, at the same time, her guilt for being pregnant while the patient is trying to conceive is psychologically exhausting (L. Covington & Jaffe, 2022). It can be unsettling to be confronted with anger. Depending on the extent of the practice, whether it deals exclusively with reproductive patients or not, it can feel overwhelming to be repeatedly on the receiving end of hostility. Likewise, if clients terminate therapy because of the therapist's pregnancy, her confidence in her abilities may suffer. Hard as she may try, the therapeutic rupture caused by the therapist's pregnancy may be one where a repair is not possible.

One of the consistent findings in the literature is that clinicians feel lost in knowing how to manage their pregnancy with clients in general, with hardly any supervision available. While pregnancies are experienced in clinical practice all the time, little has been studied (Wolfe, 2013). As noted by Way et al. (2019), there is a lack of pregnancy-specific guidance and supervision, "highlighting that professional issues relating to pregnancy continue to be overlooked" (p. 461). All this is magnified in the field of reproductive psychology, where the impact of the clinician's pregnancy is felt on a completely different, more intense level. More research and attention to this specific therapeutic area will no doubt continue to develop.

SUMMARY

As fertility counselors, we have reproductive stories of our own. Some of us may have dealt with reproductive trauma and loss, while others have not. Reproductive stories become visible, quite literally, when a therapist becomes pregnant. When working with reproductive patients, our fertility status shifts from neutral to being front and center in the counseling space, whether in person or virtually. Like a volcanic eruption, a multitude of feelings can come flowing out—not only for patients but also for us. How a pregnant therapist manages the intersection of her personal life with her professional one and how she manages clients' feelings about her pregnancy is complicated. There is not a "one-size-fits-all" solution; rather, a nuanced, individualized approach is needed based on the client, their reproductive story, and the trauma they have experienced.

Because there is a lack of guidelines for pregnant therapists, especially when counseling reproductive clients, the emotional strain can take a toll. This is a perfect segue to discuss the importance and need for self-care. In the following chapter, we discuss the impact this work can have on us and our mental health needs and how to cope with these stressors.

12 REPRODUCTIVE THERAPIST SELF-CARE

Taking Care of Ourselves While Taking Care of Others

In dealing with those who are undergoing great suffering, if you feel "burnout" setting in, if you feel demoralized and exhausted, it is best, for the sake of everyone, to withdraw and restore yourself. The point is to have a long-term perspective.

—Dalai Lama

Although this chapter appears at the end of this volume, it by no means implies that therapist self-care should be considered last. If you feel compelled to skip this chapter, you are not alone. As often happens when caring for others, people may overlook their own needs, putting self-care "at the end of a practitioner's to-do list, rather than being made a priority" (Posluns & Gall, 2020, p. 2). Self-care, important in all caregiving roles, is especially so in the field of reproductive medicine and counseling. Although it can be rewarding work to help clients reach their parenting goals, we are also confronted with trauma and loss daily. As discussed later, this can be particularly difficult if the therapist and client have had a similar experience.

https://doi.org/10.1037/0000400-012
Reproductive Trauma: Psychotherapy With Clients Experiencing Infertility and Pregnancy Loss, Second Edition, by J. Jaffe

This chapter describes compassion fatigue, burnout, and vicarious trauma and offers suggestions for preventing these from interfering with our work and personal lives.

COMPASSION FATIGUE, BURNOUT, AND VICARIOUS TRAUMA: DEFINITIONS

Therapeutic work is stressful; clients present with emotional material that may be difficult to navigate, with emotions ranging from depression, anxiety, anger, and the possibility of suicidal ideation. Depending on one's work environment, the practical demands of high caseloads, the abundance of paperwork, and professional isolation can be additional stressors for clinicians and trainees (El-Ghoroury et al., 2012; Posluns & Gall, 2020). El-Ghoroury et al. (2012) found that over 70% of psychology graduate students reported that stressors negatively impacted their overall functioning. The toll on clinicians who work with trauma patients was reported to affect mood, sleep, and ability to concentrate (Killian, 2008).

Compassion fatigue occurs when therapists are overexposed to client suffering. In essence, it refers to a therapist who is tired of caring. "Therapists who experience compassion fatigue absorb the emotional weight of their clients' traumatic experiences that negatively impact both their professional identities and personal lives" (Berzoff & Kita, 2010, p. 342). It is the physical, emotional, and psychological exhaustion that comes from helping others cope with their feelings of trauma and stress. Some symptoms caregivers can experience are shifts in their mood, including depression, irritability, impatience, and feeling worn out or depleted. Clinicians may also suffer somatic symptoms such as headaches and sleep disturbances. The implication for clinical work is that therapists may be less available to process patients' issues (Figley, 2002).

Burnout is a concept people use in the vernacular all the time. When someone says, "I am totally burnt out," it usually means they feel overworked and underappreciated. Although similar to compassion fatigue, burnout has more to do with problems in the workplace rather than the overload of caring too much (Pehlivan & Guner, 2018). Burnout may cause some of the same symptoms as compassion fatigue: dysphoric mood and somatic symptoms.

Vicarious trauma may also be confused with compassion fatigue. It can be defined as the effect on a therapist after hearing a client's story of trauma, whereby the therapist feels traumatized as well. Saakvitne (2002) differentiated three types of trauma: direct or primary, secondary, and vicarious. *Direct* or *primary trauma* refers to a situation that directly happens to the therapist. *Secondary trauma* is witnessing the traumatization of others one cares for, whereas *vicarious trauma* is the internal transformation of the therapist as a result of engaging with traumatized patients. It is "a direct reaction to traumatic client material" (Trippany et al., 2004, p. 32). In a sense, a patient's traumatic experience can "rub off" on the clinician. Berzoff and Kita (2010) differentiated vicarious trauma and compassion fatigue: In vicarious trauma, "the therapist experiences the same post-traumatic stress symptoms of the client," whereas compassion fatigue has "a more global and diffuse impact" (p. 344).

The feelings therapists experience after hearing details of a miscarriage or seeing images of a baby who has died can leave them feeling traumatized. We take on the client's story and have our own traumatic reactions to it. This can be particularly difficult if the therapist has had a similar reproductive loss. The client's trauma can act as a trigger in bringing up issues for the therapist. Vicarious trauma can also occur before the therapist attempts pregnancy. Hearing stories of infertility and loss can raise anxiety, even though those events may never happen to the therapist. As discussed in the following section, when the therapist and client share a similar traumatic event, it changes our normal therapeutic stance. In this heightened emotional state, we may feel an overabundance of empathy but may also feel unsure of how to manage the client's needs and our own.

It should be noted that at the time of this writing, we are collectively living through difficult times. While COVID-19 may be subsiding, the toll it has taken still lingers for our patients, their families, and ours (Norcross & Phillips, 2020). The political climate in the United States and around the world is filled with anger and vitriol, with war raging and the threat of nuclear disaster looming. Issues pertaining to climate change present an existential threat to humanity. Racial inequities persist, and attitudes toward the LGBTQ+ community are becoming more politically charged and divisive. Reproductive rights continue to erode, directly affecting us in the field of reproductive psychology. It is important to be aware of this communally shared trauma—which may change over time and the course of historical events and may increase the risk of burnout not only for ourselves but also for our patients. These are shared traumas; they may not be seen as presenting problems but are living in the background for all of us.

A SHARED EXPERIENCE

What is important for assessing self-care is the recognition that clinicians—whether working in a medical clinic, working in private practice, or conducting evaluations—can feel overburdened and stressed. Fertility counselors are exposed to stories that are difficult to hear. They leave their mark on us, and to do our job effectively, we need to be present and receptive to their trauma and remove ourselves from it. We need to keep one foot in their world and the other in ours.

Straddling that clinical line becomes more complicated depending on one's reproductive story. Is the client's story triggering our own? Are our reproductive issues stressing us as we try to help clients navigate theirs? It is only natural for therapists to compare their experiences with those of their clients. A shared experience of infertility, for example, would naturally prompt the therapist to reflect on their own struggles caused by the condition, whether this has been disclosed or not. With a shared trauma, we must remain conscious of our vulnerability while tracking the patient's affect (Saakvitne, 2002). To be clear, the therapist is not offering advice on how they managed their trauma; rather, they are using their history of illness and loss to help clients reflect on the struggles in their lives. "Using the common ground as a springboard for generating questions" can help patients through their journey (McDaniel et al., 2009, p. 4).

Having a shared experience can enhance the connection and empathy therapists feel toward their patients. So many reproductive patients have expressed that they want and need us to understand what they are going through. Reproductive trauma is not only a psychological crisis but also a medical one. Although therapists can learn about the multitude of medical interventions available, with a shared experience, the therapist knows firsthand what it feels like. A shared experience of a reproductive trauma—even if it is not exactly the same as a client's—allows us to connect with their deep affective hardships.

We may also be better able to understand patients' need to know if we have children or not. The shared experience of feeling a divide in the world—between those who have children and those who do not—is something a therapist can understand from the inside if they, too, have struggled with infertility or pregnancy loss. The expectation that one will be invited to the party and then wait hopefully for an invitation that never comes is devastating. Maybe knowing this in our bones allows us to answer, "Do you have kids?" in a way that conveys the deepest understanding of what it means. Perhaps the answer conveys the message, "I know what it feels like to wonder which side of the fence someone is standing on. The gate had been closed for me too."

There are risks involved in having a shared experience as well. We may overidentify with the client and assume that strategies we used and benefited from will work for them as well. For example, if the therapist was able to build their family through adoption, they may be more inclined to suggest their client do the same. Likewise, if a therapist has found solace through religious beliefs, they may encourage clients to explore that path. While urging explorations of many options is desirable, awareness of our biases is important to keep in mind.

Another danger in having a shared experience is that it can have a direct negative impact on our well-being. Hearing the emotional and physical pain patients need to discuss may trigger our own intrusive thoughts, memories, or imagery, and our defenses may be overwhelmed. We may lose perspective and be less effective in our therapeutic work. When working with infertility patients who have come to the end of their treatment choices, for example, I have been aware of my biases in encouraging them to pursue other avenues to parenthood. Because of my own story and the positive outcome I experienced, I wish the same for them. When one patient said, "I know you want me to have a baby, but . . ." I realized that I needed to stay neutral and support her in decisions to remain child free. We can learn a great deal about ourselves by observing our reactions, emotions, and coping when attuned to clients' dilemmas.

"HOW AM I DOING?"

This simple question, "How Am I Doing?" might easily be ignored and has been recommended for each of us to ask ourselves regularly (Saakvitne, 2002). The importance of taking care of ourselves cannot be stressed enough. Our psychological health and welfare must be addressed for us to be available to help patients. Caregivers tend to overlook themselves in the process of helping others. Assessing our well-being is necessary to stay present and available to patients. Wise et al. (2012) made the case that "self-care is an ethical imperative as it relates to competence" (p. 487). A self-assessment that is showing cracks—feelings of low self-worth, anxiety, moodiness, or irritability—needs to be addressed with a desire for improvement, not in a punitive manner. Rather than feeling bad about ourselves, we can look at negative emotions as a kind of alarm system—warning signs that more time and energy needs to be spent on caring about and for the caregiver.

If therapist stress is not addressed, it can impair functioning. This is emotionally exhausting work (S. L. Shapiro et al., 2007). Not returning phone calls, being late for appointments, or crossing ethical boundaries are example indicators of caregivers feeling overwhelmed. In this sense, it is an ethical violation not to take care of oneself (Wise et al. 2012). The good news is that a great deal of research has been done into how therapists can and do take care of themselves. Saakvitne (2002) categorized these strategies into protection, self-care, and transformation. *Protection* refers to being aware of signs of feeling overwhelmed, such as chronic fatigue, somatic symptoms, emotional overload, feelings of being disconnected, or the loss of joy or satisfaction with the work. *Self-care* refers to the understanding that we need to keep ourselves physically and emotionally healthy; it is about building in emotional escape hatches for ourselves. Last, *transformation* refers to the need for meaningfulness in our work. It is important to recognize if we are feeling jaded, negative, or depleted. While it is normal to feel tired at the end of a clinical day, we need to find ways to feel rejuvenated. The next section delineates practical solutions for how we can promote our well-being.

SELF-CARE STRATEGIES

Because it has been suggested that the therapist's self is among the most important instruments in therapeutic work, it stands to reason that taking care of oneself is of primary importance (Thériault et al., 2015). While all mental health practitioners would be advised to take care of their physical and mental well-being, it is particularly true for clinicians in the reproductive field. Given the extent of the losses and trauma that clients undergo and the profound loss of their reproductive story so deeply embedded in their sense of self, it is not surprising that it can take its toll. In addition, because many providers have also had reproductive challenges, we may be particularly vulnerable to the pitfalls of providing care to this population. Indeed, if a clinician is going through in vitro fertilization (IVF) or pregnancy demise, focusing on oneself is necessary. The following are suggestions based on the literature for how to care for ourselves as we care for clients.

Basic Health Needs

How often have you skipped lunch to fit in another client? How much water do you drink in a day? Are you too tired to exercise after seeing clients? Is your office chair causing back pain? Are you too hot or too cold? Is there noise or distraction from other areas in your work setting?

As basic as it may seem, nutrition, hydration, and exercise are critical components in providing effective care for patients. If your work environment is unpleasant, it can directly impact your ability to concentrate. One therapist was so cold (the thermostat was controlled in another part of the building) that she had to bring a portable heater to her office to be comfortable. She described feeling a little like Goldilocks, but to focus on her clients, she needed to create an environment that suited her.

Posluns and Gall (2020) stated that being aware of the mental, emotional, and physical hazards associated with this work allows us to care for ourselves.

Because the nature of the work is sedentary, taking care of our physical needs is essential. It may be as simple as getting up between clients and stretching. Even a walk to the restroom can provide a physical break from sitting. Practitioners should keep in mind the need to refuel; if a particular client has presented challenging or draining material, the therapist's "tank" may be running on empty. One problem is that we may not realize how drained we are until it is too late. We may have another client waiting and cannot give ourselves the break we need. While we may be able to power through, the consequences of continually doing so can do harm.

Balance

Finding a balance between one's professional and personal life is a large component of self-care: "As a profession we tend to neglect the importance of creating a sustainable balance between caring for our clients and caring for ourselves" (Wise et al., 2012, p. 487). Putting others' needs in front of our own is part of being in a helping profession, but it can backfire if it depletes us. Poor work–life balance has been linked to physical exhaustion, high levels of stress and anxiety, and emotional fatigue. In Posluns and Gall's (2020) review of the literature, they found that maintaining a balance between work and personal life led to greater career satisfaction and a lower risk of burnout.

Balance can be promoted by cultivating professional goals outside of direct clinical work, such as teaching, writing, or supervising. Engaging in nonwork-related interests—whatever they may be—is just as important; they should not get shunted aside because of the demands of work. It is not just work–life balance that needs to be considered; equally significant is the balance within one's workday itself. If possible, building in breaks in the day—taking a lunch break or finding time to exercise—can be restorative. One therapist took time in the day to practice playing the guitar; another used a break to learn Spanish. Again, if possible, try to schedule clients in a way that is not draining. For example, back-to-back patients who have recently had a pregnancy loss may be too emotionally challenging. Paying attention to the impact of the client's emotional demands on you can help you manage your own needs.

Social Support

As a graduate student, it was drummed into me never to do clinical work in a vacuum. The need for connection with others—colleagues, supervisors, family, or friends—is an essential element for the well-being of practitioners. Our work is often done in isolation; our interactions are with clients struggling with difficult life issues, especially reproductive clients. Talking with peers or supervisors can increase professional development and reduce the risk of negative outcomes (Posluns & Gall, 2020). In particular, practitioners dealing with burnout, compassion fatigue, or vicarious trauma can get support from colleagues by talking it out. This is especially true if the therapist and client have a shared experience. Indeed, professional and peer supervision has been ranked as one of the most important strategies for managing self-care (Thériault et al., 2015). Professional consultation is especially recommended for cases touching on a therapist's reproductive loss.

Aside from professional support, nurturance on a personal level is also necessary. Spending time with family and friends and not talking about clinical issues is a way to enhance work–life balance. As mentioned, it is important to cultivate interests and relationships that are not work related, such as socializing with others and engaging in activities that are pleasurable, bring joy, and/or allow us to escape: "To balance the cost of bearing witness, we need opportunities that allow us to turn away, to escape from harsh reality into fantasy, imagination, art, music, creativity, and sheer foolishness" (Saakvitne, 2002). There is nothing like a good belly laugh with friends to brighten the soul.

Another source of emotional support can come from personal therapy. Gaining insight into our anxieties and insecurities, learning better coping strategies, and being aware of personal frustrations can increase our capability to help others. The more we know ourselves—our strengths and pitfalls— and the healthier we are, the more we can be present for patients.

Mindfulness

Therapist self-care also encompasses maintaining a sense of purpose. Some have categorized this as a spiritual connection to the need for something larger and meaningful (Harrison & Westwood, 2009). Managing self-care through mindfulness and gratitude practices are ways for practitioners to engage in and sustain the meaningfulness of our work.

Mindfulness, as previously discussed as a therapeutic tool for patients, is equally effective for therapists. It has been defined as paying attention "moment by moment and day by day in how we respond to the world we inhabit" (Kabat-Zinn, 2021, p. 1556). The mindfulness-based stress reduction program (MBSR), first developed by Kabat-Zinn,[1] has been shown to reduce distress and enhance well-being in patient populations and health care

---

[1] For the authorized curriculum guide for MBSR, see Santorelli et al. (2017).

professionals (S. L. Shapiro et al., 2007). Using a combination of meditation, breathing techniques, and yoga practices, practitioners focus on the here and now without judgment. In restoring awareness of the present, studies of mental health therapist trainees found that mindfulness counteracted caregiver burnout, decreased stress, increased compassion for self and others, and allowed them to slow down and feel a greater connection (Dorian & Killebrew, 2014; S. L. Shapiro et al., 2007).

Norcross and Phillips (2020) described the additional stressors on mental health providers during the pandemic. Certainly, at the height of it, the collective stress was debilitating for everyone. Therapists could not distance themselves from the trauma because it was happening to all of us. This shared experience of living through an unprecedented time revealed our vulnerability and humanity. Norcross and Phillips suggested several strategies for self-care that go beyond use in the pandemic. One helpful idea is to take "mindful moments" (Norcross & Phillips, 2020, p. 61). Based on MBSR, it "minds the body, sets boundaries between your client focus and your self-care, restructures your monkey brain thoughts, and represents at least a momentary escape from usual professional activity" (Norcross & Phillips, 2020, p. 61). A simple way to take a "mindful moment" is to sit quietly and really look at something, perhaps a piece of artwork you have hanging in your office or home, or listen closely to the sounds around you. At first, you might not hear anything, but as you concentrate, you will begin to hear the subtle sounds around you, perhaps just your own breathing. On a bathroom break, you can pay attention to the sensation of the water as you wash your hands, the smell of the soap, or the feel of the towel as you dry off. Focusing on the here and now, even for 30 seconds, is a way of cleansing the palate, so to speak; it is a small pause to center yourself and prepare for the next client interaction.

Norcross and Phillips (2020) also suggested practicing daily gratitude. Research has suggested that the regular expression of gratitude enhances physical health and well-being (Wise et al., 2012). Seligman et al. (2005) purported that the practice of optimistic thinking can improve the quality of one's life. A meta-analysis of 419 studies found that mindfulness-based and positive psychological interventions were effective in both clinical and nonclinical populations (van Agteren et al., 2021). A classic gratitude exercise is to take note of three good things that happened during the day. These can be written down in a gratitude journal or perhaps just thought about as one prepares for sleep. At the end of a workday, reflecting on a positive client interaction is a good way to remember one's purpose. It can also be helpful to think about the numerous things you accomplished that day versus the list of things that did not get done. Negative emotions often overwhelm positive ones; it takes effort to have the positive ones stand out, but doing so can decrease negative affect and promote self-care. Taking mindful moments and practicing gratitude are two simple exercises that can be done anywhere at any time.

These practices can be especially helpful when working with reproductive clients. As discussed throughout this volume, the feelings that arise from the trauma and loss of a baby or a longed-for baby are intense, not only for clients but also for us. Likewise, these methods of self-care can be introduced to patients to help manage their stressors. One patient described a mindful moment when giving herself shots for an upcoming IVF cycle. "I paused before the injection," she said, "paying attention to the objects in the room, the things I had lovingly chosen to decorate my home with. It reminded me of who I am and what I have to offer; it helped to calm me down."

Meaning-Making

Therapist self-care also involves meaning-making. There may be times when we doubt the meaning of our work: Are we really helping? When it appears that a client is not making any progress in treatment, clinicians may doubt the effectiveness of the treatment. It is essential to pay attention to our attitude; if it becomes jaded and negative, we must recognize the possibility of burnout, compassion fatigue, or vicarious trauma (Saakvitne, 2002). It can be helpful to remind ourselves what motivated us to pursue this career in the first place.

A meaning-making model, composed of global and situational levels, has been proposed (Park, 2010). *Global meaning* refers to an overall set of beliefs, while *situational meaning* comprises the understanding and appraisal of a specific event. The discrepancy between an individual's global beliefs and their evaluation of a particular situation can create distress (Park, 2013). The objective of reducing this discrepancy can serve as another pathway to self-care (Posluns & Gall, 2020).

For reproductive patients, core beliefs, as discussed in Chapter 3, have been shattered. Fertility challenges violate the global beliefs of fairness, predictability of the world, and benevolence. Goals are disrupted, and the appraisal of life's purpose and control may be seriously questioned. By creating a new narrative, editing, and redrafting their reproductive story, patients may be able to find new meaning for themselves. Meaning and well-being may come in exploring avenues that lead to posttraumatic growth. Meaning can also be made through spiritual beliefs to address existential issues (Park,

2013; Posluns & Gall, 2020). Questioning the reasons for their reproductive trauma can promote a new appraisal of personal values and beliefs.

The process of finding meaning for therapists is parallel to that of reproductive patients. Although we may not be able to measure the effects and benefits of clinical work precisely, it is important to remember that it is extremely valuable. As we assist patients in finding meaning from the reproductive trauma they have experienced, we, too, can find value in our work and consequently promote our own well-being. Posluns and Gall (2020) cited research that suggested meaning-making for therapists is associated with less depression, stress, and burnout and greater social support and career satisfaction. With the many avenues to self-care available and the therapist's awareness of the potential adverse outcomes of working with reproductive clients, a downward spiral of negativity can be reversed to promote positive feelings regarding the work and one's well-being.

SUMMARY

Therapists are often drawn into the field of reproductive psychology because of their difficulties in having children. It can be especially gratifying to follow the lives of clients as they grow from the reproductive trauma they have endured, whether the end of their story results in creating a family or remaining child free. Having a shared experience can be a valuable resource; therapists can tap into their own lives to better empathize with patients. However, hearing patients' stories of grief and loss may trigger the therapist's helplessness and sadness; this can be extremely difficult and interfere with therapy, depending on where the clinician is in their reproductive story.

Seeking consultation with peers and/or supervisors ensures that the mental health professional is not going it alone. Putting into practice any—or perhaps all—of the self-care strategies described in this chapter—especially if feeling vulnerable, exhausted, or traumatized—will prove beneficial not only to oneself but also to clients. Being mindful of our needs influences how we are with others and in the world. Acknowledging our humanness—our strengths and frailties—highlights the importance of taking care of ourselves as we care for patients.

EPILOGUE

Giving Voice to Patients' and Therapists' Reproductive Stories

The second edition of *Reproductive Trauma* has focused on many of the new developments in reproductive medicine, which have enabled more and more people to create families. While new medical technology continues to offer ways to create a family that seemed impossible just a few years ago, the desire to have children has been a constant throughout and cuts across gender, sexual identity, culture, and religion.

Across the board, people have unique reproductive stories, whether they have children or not and whether they want children or not. Working in the field of reproductive psychology allows therapists to bear witness to these stories. The phenomenon that has not changed with time is the crushing defeat when a longed-for baby dies, whether due to a miscarriage, stillbirth, or other perinatal loss. Equally as devastating is the emotional injury caused by infertility, when month after month, cycle after cycle, people trudge through the succession of hope and despair over and over again.

Largely because of the disenfranchised losses they have experienced, reproductive patients crave acknowledgment and validation. So often, they feel invisible and are given the message to move on. We, as reproductive therapists, allow clients to give voice to their stories and feelings about the trauma they have suffered. Even just labeling their experience as a trauma allows them to understand why they feel as they do and are affected so deeply. Bringing to light their early reproductive story and its connection with their reproductive trauma can give rise to a deeper understanding of other parts of their lives: childhood conflicts, relationships within their family of origin, and concepts regarding their sense of self and the impact it can have on intimate relationships. It can also give rise to remarkable explorations of ways to edit, rewrite, and grow from the trauma.

As therapists in this field, we also have reproductive stories that sometimes align with those of the clients we see. As we engage with clients and hear their stories, we must also be aware of our own. This self-reflection not only enhances the therapeutic relationship with clients but also contributes to our own growth. My interest in the therapeutic relationship and the interplay between the therapist's story and the client's has been part of my own growth and has largely fueled Part II of this volume.

Finally, I would like to thank you, the reader, for the work you do. The psychological care you provide for reproductive clients is so necessary. Your attention to their needs during this life-altering crisis allows them to move forward through their grief and loss. While there are no guarantees to predict how a client's story will end, you can guide them to recognize how their reproductive trauma has forged new stories and promoted psychological growth.

References

Abhari, S., & Kawwass, J. F. (2021). Pregnancy and neonatal outcomes after transfer of mosaic embryos: A review. *Journal of Clinical Medicine, 10*(7), 1369. https://doi.org/10.3390/jcm10071369

Abrams, Z. (2022, September). The facts about abortion and mental health. *Monitor on Psychology, 53*(6), 40. https://www.apa.org/monitor/2022/09/news-facts-abortion-mental-health

Adams, H. B. (2017). Rhetorics of unwed motherhood and shame. *Women's Studies in Communication, 40*(1), 91–110. https://doi.org/10.1080/07491409.2016.1247401

American College of Obstetricians & Gynecologists. (2015). *Abortion care: Does having an abortion affect your future health?* http://www.acog.org/womens-health/faqs/induced-abortion

American Counseling Association. (2014). *2014 ACA code of ethics*. https://www.counseling.org/knowledge-center

American Psychiatric Association. (2022). *Diagnostic and statistical manual of mental disorders* (5th ed., text rev.). https://doi.org/10.1176/appi.books.9780890425787

American Psychological Association. (2017). *Ethical principles of psychologists and code of conduct* (2002, amended June 1, 2010, and January 1, 2017). https://www.apa.org/ethics/code/index.aspx

American Society for Reproductive Medicine. (2017). *Quick facts about infertility*. https://connect.asrm.org/srs/about/new-item9?ssopc=1

American Society for Reproductive Medicine. (2023). *ASRM publishes a new, more inclusive, definition of "infertility."* https://www.reproductivefacts.org/

news-and-publications/fertility-in-the-news/new-definition-infertility/?_t_id=
TFtWrxixEEchybudFbn4RQ%3d%3d&_t_uuid=7inAwiooS0mAAhBHbYhONA&_
t_q=ASRM+Publishes+a+New%2c+More+Inclusive+Definition+of+Infertility&_
t_tags=siteid%3adb69d13f-2074-446c-b7f0-d15628807d0c%2clanguage%
3aen%2candquerymatch&_t_hit.id=ASRM_Models_Pages_ContentPage/
_f6451e75-3bae-4185-83d8-27d873da5afe_en&_t_hit.pos=1

Angarita, A. M., Johnson, C. A., Fader, A. N., & Christianson, M. S. (2016).
Fertility preservation: A key survivorship issue for young women with cancer.
Frontiers in Oncology, 6(6), 102. https://doi.org/10.3389/fonc.2016.00102

Anonymous. (2007). The impact that changed my life. *Professional Psychology:
Research and Practice, 38*(6), 561–570. https://doi.org/10.1037/0735-7028.
38.6.561

Aoun, A., Khoury, V. E., & Malakieh, R. (2021). Can nutrition help in the treatment of infertility? *Preventive Nutrition and Food Science, 26*(2), 109–120.
https://doi.org/10.3746/pnf.2021.26.2.109

Applegarth, L. D. (2000). Individual counseling and psychotherapy. In L. H. Burns
& S. N. Covington (Eds.), *Infertility counseling: A comprehensive handbook for
clinicians* (pp. 85–101). The Parthenon Publishing Group.

Applegarth, L. D., & Riddle, M. P. (2007). What do we know and what can
we learn from families created through egg donation? *Journal of Infant,
Child and Adolescent Psychotherapy, 6*(2), 90–96. https://doi.org/10.1080/
15289160701624274

Arnason, A. (2012). Individuals and relationships: On the possibilities and
impossibilities of presence. In D. J. Davies & C. Park (Eds.), *Emotion, identity
and death: Mortality across disciplines* (pp. 59–70). Ashgate.

Arnett, J. J. (2000). Emerging adulthood. A theory of development from the
late teens through the twenties. *American Psychologist, 55*(5), 469–480.
https://doi.org/10.1037/0003-066X.55.5.469

Avelin, P., Rådestad, I., Säflund, K., Wredling, R., & Erlandsson, K. (2013).
Parental grief and relationships after the loss of a stillborn baby. *Midwifery,
29*(6), 668–673. https://doi.org/10.1016/j.midw.2012.06.007

Ayaltu, E. D. E., & Bayraktar, S. (2017). Examination of factors related with
posttraumatic growth in infertile individuals. *International Journal of Social
Science and Education Research, 3*, 1216–1232. https://doi.org/10.24289/
ijsser.321913

Baden, A., & Wiley, M. O. (2007). Birth parents in adoption: Using research to
inform practice. In R. A. Javier, A. L. Baden, F. A. Biafora, & A. Camacho-
Gingerich (Eds.), *Handbook of adoption: Implications for researchers, practitioners, and families* (pp. 425–444). Sage Publications.

Baetens, P., Devroey, P., Camus, M., Van Steirteghem, A. C., & Ponjaert-
Kristoffersen, I. (2000). Counselling couples and donors for oocyte donation:
The decision to use either known or anonymous oocytes. *Human Reproduction,
15*(2), 476–484. https://doi.org/10.1093/humrep/15.2.476

Bak, W. (2015). Possible selves: Implications for psychotherapy. *International Journal of Mental Health and Addiction, 13*(5), 650–658. https://doi.org/10.1007/s11469-015-9553-2

Bakhbakhi, D., Burden, C., Storey, C., & Siassakos, D. (2017). Care following stillbirth in high-resource settings: Latest evidence, guidelines, and best practice points. *Seminars in Fetal & Neonatal Medicine, 22*(3), 161–166. https://doi.org/10.1016/j.siny.2017.02.008

Barnett, J. E. (2011). Psychotherapist self-disclosure: Ethical and clinical considerations. *Psychotherapy, 48*(4), 315–321. https://doi.org/10.1037/a0026056

Barnett, M. (2007). What brings you here? An exploration of the unconscious motivations of those who choose to train and work as psychotherapists and counselors. *Psychodynamic Practice, 13*(3), 257–274. https://doi.org/10.1080/14753630701455796

Barrett, M. S., & Berman, J. S. (2001). Is psychotherapy more effective when therapists disclose information about themselves? *Journal of Consulting and Clinical Psychology, 69*(4), 597–603. https://doi.org/10.1037/0022-006X.69.4.597

Bartlik, B., Greene, K., Graf, M., Sharma, G., & Melnick, H. (1997). Examining PTSD as a complication of infertility. *Medscape Women's Health, 2*(3), 1.

Batra, S. (2013). The psychosocial development of children: Implications for education and society—Erik Erikson in context. *Contemporary Education Dialogue, 10*(2), 249–278. https://doi.org/10.1177/0973184913485014

Beauchamp, T. L., & Childress, J. F. (1979). *Principles of biomedical ethics*. Oxford University Press.

Beck, C. T. (2006). Postpartum depression: It isn't just the blues. *The American Journal of Nursing, 106*(5), 40–50. https://doi.org/10.1097/00000446-200605000-00020

Beech, H. (2022, November 27). When surrogacy becomes a crime. *The New York Times*.

Bellieni, C. V., & Buonocore, G. (2013). Abortion and subsequent mental health: Review of the literature. *Psychiatry and Clinical Neurosciences, 67*(5), 301–310. https://doi.org/10.1111/pcn.12067

Benedek, T. (1952). Infertility as a psychosomatic defense. *Fertility and Sterility, 3*(6), 527–541. https://doi.org/10.1016/S0015-0282(16)31084-6

Benedek, T. (1959). Parenthood as a developmental phase; a contribution to the libido theory. *Journal of the American Psychoanalytic Association, 7*(3), 389–417. https://doi.org/10.1177/000306515900700301

Bennett, S. M., Litz, B. T., Lee, B. S., & Maguen, S. (2005). The scope and impact of perinatal loss: Current status and future directions. *Professional Psychology: Research and Practice, 36*(2), 180–187. https://doi.org/10.1037/0735-7028.36.2.180

Benward, J. M. (2015). Disclosure: Helping families talk about assisted reproduction. In S. N. Covington (Ed.), *Fertility counseling: Clinical guide and case studies* (pp. 252–264). Cambridge University Press. https://doi.org/10.1017/CBO9781107449398.019

Berzoff, J., & Kita, E. (2010). Compassion fatigue and countertransference: Two different concepts. *Clinical Social Work Journal, 38*(3), 341–349. https://doi.org/10.1007/s10615-010-0271-8

Bewkes, F. J. (2014). Surrogate or "mother"? The problem of traditional surrogacy. *Tennessee Journal of Race, Gender, & Social Justice, 3*(2), 144–172. https://ir.law.utk.edu/cgi/viewcontent.cgi?article=1057&context=rgsj

Bhat, A., & Byatt, N. (2016). Infertility and perinatal loss: When the bough breaks. *Current Psychiatry Reports, 18*(3), 31. https://doi.org/10.1007/s11920-016-0663-8

Białek, K. I., & Malmur, M. (2020). Risk of post-traumatic stress disorder in women after miscarriage. *Medicine Studies, 36*(2), 134–141. https://doi.org/10.5114/ms.2020.96794

Bibring, G. (1959). Some consideration of the psychological processes in pregnancy. *The Psychoanalytic Study of the Child, 14*(1), 113–121. https://doi.org/10.1080/00797308.1959.11822824

Bindeman, J. (2019). Reproductive trauma as a catalyst for clinician transformation. *Journal of Psychotherapy Integration, 29*(2), 84–94. https://doi.org/10.1037/int0000155

Bitler, M., & Zavodny, M. (2002). Did abortion legalization reduce the number of unwanted children? Evidence from adoptions. *Perspectives on Sexual and Reproductive Health, 34*(1), 25–33. https://doi.org/10.2307/3030229

Bloomgarden, A., & Mennuti, R. B. (2009). Therapist self-disclosure: Beyond the taboo. In A. Bloomgarden & R. B. Mennuti (Eds.), *Psychotherapist revealed* (pp. 3–15). Routledge.

Blos, P. (1967). The second individuation process of adolescence. *The Psychoanalytic Study of the Child, 22*(1), 162–186. https://doi.org/10.1080/00797308.1967.11822595

Bogdan-Lovis, E., Zhuang, J., Goldbort, J., Shareef, S., Bresnahan, M., Kelly-Blake, K., & Elam, K. (2023). Do Black birthing persons prefer a Black health care provider during birth? Race concordance in birth. *Birth, 50*(2), 310–318. https://doi.org/10.1111/birt.12657

Boivin, J. (2003). A review of psychosocial interventions in infertility. *Social Science & Medicine, 57*(12), 2325–2341. https://doi.org/10.1016/S0277-9536(03)00138-2

Boivin, J., & Schmidt, L. (2009). Use of complementary and alternative medicines associated with a 30% lower ongoing pregnancy/live birth rate during 12 months of fertility treatment. *Human Reproduction, 24*(7), 1626–1631. https://doi.org/10.1093/humrep/dep077

Bordin, E. (1979). The generalizability of the psychoanalytic concept of the working alliance. *Psychotherapy: Theory, Research & Practice, 16*(3), 252–260. https://doi.org/10.1037/h0085885

Bortoletto, P. (2020). Impending ice age of assisted reproductive technology. *F&S Reports, 1*(2), 60. https://doi.org/10.1016/j.xfre.2020.06.001

Braverman, A. M. (2015). Mental health counseling in third-party reproduction in the United States: Evaluation, psychoeducation, or ethical gatekeeping? *Fertility and Sterility, 104*(3), 501–506. https://doi.org/10.1016/j.fertnstert.2015.06.023

Brigance, C. A., Brown, E. C., & Cottone, R. R. (2021). Therapeutic intervention for couples experiencing infertility: An emotionally focused couples therapy approach. *The Family Journal, 29*(1), 72–79. https://doi.org/10.1177/1066480720973420

Brody, L. S. (2017). *The fifth trimester: The working mom's guide to style, sanity, and big success after baby.* Doubleday.

Brodzinsky, D., & Smith, S. L. (2014). Post-placement adjustment and the needs of birthmothers who place an infant for adoption. *Adoption Quarterly, 17*(3), 165–184. https://doi.org/10.1080/10926755.2014.891551

Brownlee, K., & Oikonen, J. (2004). Toward a theoretical framework for perinatal bereavement. *British Journal of Social Work, 34*(4), 517–529. https://doi.org/10.1093/bjsw/bch063

Buluc-Halper, E., & Griffin, P. W. (2015). Multicultural considerations in infertility counseling. *Ideas and Research You Can Use: Vistas 2016,* Article 18. https://www.counseling.org/docs/default-source/vistas/article_18f0bf24f16116603abcacff0000bee5e7.pdf?sfvrsn=4

Burton, N. (2021, February 20). The myth of Chiron, the wounded healer. *Psychology Today.* https://www.psychologytoday.com/ca/blog/hide-and-seek/202102/the-myth-chiron-the-wounded-healer

Cann, A., Calhoun, L. G., Tedeschi, R. G., Kilmer, R. P., Gil-Rivas, V., Vishnevsky, T., & Danhauer, S. C. (2010). The Core Beliefs Inventory: A brief measure of disruption in the assumptive world. *Anxiety, Stress & Coping, 23*(1), 19–34. https://doi.org/10.1080/10615800802573013

Capitulo, K. L. (2004). Perinatal grief online. *The American Journal of Maternal Child Nursing, 29*(5), 305–311. https://doi.org/10.1097/00005721-200409000-00008

Capitulo, K. L. (2005). Evidence for healing interventions with perinatal bereavement. *The American Journal of Maternal Child Nursing, 30*(6), 389–396. https://doi.org/10.1097/00005721-200511000-00007

Carlson, R., Lammert, C., & O'Leary, J. M. (2012). The evolution of group and online support for families who have experienced perinatal or neonatal loss. *Illness, Crisis, & Loss, 20*(3), 275–293. https://doi.org/10.2190/IL.20.3.e

Carone, N., Baiocco, R., & Lingiardi, V. (2017). Single fathers by choice using surrogacy: Why men decide to have a child as a single parent. *Human Reproduction, 32*(9), 1871–1879. https://doi.org/10.1093/humrep/dex245

Carpenter, E. (2021). "The health system just wasn't built for us": Queer cisgender women and gender-expansive individuals' strategies for navigating reproductive healthcare. *Women's Health Issues, 31*(5), 478–484. https://doi.org/10.1016/j.whi.2021.06.004

Casillas, F., Retana-Marquez, S., Ducolomb, Y., & Betancourt, M. (2015). New trends in assisted reproduction techniques: Cryopreservation, in vitro fertilization, intracytoplasmic sperm injection and physiological intracytoplasmic sperm infection. *Anatomy and Physiology, 5*(4), Article 184. https://doi.org/10.4172/2161-0940.1000184

Cedars, M. I. (2022). Evaluation of female fertility—AMH and ovarian reserve testing. *The Journal of Clinical Endocrinology and Metabolism, 107*(6), 1510–1519. https://doi.org/10.1210/clinem/dgac039

Chavarro, J. E., Rich-Edwards, J. W., Rosner, B. A., & Willett, W. C. (2007). Diet and lifestyle in the prevention of ovulatory disorder infertility. *Obstetrics and Gynecology, 110*(5), 1050–1058. https://doi.org/10.1097/01.AOG.0000287293.25465.e1

Chavarro, J. E., Rich-Edwards, J. W., Rosner, B. A., & Willett, W. C. (2008). Use of multivitamins, intake of B vitamins, and risk of ovulatory infertility. *Fertility and Sterility, 89*(3), 668–676. https://doi.org/10.1016/j.fertnstert.2007.03.089

Cheng, P. J., Pastuszak, A. W., Myers, J. B., Goodwin, I. A., & Hotaling, J. M. (2019). Fertility concerns of the transgender patient. *Translational Andrology and Urology, 8*(3), 209–218. https://doi.org/10.21037/tau.2019.05.09

Cheong, Y. C., Dix, S., Hung Yu Ng, E., Ledger, W. L., & Farquhar, C. (2013). Acupuncture and assisted reproductive technology. *Cochrane Database of Systematic Reviews*. Advance online publication. https://doi.org/10.1002/14651858.CD006920.pub3

Chiorino, V., Cattaneo, M. C., Macchi, E. A., Salerno, R., Roveraro, S., Bertolucci, G. G., Mosca, F., Fumagalli, M., Cortinovis, I., Carletto, S., & Fernandez, I. (2020). The EMDR Recent Birth Trauma Protocol: A pilot randomised clinical trial after traumatic childbirth. *Psychology & Health, 35*(7), 795–810. https://doi.org/10.1080/08870446.2019.1699088

Christianson, M. S., Stern, J. E., Sun, F., Zhang, H., Styer, A. K., Vitek, W., & Polotsky, A. J. (2020). Embryo cryopreservation and utilization in the United States from 2004–2013. *F & S Reports, 1*(2), 71–77. https://doi.org/10.1016/j.xfre.2020.05.010

Cil, A. P., Bang, H., & Oktay, K. (2013). Age-specific probability of live birth with oocyte cryopreservation: An individual patient data meta-analysis. *Fertility and Sterility, 100*(2), 492–499. https://doi.org/10.1016/j.fertnstert.2013.04.023

Clapton, G. (2019). Against all odds? Birth fathers and enduring thoughts of the child lost to adoption. *Genealogy, 3*(2), Article 13. https://doi.org/10.3390/genealogy3020013

Clapton, G., & Clifton, J. (2016). The birth fathers of adopted children: Differences and continuities over a 30-year period. *Adoption & Fostering, 40*(2), 153–166. https://doi.org/10.1177/0308575916641616

Clutter, L. B. (2020). Perceptions of birth fathers about their open adoption. *The American Journal of Maternal/Child Nursing, 45*(1), 26–32. https://doi.org/10.1097/NMC.0000000000000591

Cohen, I. G., & Adashi, E. Y. (2013). Made-to-order embryos for sale—A brave new world? *The New England Journal of Medicine, 368*(26), 2517–2519. https://doi.org/10.1056/NEJMsb1215894

Colarusso, C. A. (1990). The third individuation: The effect of biological parenthood on separation-individuation processes in adulthood. *The Psychoanalytic Study of the Child, 45*(1), 179–194. https://doi.org/10.1080/00797308.1990.11823516

Coleman, E., Bockting, W., Botzer, M., Cohen-Kettenis, P., DeCuypere, G., Feldman, J., Fraser, L., Green, J., Knudson, G., Meyer, W. J., Monstrey, S., Adler, R. K., Brown, G. R., Devor, A. H., Ehrbar, R., Ettner, R., Eyler, E., Garofalo, R., Karasic, D. H., . . . Zucker, K. (2012). Standards of care for the health of transsexual, transgender, and gender-nonconforming people, version 7. *International Journal of Transgenderism, 13*(4), 165–232. https://doi.org/10.1080/15532739.2011.700873

Coleman, P. K. (2011). Abortion and mental health: Quantitative synthesis and analysis of research published 1995–2009. *The British Journal of Psychiatry, 199*(3), 180–186. https://doi.org/10.1192/bjp.bp.110.077230

Comstock, D. L. (2009). Confronting life's adversities: Self-disclosure in print and in session. In A. Bloomgarden & R. B. Mennuti (Eds.), *Psychotherapist revealed* (pp. 257–2730). Routledge.

Condon, J., Corkindale, C., Boyce, P., & Gamble, E. (2013). A longitudinal study of father-to-infant attachment: Antecedents and correlates. *Journal of Reproductive and Infant Psychology, 31*(1), 15–30. https://doi.org/10.1080/02646838.2012.757694

Conway, P., & Valentine, D. (1988). Reproductive losses and grieving. *Journal of Social Work & Human Sexuality, 6*(1), 43–64. https://doi.org/10.1300/J291v06n01_05

Cornefert, P. A. (2021). *Australian birth fathers of adopted children: Their perspectives, feelings, and experiences about the adoption of their child* [Doctoral dissertation, UNSW Sydney]. UNSW Sydney Library. https://doi.org/10.26190/unsworks/22572

Cornell, W. F. (2007). The intricate intimacies of psychotherapy and questions of self-disclosure. *European Journal of Psychotherapy and Counselling, 9*(1), 51–61. https://doi.org/10.1080/13642530601164372

Côté-Arsenault, D. (2003). Weaving babies lost in pregnancy into the fabric of the family. *Journal of Family Nursing, 9*(1), 23–37. https://doi.org/10.1177/1074840702239489

Cougle, J. R., Reardon, D. C., & Coleman, P. K. (2003). Depression associated with abortion and childbirth: A long-term analysis of the NLSY cohort. *Medical Science Monitor, 9*(4), CR105–CR112.

Covington, L., & Jaffe, J. (2022). Walking the tightrope: The pregnant fertility counselor. In S. N. Covington (Ed.), Fertility counseling: Clinical guide (2nd ed., pp. 245–253). Cambridge University Press. https://doi.org/10.1017/9781009030151.025

Covington, S. N. (2006). Group approaches to infertility counseling. In S. N. Covington & L. H. Burns (Eds.), Infertility counseling: A comprehensive handbook for clinicians (2nd ed., pp. 156–168). Cambridge University Press.

Covington, S. N., & Adamson, G. D. (2015). Collaborative reproductive healthcare model: A patient-centered approach to medical and psychosocial care. In S. N. Covington (Ed.), Fertility counseling: Clinical guide and case studies (pp. 1–44). Cambridge University Press. https://doi.org/10.1017/CBO9781107449398.002

Covington, S. N., & Marosek, K. R. (1999, September 25–30). Personal infertility experience among nurses and mental health professionals working in reproductive medicine [Paper presentation]. American Society for Reproductive Medicine meeting, Toronto, Canada.

Covington, S. N., & Patrizio, P. (2013). Gestational carriers and surrogacy. In M. Sauer (Ed.), Principles of oocyte and embryo donation (pp. 277–288). Springer. https://doi.org/10.1007/978-1-4471-2392-7_21

Craven, C., & Peel, E. (2014). Stories of grief and hope: Queer experiences of reproductive loss. In M. F. Gibson (Ed.), Queering maternity and motherhood: Narrative and theoretical perspectives on queer conception, birth and parenting (pp. 97–110). Demeter Press.

Cudmore, L. (2005). Becoming parents in the context of loss. Sexual and Relationship Therapy, 20(3), 299–308. https://doi.org/10.1080/14681990500141204

D'Aulaire, I., & D'Aulaire, E. P. (1962). D'Aulaires' book of Greek myths. Bantam Doubleday Dell.

Daneault, S. (2008). The wounded healer: Can this idea be of use to family physicians? Canadian Family Physician, 54(9), 1218–1219, 1223–1225.

Daniluk, J. C., & Hurtig-Mitchell, J. (2003). Themes of hope and healing: Infertile couples' experience of adoption. Journal of Counseling & Development, 81(4), 389–399. https://doi.org/10.1002/j.1556-6678.2003.tb00265.x

Darbandi, S., Darbandi, M., Khorram Khorshid, H. R., & Sadeghi, M. R. (2018). Yoga can improve assisted reproduction technology outcomes in couples with infertility. Alternative Therapies in Health and Medicine, 24(4), 50–55.

Davoudian, T., & Covington, L. (2022). Pregnancy and postpartum adjustment in fertility counseling. In S. N. Covington (Ed.), Fertility counseling: Clinical guide (2nd ed., pp. 234–244). Cambridge University Press. https://doi.org/10.1017/9781009030151.024

DeFrain, J. (1991). Learning about grief from normal families: SIDS, stillbirth and miscarriage. Journal of Marital and Family Therapy, 17(3), 215–232. https://doi.org/10.1111/j.1752-0606.1991.tb00890.x

de Lacey, S. (2007). Decisions for the fate of frozen embryos: Fresh insights into patients' thinking and their rationales for donating or discarding embryos.

Human Reproduction, 22(6), 1751–1758. https://doi.org/10.1093/humrep/dem056

de Liz, T. M., & Strauss, B. (2005). Differential efficacy of group and individual/couple psychotherapy with infertile patients. *Human Reproduction, 20*(5), 1324–1332. https://doi.org/10.1093/humrep/deh743

deMontigny, F., Verdon, C., Meunier, S., & Dubeau, D. (2017). Women's persistent depressive and perinatal grief symptoms following a miscarriage: The role of childlessness and satisfaction with healthcare services. *Archives of Women's Mental Health, 20*(5), 655–662. https://doi.org/10.1007/s00737-017-0742-9

De Simone, M. (1996). Birth mother loss: Contributing factors to unresolved grief. *Clinical Social Work Journal, 24*(1), 65–76. https://doi.org/10.1007/BF02189942

Deutsch, H. (1945). *The psychology of women: Motherhood* (Vol. 2). Grune & Stratton.

de Ziegler, D., & Toner, J. P. (2022). Fertility workups: The times they are a-changin'. *Fertility and Sterility, 118*(1), 5–7. https://doi.org/10.1016/j.fertnstert.2022.05.007

Dickenson, D. (2008). *Body shopping: The economy fuelled by flesh and blood.* Oneworld.

Dobbs v. Jackson Women's Health Organization, 597 U.S. _, No. 19–1392. (2022).

Doka, K. J. (1989). Disenfranchised grief. In K. J. Doka (Ed.), *Disenfranchised grief: Recognizing hidden sorrow* (pp. 3–11). Lexington Books/Free Press.

Doka, K. J., & Martin, T. L. (2011). Grieving styles: Gender and grief. *Grief Matters: The Australian Journal for Grief and Bereavement, 14,* 42–45.

Domar, A. D., Clapp, D., Slawsby, E., Kessel, B., Orav, J., & Freizinger, M. (2000). The impact of group psychological interventions on distress in infertile women. *Health Psychology, 19*(6), 568–575. https://doi.org/10.1037/0278-6133.19.6.568

Domar, A. D., Conboy, L., Denardo-Roney, J., & Rooney, K. L. (2012). Lifestyle behaviors in women undergoing in vitro fertilization: A prospective study. *Fertility and Sterility, 97*(3), 697–701. https://doi.org/10.1016/j.fertnstert.2011.12.012

Dombo, E., & Flood, M. (2022). "Be fruitful and multiply": Addressing spirituality in fertility counseling. In S. N. Covington (Ed.), *Fertility counseling: Clinical guide* (2nd ed., pp. 88–95). Cambridge University Press. https://doi.org/10.1017/9781009030151.009

Dombo, E. A., & Bass, A. (2013). Caring for your clients while caring for your baby: Responsible and ethical planning for parental leave. *Professional Development: The International Journal of Continuing Social Work Education, 16*(2), 56–64.

Dondorp, W. J., De Wert, G. M., & Janssens, P. M. W. (2010). Shared lesbian motherhood: A challenge of established concepts and frameworks. *Human Reproduction, 25*(4), 812–814. https://doi.org/10.1093/humrep/deq012

Donnez, J., Dolmans, M. M., Pellicer, A., Diaz-Garcia, C., Sanchez Serrano, M., Schmidt, K. T., Ernst, E., Luyckx, V., & Andersen, C. Y. (2013). Restoration of ovarian activity and pregnancy after transplantation of cryopreserved ovarian tissue: A review of 60 cases of reimplantation. *Fertility and Sterility, 99*(6), 1503–1513. https://doi.org/10.1016/j.fertnstert.2013.03.030

Dorian, M., & Killebrew, J. E. (2014). A study of mindfulness and self-care: A path to self-compassion for female therapists in training. *Women & Therapy, 37*(1–2), 155–163. https://doi.org/10.1080/02703149.2014.850345

Dumbala, S., Bhargav, H., Satyanarayana, V., Arasappa, R., Varambally, S., Desai, G., & Bangalore, G. N. (2020). Effect of yoga on psychological distress among women receiving treatment for infertility. *International Journal of Yoga, 13*(2), 115–119. https://doi.org/10.4103/ijoy.IJOY_34_19

Edwards, R. G. (2001). The bumpy road to human in vitro fertilization. *Nature Medicine, 7*(10), 1091–1094. https://doi.org/10.1038/nm1001-1091

El-Ghoroury, N. H., Galper, D. I., Sawaqdeh, A., & Bufka, L. F. (2012). Stress, coping, and barriers to wellness among psychology graduate students. *Training and Education in Professional Psychology, 6*(2), 122–134. https://doi.org/10.1037/a0028768

Erikson, E. H. (1963). *Childhood and society* (2nd ed.). Norton.

Esfandiari, N., Bunnell, M. E., & Casper, R. F. (2016). Human embryo mosaicism: Did we drop the ball on chromosomal testing? *Journal of Assisted Reproduction and Genetics, 33*(11), 1439–1444. https://doi.org/10.1007/s10815-016-0797-y

ESHRE PGT Consortium Steering Committee, Carvalho, F., Coonen, E., Goossens, V., Kokkali, G., Rubio, C., Meijer-Hoogeveen, M., Moutou, C., Vermeulen, N., & De Rycke, M. (2020). ESHRE PGT Consortium good practice recommendations for the organization of PGT. *Human Reproduction Open, 2020*(3), Article hoaa021. https://doi.org/10.1093/hropen/hoaa021

Eskew, A. M., & Jungheim, E. S. (2017). A history of developments to improve *in vitro* fertilization. *Missouri Medicine, 114*(3), 156–159.

Ethics Committee of the American Society for Reproductive Medicine. (2009). Interests, obligations, and rights of the donor in gamete donation. *Fertility and Sterility, 91*(1), 22–27. https://doi.org/10.1016/j.fertnstert.2008.09.062

Ethics Committee of the American Society for Reproductive Medicine. (2013a). Disposition of abandoned embryos: A committee opinion. *Fertility and Sterility, 99*(7), 1848–1849. https://doi.org/10.1016/j.fertnstert.2013.02.024

Ethics Committee of the American Society for Reproductive Medicine. (2013b). Informing offspring of their conception by gamete or embryo donation: A committee opinion. *Fertility and Sterility, 100*(1), 45–49. https://doi.org/10.1016/j.fertnstert.2013.02.028

Ethics Committee of the American Society for Reproductive Medicine. (2015). Access to fertility services by transgender persons: An Ethics Committee opinion. *Fertility and Sterility, 104*(5), 1111–1115. https://doi.org/10.1016/j.fertnstert.2015.08.021

Ethics Committee of the American Society for Reproductive Medicine. (2017). Using family members as gamete donors or gestational carriers. *Fertility and Sterility, 107*(5), 1136–1142. https://doi.org/10.1016/j.fertnstert.2017.02.118

Ethics Committee of the American Society for Reproductive Medicine. (2018a). Informing offspring of their conception by gamete or embryo donation: An Ethics Committee opinion. *Fertility and Sterility, 109*(4), 601–605. https://doi.org/10.1016/j.fertnstert.2018.01.001

Ethics Committee of the American Society for Reproductive Medicine. (2018b). Planned oocyte cryopreservation for women seeking to preserve future reproductive potential: An Ethics Committee opinion. *Fertility and Sterility, 110*(6), 1022–1028. https://doi.org/10.1016/j.fertnstert.2018.08.027

Ethics Committee of the American Society for Reproductive Medicine. (2018c). Use of preimplantation genetic testing for monogenic defects (PGT-M) for adult-onset conditions: An Ethics Committee opinion. *Fertility and Sterility, 109*(6), 989–992. https://doi.org/10.1016/j.fertnstert.2018.04.003

Ethics Committee of the American Society for Reproductive Medicine. (2020). Compassionate transfer: Patient requests for embryo transfer for nonreproductive purposes. *Fertility and Sterility, 113*(1), 62–65. https://doi.org/10.1016/j.fertnstert.2019.10.013

Eubanks, C. F., Muran, J. C., & Safran, J. D. (2018). Alliance rupture repair: A meta-analysis. *Psychotherapy, 55*(4), 508–519. https://doi.org/10.1037/pst0000185

Facchinetti, F., Pedrielli, G., Benoni, G., Joppi, M., Verlato, G., Dante, G., Balduzzi, S., & Cuzzolin, L. (2012). Herbal supplements in pregnancy: Unexpected results from a multicentre study. *Human Reproduction, 27*(11), 3161–3167. https://doi.org/10.1093/humrep/des303

Fallon, A. E., & Brabender, V. M. (2003). *Awaiting the therapist's baby: A guide for expectant parent-practitioners.* Erlbaum. https://doi.org/10.4324/9781410606846

Faramarzi, M., Pasha, H., Esmailzadeh, S., Kheirkhah, F., Heidary, S., & Afshar, Z. (2013). The effect of the cognitive behavioral therapy and pharmacotherapy on infertility stress: A randomized controlled trial. *International Journal of Fertility & Sterility, 7*(3), 199–206.

Fard, T. R., Kalantarkousheh, M., & Faramarzi, M. (2018). Effect of mindfulness-based cognitive infertility stress therapy on psychological well-being of women with infertility. *Middle East Fertility Society Journal, 23*(4), 476–481. https://doi.org/10.1016/j.mefs.2018.06.001

Farzaneh, F., & Khalili, M. (2019). Prevalence of celiac in infertile women due to unexplained infertility. *Prensa Medica Argentina, 105*(5), 317–319. https://prensamedica.com.ar/LPMA_V105_N05_P317.pdf

Fenster, S., Phillip, S. B., & Rapoport, E. R. G. (1986). *The therapist's pregnancy: Intrusion in the analytic space.* The Analytic Press.

Figley, C. R. (2002). Compassion fatigue: Psychotherapists' chronic lack of self care. *Journal of Clinical Psychology, 58*(11), 1433–1441. https://doi.org/10.1002/jclp.10090

Figueiredo, B., Costa, R., Pacheco, A., & Pais, A. (2007). Mother-to-infant and father-to-infant initial emotional involvement. *Early Child Development and Care, 177*(5), 521–532. https://doi.org/10.1080/03004430600577562

Foote, R. H. (2002). The history of artificial insemination: Selected notes and notables. *Journal of Animal Science, 80*(E-suppl_2), 1–10. https://doi.org/10.2527/animalsci2002.80E-Suppl_21a

Fravel, D. L., McRoy, R. G., & Grotevant, H. D. (2000). Birthmother perceptions of the psychologically present adopted child: Adoption openness and boundary ambiguity. *Family Relations, 49*(4), 425–432. https://doi.org/10.1111/j.1741-3729.2000.00425.x

Freeman, T. (2015). Gamete donation, information sharing and the best interests of the child: An overview of the psychosocial evidence. *Monash Bioethics Review, 33*(1), 45–63. https://doi.org/10.1007/s40592-015-0018-y

Freud, E. L. (Ed.). (1960). *Letters of Sigmund Freud*. Basic Books.

Freud, S. (2000). Recommendations to physicians practicing psycho-analysis. In J. Strachey (Ed. & Trans.), *The standard edition of the psychological works of Sigmund Freud* (pp. 1–120). Hogarth Press. (Original work published 1912)

Frey, L. L. (2013). Relational-cultural therapy: Theory, research, and application to counseling competencies. *Professional Psychology: Research and Practice, 44*(3), 177–185. https://doi.org/10.1037/a0033121

Friedman, C. (2007). First comes love, then comes marriage, then comes baby carriage: Perspectives on gay parenting and reproductive technology. *Journal of Infant, Child & Adolescent Psychotherapy, 6*(2), 111–123. https://doi.org/10.1080/15289160701624407

Frith, L., & Blyth, E. (2013). They can't have my embryo: The ethics of conditional embryo donation. *Bioethics, 27*(6), 317–324. https://doi.org/10.1111/bioe.12034

Frith, L., Blyth, E., Crawshaw, M., & van den Akker, O. (2018). Secrets and disclosure in donor conception. *Sociology of Health & Illness, 40*(1), 188–203. https://doi.org/10.1111/1467-9566.12633

Galic, I., Negris, O., Warren, C., Brown, D., Bozen, A., & Jain, T. (2021). Disparities in access to fertility care: Who's in and who's out. *F & S Reports, 2*(1), 109–117. https://doi.org/10.1016/j.xfre.2020.11.001

Galst, J. P. (2018). The elusive connection between stress and infertility: A research review with clinical implications. *Journal of Psychotherapy Integration, 28*(1), 1–13. https://doi.org/10.1037/int0000081

Galst, J. P., & Horowitz, J. E. (2015). Ethical aspects of fertility counseling. In S. N. Covington (Ed.), *Fertility counseling: Clinical guide and case studies* (pp. 281–295). Cambridge University Press. https://doi.org/10.1017/CBO9781107449398.021

Garner, C. H. (1985). Pregnancy after infertility. *Journal of Obstetric, Gynecologic, and Neonatal Nursing, 14*(Suppl. 6), S58–S62. https://doi.org/10.1111/j.1552-6909.1985.tb02802.x

Garvin, S. E., Chatzicharalampous, C., & Puscheck, E. (2019). Reflections on preimplantation genetic testing for aneuploidy and mosaicism: How did we get here, and what does it mean clinically? *Fertility and Sterility, 111*(1), 45–47. https://doi.org/10.1016/j.fertnstert.2018.11.006

Gaskins, A. J., & Chavarro, J. E. (2018). Diet and fertility: A review. *American Journal of Obstetrics and Gynecology, 218*(4), 379–389. https://doi.org/10.1016/j.ajog.2017.08.010

Gates, G. J. (2015). Marriage and family: LGBT individuals and same-sex couples. *The Future of Children, 25*(2), 67–87. https://doi.org/10.1353/foc.2015.0013

Ge, X., Natsuaki, M. N., Martin, D. M., Leve, L. D., Neiderhiser, J. M., Shaw, D. S., Villareal, G., Scaramella, L., Reid, J. B., & Reiss, D. (2008). Bridging the divide: Openness in adoption and postadoption psychosocial adjustment among birth and adoptive parents. *Journal of Family Psychology, 22*(4), 529–540. https://doi.org/10.1037/a0012817

Geller, P. A., Psaros, C., & Kornfield, S. L. (2010). Satisfaction with pregnancy loss aftercare: Are women getting what they want? *Archives of Women's Mental Health, 13*(2), 111–124. https://doi.org/10.1007/s00737-010-0147-5

Gelso, C. J. (2011). *The real relationship in psychotherapy: The hidden foundation of change*. American Psychological Association. https://doi.org/10.1037/12349-000

Gelso, C. J., & Hayes, J. A. (2007). *Countertransference and the therapist's inner experience: Perils and possibilities*. Erlbaum. https://doi.org/10.4324/9780203936979

Gerson, B. (2009). An analyst's pregnancy loss and its effect on treatment. In B. Gerson (Ed.), *The therapist as a person: Life crises, life choices, life experiences, and their effects on treatment* (pp. 55–69). Routledge. (Original work published 1996)

Gibson, M. F. (2012). Opening up: Therapist self-disclosure in theory, research, and practice. *Clinical Social Work Journal, 40*(3), 287–296. https://doi.org/10.1007/s10615-012-0391-4

Gilbert, K. R. (1996). "We've had the same loss, why don't we have the same grief?" Loss and differential grief in families. *Death Studies, 20*(3), 269–283. https://doi.org/10.1080/07481189608252781

Gillies, J., & Neimeyer, R. A. (2006). Loss, grief, and the search for significance: Toward a model of meaning reconstruction in bereavement. *Journal of Constructivist Psychology, 19*(1), 31–65. https://doi.org/10.1080/10720530500311182

Gleicher, N., & Caplan, A. L. (2018). An alternative proposal to the destruction of abandoned human embryos. *Nature Biotechnology, 36*(2), 139–141. https://doi.org/10.1038/nbt.4070

Glimberg, I., Haggård, L., Lebwohl, B., Green, P. H. R., & Ludvigsson, J. F. (2021). The prevalence of celiac disease in women with infertility—A systematic review with meta-analysis. *Reproductive Medicine and Biology, 20*(2), 224–233. https://doi.org/10.1002/rmb2.12374

Goedeke, S., Daniels, K., Thorpe, M., & Du Preez, E. (2015). Building extended families through embryo donation: The experiences of donors and recipients. *Human Reproduction, 30*(10), 2340–2350. https://doi.org/10.1093/humrep/dev189

Gold, K. J., Boggs, M. E., Mugisha, E., & Palladino, C. L. (2012). Internet message boards for pregnancy loss: Who's on-line and why? *Women's Health Issues, 22*(1), e67–e72. https://doi.org/10.1016/j.whi.2011.07.006

Gold, K. J., Leon, I., Boggs, M. E., & Sen, A. (2016). Depression and posttraumatic stress symptoms after perinatal loss in a population-based sample. *Journal of Women's Health, 25*(3), 263–269. https://doi.org/10.1089/jwh.2015.5284

Goldbach, K. R., Dunn, D. S., Toedter, L. J., & Lasker, J. N. (1991). The effects of gestational age and gender on grief after pregnancy loss. *American Journal of Orthopsychiatry, 61*(3), 461–467. https://doi.org/10.1037/h0079261

Goldberg, A. E., Downing, J. B., & Richardson, H. B. (2009). The transition from infertility to adoption: Perceptions of lesbian and heterosexual couples. *Journal of Social and Personal Relationships, 26*(6–7), 938–963. https://doi.org/10.1177/0265407509345652

Goldberg, S. K., & Conron, K. J. (2018). How many same-sex couples in the U.S. are raising children? *The Williams Institute UCLA School of Law.* https://williamsinstitute.law.ucla.edu/wp-content/uploads/Same-Sex-Parents-Jul-2018.pdf

Goldfried, M. R., Burckell, L. A., & Eubanks-Carter, C. (2003). Therapist self-disclosure in cognitive-behavior therapy. *Journal of Clinical Psychology, 59*(5), 555–568. https://doi.org/10.1002/jclp.10159

Golombok, S., Blake, L., Casey, P., Roman, G., & Jadva, V. (2013). Children born through reproductive donation: A longitudinal study of psychological adjustment. *Journal of Child Psychology and Psychiatry, 54*(6), 653–660. https://doi.org/10.1111/jcpp.12015

Golombok, S., Cook, R., Bish, A., & Murray, C. (1995). Families created by the new reproductive technologies: Quality of parenting and social and emotional development of the children. *Child Development, 66*(2), 285–298. https://doi.org/10.2307/1131578

Golombok, S., Murray, C., Jadva, V., Lycett, E., MacCallum, F., & Rust, J. (2006). Non-genetic and non-gestational parenthood: Consequences for parent–child relationships and the psychological well-being of mothers, fathers and children at age 3. *Human Reproduction, 21*(7), 1918–1924. https://doi.org/10.1093/humrep/del039

Golombok, S., Murray, C., Jadva, V., MacCallum, F., & Lycett, E. (2004). Families created through surrogacy arrangements: Parent-child relationships in the 1st year of life. *Developmental Psychology, 40*(3), 400–411. https://doi.org/10.1037/0012-1649.40.3.400

Golombok, S., Zadeh, S., Freeman, T., Lysons, J., & Foley, S. (2021). Single mothers by choice: Parenting and child adjustment in middle childhood. *Journal of Family Psychology, 35*(2), 192–202. https://doi.org/10.1037/fam0000797

Golombok, S., Zadeh, S., Imrie, S., Smith, V., & Freeman, T. (2016). Single mothers by choice: Mother–child relationships and children's psychological adjustment. *Journal of Family Psychology, 30*(4), 409–418. https://doi.org/10.1037/fam0000188

González-Ramos, Z., Zuriguel-Pérez, E., Albacar-Riobóo, N., & Casadó-Marín, L. (2021). The emotional responses of women when terminating a pregnancy for medical reasons: A scoping review. *Midwifery, 103*, Article 103095. https://doi.org/10.1016/j.midw.2021.103095

Greenfeld, D. A., Diamond, M. P., & DeCherney, A. H. (1988). Grief reactions following in-vitro fertilization treatment. *Journal of Psychosomatic Obstetrics & Gynecology, 8*(3), 169–174. https://doi.org/10.3109/01674828809016784

Grocher, K., & Gerrits, T. (2022). A racially and culturally sensitive approach to fertility counseling. In S. N. Covington (Ed.), *Fertility counseling: Clinical guide* (2nd ed., pp. 183–194). Cambridge University Press. https://doi.org/10.1017/9781009030151.019

Guy, B. (2018). I poems on abortion: Women's experiences with terminating their pregnancies for medical reasons. *Women's Reproductive Health, 5*(4), 262–276. https://doi.org/10.1080/23293691.2018.1523115

Hacham-Lynch, R. (2014). *The pregnant therapist: An exploration of counter-transference issues and their impact on the therapeutic relationship* [Undergraduate thesis, Dublin Business School]. DBS eSource. https://esource.dbs.ie/bitstream/handle/10788/1880/ba_lynch_r_2014.pdf?sequence=1

Hadley, E., & Stuart, J. (2009). The expression of parental identifications in lesbian mothers' work and family arrangements. *Psychoanalytic Psychology, 26*(1), 42–68. https://doi.org/10.1037/a0014676

Hamama, L., Rauch, S. A. M., Sperlich, M., Defever, E., & Seng, J. S. (2010). Previous experience of spontaneous or elective abortion and risk for post-traumatic stress and depression during subsequent pregnancy. *Depression and Anxiety, 27*(8), 699–707. https://doi.org/10.1002/da.20714

Hammond, H. (2015). Social interest, empathy, and online support groups. *The Journal of Individual Psychology, 71*(2), 174–184. https://doi.org/10.1353/jip.2015.0008

Hanson, J. (2005). Should your lips be sealed? How therapist self-disclosure and non-disclosure affects clients. *Counselling & Psychotherapy Research, 5*(2), 96–104. https://doi.org/10.1080/17441690500226658

Harper, J. C., Kennett, D., & Reisel, D. (2016). The end of donor anonymity: How genetic testing is likely to drive anonymous gamete donation out of business. *Human Reproduction, 31*(6), 1135–1140. https://doi.org/10.1093/humrep/dew065

Harrison, R. L., & Westwood, M. J. (2009). Preventing vicarious traumatization of mental health therapists: Identifying protective practices. *Psychotherapy: Theory, Research, Practice, Training, 46*(2), 203–219. https://doi.org/10.1037/a0016081

Hart, V. A. (2002). Infertility and the role of psychotherapy. *Issues in Mental Health Nursing, 23*(1), 31–41. https://doi.org/10.1080/01612840252825464

Hathaway, S. R., & McKinley, J. C. (1940). *The MMPI manual*. Psychological Corporation.

Hazen, M. A. (2006). Silences, perinatal loss, and polyphony: A post-modern perspective. *Journal of Organizational Change Management, 19*(2), 237–249. https://doi.org/10.1108/09534810610648933

Herman, J. L., Flores, A. R., & O'Neill, K. K. (2022). *How many adults and youth identify as transgender in the United States?* The Williams Institute, UCLA School of Law.

Hershberger, P., Klock, S. C., & Barnes, R. B. (2007). Disclosure decisions among pregnant women who received donor oocytes: A phenomenological study. *Fertility and Sterility, 87*(2), 288–296. https://doi.org/10.1016/j.fertnstert.2006.06.036

Hill, C. E., & Knox, S. (2001). Self-disclosure. *Psychotherapy: Theory, Research, Practice, Training, 38*(4), 413–417. https://doi.org/10.1037/0033-3204.38.4.413

Ho, W. L. C., Bourne, H., Gook, D., Clarke, G., Kemertzis, M., Stern, K., Agresta, F., Heloury, Y., Clark, H., Orme, L., Jayasinghe, Y., Zacharin, M. R., & the Paediatric & Adolescent Fertility Preservation Task Force, Melbourne. (2017). A short report on current fertility preservation strategies for boys. *Clinical Endocrinology, 87*(3), 279–285. https://doi.org/10.1111/cen.13377

Hoffkling, A., Obedin-Maliver, J., & Sevelius, J. (2017). From erasure to opportunity: A qualitative study of the experiences of transgender men around pregnancy and recommendations for providers. *BMC Pregnancy and Childbirth, 17*(Suppl. 2), Article 332. https://doi.org/10.1186/s12884-017-1491-5

Hoffman, D. I., Zellman, G. L., Fair, C. C., Mayer, J. F., Zeitz, J. G., Gibbons, W. E., Turner, T. G., Jr., & the Society for Assisted Reproduction Technology (SART) and RAND. (2003). Cryopreserved embryos in the United States and their availability for research. *Fertility and Sterility, 79*(5), 1063–1069. https://doi.org/10.1016/S0015-0282(03)00172-9

Hosaka, T., Matsubayashi, H., Sugiyama, Y., Izumi, S., & Makino, T. (2002). Effect of psychiatric group intervention on natural-killer cell activity and pregnancy rate. *General Hospital Psychiatry, 24*(5), 353–356. https://doi.org/10.1016/S0163-8343(02)00194-9

Huang, S. T., & Chen, A. P. C. (2008). Traditional Chinese medicine and infertility. *Current Opinion in Obstetrics & Gynecology, 20*(3), 211–215. https://doi.org/10.1097/GCO.0b013e3282f88e22

Hughes, P., Turton, P., Hopper, E., & Evans, C. D. H. (2002). Assessment of guidelines for good practice in psychosocial care of mothers after stillbirth: A cohort study. *The Lancet, 360*(9327), 114–118. https://doi.org/10.1016/S0140-6736(02)09410-2

Hullender Rubin, L. E., Opsahl, M. S., Wiemer, K. E., Mist, S. D., & Caughey, A. B. (2015). Impact of whole systems traditional Chinese medicine on in-vitro fertilization outcomes. *Reproductive Biomedicine Online, 30*(6), 602–612. https://doi.org/10.1016/j.rbmo.2015.02.005

Hutto, D. D., & Gallagher, S. (2017). Re-authoring narrative therapy: Improving our selfmanagement tools. *Philosophy, Psychiatry, & Psychology, 24*(2), 157–167. https://doi.org/10.1353/ppp.2017.0020

Hydén, L. C. (2010). Identity, self, narrative. In M. Hyvärinen, L. C. Hydén, & M. Saarenheimo (Eds.), *Beyond narrative coherence* (pp. 33–47). John Benjamins. https://doi.org/10.1075/sin.11.03hyd

Hynie, M., & Burns, L. (2006). Cross-cultural issues in infertility counseling. In S. N. Covington & L. Burns (Eds.), *Infertility counseling: A comprehensive handbook for clinicians* (2nd ed., pp. 61–82). Cambridge University Press.

Ilioi, E., Blake, L., Jadva, V., Roman, G., & Golombok, S. (2017). The role of age of disclosure of biological origins in the psychological wellbeing of adolescents conceived by reproductive donation: A longitudinal study from age 1 to age 14. *Journal of Child Psychology and Psychiatry, 58*(3), 315–324. https://doi.org/10.1111/jcpp.12667

Imrie, S., Jadva, V., & Golombok, S. (2020). "Making the child mine": Mothers' thoughts and feelings about the mother–infant relationship in egg donation families. *Journal of Family Psychology, 34*(4), 469–479. https://doi.org/10.1037/fam0000619

Jadva, V., Badger, S., Morrissette, M., & Golombok, S. (2009). 'Mom by choice, single by life's circumstance . . .' Findings from a large scale survey of the experiences of single mothers by choice. *Human Fertility, 12*(4), 175–184. https://doi.org/10.3109/14647270903373867

Jadva, V., Freeman, T., Kramer, W., & Golombok, S. (2009). The experiences of adolescents and adults conceived by sperm donation: Comparisons by age of disclosure and family type. *Human Reproduction, 24*(8), 1909–1919. https://doi.org/10.1093/humrep/dep110

Jadva, V., Freeman, T., Tranfield, E., & Golombok, S. (2018). Why search for a sperm donor online? The experiences of women searching for and contacting sperm donors on the internet. *Human Fertility, 21*(2), 112–119. https://doi.org/10.1080/14647273.2017.1315460

Jadva, V., Imrie, S., & Golombok, S. (2015). Surrogate mothers 10 years on: A longitudinal study of psychological well-being and relationships with the parents and child. *Human Reproduction, 30*(2), 373–379. https://doi.org/10.1093/humrep/deu339

Jadva, V., Murray, C., Lycett, E., MacCallum, F., & Golombok, S. (2003). Surrogacy: The experiences of surrogate mothers. *Human Reproduction, 18*(10), 2196–2204. https://doi.org/10.1093/humrep/deg397

Jaffe, J. (2015). The view from the fertility counselor's chair. In S. N. Covington (Ed.), *Fertility counseling: Clinical guide and case studies* (pp. 239–251). Cambridge University Press. https://doi.org/10.1017/CBO9781107449398.018

Jaffe, J. (2017). Reproductive trauma: Psychotherapy for pregnancy loss and infertility clients from a reproductive story perspective. *Psychotherapy, 54*(4), 380–385. https://doi.org/10.1037/pst0000125

Jaffe, J. (2019). Trauma and the reproductive story. *Psychotherapy.net*. https://www.psychotherapy.net/article/grief/trauma-and-the-reproductive-story

Jaffe, J. (2022). Reproductive trauma and PTSD: On the battlefield of fertility counseling. In S. N. Covington (Ed.), *Fertility counseling: Clinical guide* (2nd ed., pp. 204–211). Cambridge University Press. https://doi.org/10.1017/9781009030151.021

Jaffe, J., & Diamond, M. O. (2011). *Reproductive trauma: Psychotherapy with infertility and pregnancy loss clients*. American Psychological Association. https://doi.org/10.1037/12347-000

Jaffe, J., Diamond, M. O., & Diamond, D. J. (2005). *Unsung lullabies: Understanding and coping with infertility*. St. Martin's Press.

Jain, J. K., & Paulson, R. J. (2006). Oocyte cryopreservation. *Fertility and Sterility*, *86*(Suppl. 4), 1037–1046. https://doi.org/10.1016/j.fertnstert.2006.07.1478

James-Abra, S., Tarasoff, L. A., Green, D., Epstein, R., Anderson, S., Marvel, S., Steele, L. S., & Ross, L. E. (2015). Trans people's experiences with assisted reproduction services: A qualitative study. *Human Reproduction*, *30*(6), 1365–1374. https://doi.org/10.1093/humrep/dev087

Janoff-Bulman, R. (1992). *Shattered assumptions: Towards a new psychology of trauma*. The Free Press.

Jones, C., Zadeh, S., Jadva, V., & Golombok, S. (2022). Solo fathers and mothers: An exploration of well-being, social support and social approval. *International Journal of Environmental Research and Public Health*, *19*(15), Article 9236. https://doi.org/10.3390/ijerph19159236

Jordan, J. V. (2000). The role of mutual empathy in relational/cultural therapy. *Journal of Clinical Psychology*, *56*(8), 1005–1016. https://doi.org/10.1002/1097-4679(200008)56:8<1005::AID-JCLP2>3.0.CO;2-L

Josephs, L., & Van den Broeck, U. (2015). Counseling anonymous gamete donors. In S. N. Covington (Ed.), *Fertility counseling: Clinical guide and case studies* (pp. 109–121). Cambridge University Press. https://doi.org/10.1017/CBO9781107449398.009

Jung, C. (1951). *Fundamental questions of psychotherapy*. Princeton University Press.

Jung, C. G., Jaffe, A., Winston, R., & Winston, C. (1963). *Memories, dreams, reflections*. New York, Pantheon Books.

Kabat-Zinn, J. (2003). Mindfulness-based interventions in context: Past, present, and future. *Clinical Psychology: Science and Practice*, *10*(2), 144–156. https://doi.org/10.1093/clipsy.bpg016

Kabat-Zinn, J. (2021). The liberative potential of mindfulness. *Mindfulness*, *12*(6), 1555–1563. https://doi.org/10.1007/s12671-021-01608-6

Kamel, R. M. (2013). Assisted reproductive technology after the birth of Louise Brown. *Journal of Reproduction & Infertility*, *14*(3), 96–109. https://doi.org/10.4172/2161-0932.1000156

Kennedy-Moulton, K., Miller, S., Persson, P., Rossin-Slater, M., Wherry, L., & Aldana, G. (2022). *Maternal and infant health inequality: New evidence from linked administrative data* (No. w30693). National Bureau of Economic Research. https://doi.org/10.3386/w30693

Kenny, P., Higgins, D., Soloff, C., & Sweid, R. (2012). *Past adoption experiences: National research study on the service response to past adoption practices.* Australian Institute of Family Studies.

Khoury, B., Sharma, M., Rush, S. E., & Fournier, C. (2015). Mindfulness-based stress reduction for healthy individuals: A meta-analysis. *Journal of Psychosomatic Research, 78*(6), 519–528. https://doi.org/10.1016/j.jpsychores.2015.03.009

Killian, K. D. (2008). Helping till it hurts? A multimethod study of compassion fatigue, burnout, and self-care in clinicians working with trauma survivors. *Traumatology, 14*(2), 32–44. https://doi.org/10.1177/1534765608319083

Kingdon, C., Givens, J. L., O'Donnell, E., & Turner, M. (2015). Seeing and holding baby: Systematic review of clinical management and parental outcomes after stillbirth. *Birth, 42*(3), 206–218. https://doi.org/10.1111/birt.12176

Kirkman, M. (2008). Being a 'real' mum: Motherhood through donated eggs and embryos. *Women's Studies International Forum, 31*(4), 241–248. https://doi.org/10.1016/j.wsif.2008.05.006

Klass, D. (2006). Continuing conversation about continuing bonds. *Death Studies, 30*(9), 843–858. https://doi.org/10.1080/07481180600886959

Klitzman, R., & Sauer, M. V. (2015). Creating and selling embryos for "donation": Ethical challenges. *American Journal of Obstetrics and Gynecology, 212*(2), 167–170. https://doi.org/10.1016/j.ajog.2014.10.1094

Klock, S. C., Jacob, M. C., & Maier, D. (1994). A prospective study of donor insemination recipients: Secrecy, privacy, and disclosure. *Fertility and Sterility, 62*(3), 477–484. https://doi.org/10.1016/S0015-0282(16)56934-9

Knox, S., & Hill, C. E. (2003). Therapist self-disclosure: Research-based suggestions for practitioners. *Journal of Clinical Psychology, 59*(5), 529–539. https://doi.org/10.1002/jclp.10157

Knox, S., & Hill, C. E. (2016). Introduction to a special issue on disclosure and concealment in psychotherapy. *Counselling Psychology Quarterly, 29*(1), 1–6. https://doi.org/10.1080/09515070.2015.1095156

Kolmes, K., & Taube, D. O. (2014). Seeking and finding our clients on the Internet: Boundary considerations in cyberspace. *Professional Psychology: Research and Practice, 45*(1), 3–10. https://doi.org/10.1037/a0029958

Kolmes, K., & Taube, D. O. (2016). Client discovery of psychotherapist personal information online. *Professional Psychology: Research and Practice, 47*(2), 147–154. https://doi.org/10.1037/pro0000065

Komorowski, A. S., & Feinberg, E. C. (2022). Scientific and ethical considerations in using preimplantation genetic testing for polygenic disease. *Fertility and Sterility, 117*(6), 1160–1161. https://doi.org/10.1016/j.fertnstert.2022.03.019

Koniak-Griffin, D., Logsdon, M. C., Hines-Martin, V., & Turner, C. C. (2006). Contemporary mothering in a diverse society. *Journal of Obstetric, Gynecologic, and Neonatal Nursing, 35*(5), 671–678. https://doi.org/10.1111/j.1552-6909.2006.00089.x

Korenromp, M. J., Page-Christiaens, G. C. M. L., van den Bout, J., Mulder, E. J. H., & Visser, G. H. A. (2007). Maternal decision to terminate pregnancy in case of Down syndrome. *American Journal of Obstetrics and Gynecology, 196*(2), 149.e1–149.e11. https://doi.org/10.1016/j.ajog.2006.09.013

Krahn, L., & Sullivan, R. (2015). Grief & loss resolution among birth mothers in open adoption. *Canadian Social Work Review, 32*(1–2), 27–48. https://doi.org/10.7202/1034142ar

Krawczyk, A., Kretek, A., Pluta, D., Kowalczyk, K., Czech, I., Radosz, P., & Madej, P. (2022). Gluten-free diet—Remedy for infertility or dangerous trend? *Ginekologia Polska, 93*(5), 422–426. https://doi.org/10.5603/GP.a2021.0223

Krosch, D. J., & Shakespeare-Finch, J. (2017). Grief, traumatic stress, and post-traumatic growth in women who have experienced pregnancy loss. *Psychological Trauma: Theory, Research, Practice, and Policy, 9*(4), 425–433. https://doi.org/10.1037/tra0000183

Kroth, J., Garcia, M., Hallgren, M., LeGrue, E., Ross, M., & Scalise, J. (2004). Perinatal loss, trauma, and dream reports. *Psychological Reports, 94*(3), 877–882. https://doi.org/10.2466/pr0.94.3.877-882

Kubler-Ross, E. (1969). *On death and dying*. Macmillan.

Lahl, J., Fell, K., Bassett, K., Broghammer, F. H., & Briggs, W. M. (2022). A comparison of American women's experiences with both gestational surrogate pregnancies and spontaneous pregnancies. *Dignity: A Journal of Analysis of Exploitation and Violence, 7*(3). https://doi.org/10.23860/dignity.2022.07.03.01

Larsen, E. C., Müller, J., Schmiegelow, K., Rechnitzer, C., & Andersen, A. N. (2003). Reduced ovarian function in long-term survivors of radiation- and chemotherapy-treated childhood cancer. *The Journal of Clinical Endocrinology and Metabolism, 88*(11), 5307–5314. https://doi.org/10.1210/jc.2003-030352

Lasker, J. N., & Toedter, L. J. (2000). Predicting outcomes after pregnancy loss: Results from studies using the Perinatal Grief Scale. *Illness, Crisis, & Loss, 8*(4), 350–372. https://doi.org/10.1177/105413730000800402

Lawrence, D. J. (2007). The four principles of biomedical ethics: A foundation for current bioethical debate. *Journal of Chiropractic Humanities, 14*, 34–40. https://doi.org/10.1016/S1556-3499(13)60161-8

Lee, K. (2017). What happens to the leftovers? Is compassionate transfer ethical? *Voices in Bioethics, 3*, 1–3.

Leibowitz, L. (2009). Reflections of a childless analyst. In B. Gerson (Ed.), *The therapist as a person: Life crises, life choices, life experiences, and their effects on treatment* (pp. 71–87). Routledge. (Original work published 1996)

Leon, I. G. (1990). *When a baby dies*. Yale University Press.

Leon, I. G. (1996). Reproductive loss: Barriers to psychoanalytic treatment. *Journal of the American Academy of Psychoanalysis, 24*(2), 341–352. https://doi.org/10.1521/jaap.1.1996.24.2.341

Leon, I. G. (2001). Perinatal loss. In N. L. Stotland & D. E. Stewart (Eds.), *Psychological aspects of women's healthcare: The interface between psychiatry and obstetrics and gynecology* (2nd ed., pp. 141–176). American Psychiatric Press.

Levitt, H. M., Minami, T., Greenspan, S. B., Puckett, J. A., Henretty, J. R., Reich, C. M., & Berman, J. S. (2016). How therapist self-disclosure relates to alliance and outcomes: A naturalistic study. *Counselling Psychology Quarterly, 29*(1), 7–28. https://doi.org/10.1080/09515070.2015.1090396

Lewin, T. (2007, May 22). Out of grief grows an advocacy for legal certificate of stillborn birth. *The New York Times*, A16.

Lindemann, E. (1944). Symptomatology and management of acute grief. *The American Journal of Psychiatry, 101*(2), 141–148. https://doi.org/10.1176/ajp.101.2.141

Loftus, J., & Andriot, A. L. (2012). "That's what makes a woman": Infertility and coping with a failed life course transition. *Sociological Spectrum, 32*(3), 226–243. https://doi.org/10.1080/02732173.2012.663711

Lovell, A. (2001). The changing identities of miscarriage and stillbirth: Influences on practice and ritual. *Bereavement Care, 20*(3), 37–40. https://doi.org/10.1080/02682620108657527

Lyerly, A. D., Steinhauser, K., Namey, E., Tulsky, J. A., Cook-Deegan, R., Sugarman, J., Walmer, D., Faden, R., & Wallach, E. (2006). Factors that affect infertility patients' decisions about disposition of frozen embryos. *Fertility and Sterility, 85*(6), 1623–1630. https://doi.org/10.1016/j.fertnstert.2005.11.056

MacCallum, F., Golombok, S., & Brinsden, P. (2007). Parenting and child development in families with a child conceived through embryo donation. *Journal of Family Psychology, 21*(2), 278–287. https://doi.org/10.1037/0893-3200.21.2.278

Mac Dougall, K., Becker, G., Scheib, J. E., & Nachtigall, R. D. (2007). Strategies for disclosure: How parents approach telling their children that they were conceived with donor gametes. *Fertility and Sterility, 87*(3), 524–533. https://doi.org/10.1016/j.fertnstert.2006.07.1514

Magee, L. A., Nicolaides, K. H., & von Dadelszen, P. (2022). Preeclampsia. *The New England Journal of Medicine, 386*(19), 1817–1832. https://doi.org/10.1056/NEJMra2109523

Mahalik, J. R., VanOrmer, E. A., & Simi, N. L. (2000). Ethical issues in using self-disclosure in feminist therapy. In M. M. Brabeck (Ed.), *Practicing feminist ethics in psychology* (pp. 189–201). American Psychological Association. https://doi.org/10.1037/10343-009

Mahler, M., Pine, F., & Bergman, A. (1975). *The psychological birth of the human infant*. Basic Books.

Malavé, A. (2015). Adoption. In S. N. Covington (Ed.), *Fertility counseling: Clinical guide and case studies* (pp. 197–211). Cambridge University Press. https://doi.org/10.1017/CBO9781107449398.015

Malik, S. H., & Coulson, N. S. (2008). Computer-mediated infertility support groups: An exploratory study of online experiences. *Patient Education and Counseling, 73*(1), 105–113. https://doi.org/10.1016/j.pec.2008.05.024

Malik, S., & Coulson, N. S. (2010). 'They all supported me but I felt like I suddenly didn't belong anymore': An exploration of perceived disadvantages to online support seeking. *Journal of Psychosomatic Obstetrics & Gynecology, 31*(3), 140–149. https://doi.org/10.3109/0167482X.2010.504870

Markin, R. D. (2017). An introduction to the special section on psychotherapy for pregnancy loss: Review of issues, clinical applications, and future research direction. *Psychotherapy, 54*(4), 367–372. https://doi.org/10.1037/pst0000134

Markus, H., & Nurius, P. (1986). Possible selves. *American Psychologist, 41*(9), 954–969. https://doi.org/10.1037/0003-066X.41.9.954

Marrero, S. J. (2013). The role of the psychologist in reproductive medicine. *Fertility and Sterility, 100*(3), S416. https://doi.org/10.1016/j.fertnstert.2013.07.641

Martin, P. (2011). Celebrating the wounded healer. *Counselling Psychology Review, 26*(1), 10–19. https://doi.org/10.53841/bpscpr.2011.26.1.10

Martin, T. L., & Doka, K. J. (2000). *Men don't cry . . . women do: Transcending gender stereotypes of grief*. Brunner/Mazel.

Matozzo, L. M. (2000). Impact of the therapist's pregnancy on relationships with clients: A comparative study (Publication No. WRI0279796) [Doctoral dissertation, Widener University]. Proquest Dissertations and Theses Global.

Matthews, T. J., & Hamilton, B. E. (2009). Delayed childbearing: More women are having their first child later in life. *NCHS Data Brief, 21*(21), 1–8.

Matthews, T. J., & Ventura, S. J. (1997). Birth and fertility rates by educational attainment: United States, 1994. *Monthly Vital Statistics Report, 45*(Suppl.), 10.

McAdams, D. P., Josselson, R., & Lieblich, A. (Eds.). (2006). *Identity and story: Creating self in narrative*. American Psychological Association. https://doi.org/10.1037/11414-000

McDaniel, S. H., Hepworth, J., Doherty, W. J., & McDaniel, H. (2009). *The shared experience of illness*. Basic Books.

McGee, G., Brakman, S. V., & Gurmankin, A. D. (2001). Gamete donation and anonymity: Disclosure to children conceived with donor gametes should not be optional. *Human Reproduction, 16*(10), 2033–2036. https://doi.org/10.1093/humrep/16.10.2033

McGreal, D., Evans, B. J., & Burrows, G. D. (1997). Gender differences in coping following loss of a child through miscarriage or stillbirth: A pilot study. *Stress Medicine, 13*(3), 159–165. https://doi.org/10.1002/(SICI)1099-1700(199707)13:3<159::AID-SMI734>3.0.CO;2-5

McIntyre, H. D., Catalano, P., Zhang, C., Desoye, G., Mathiesen, E. R., & Damm, P. (2019). Gestational diabetes mellitus. *Nature Reviews Disease Primers, 5*(1), 47. https://doi.org/10.1038/s41572-019-0098-8

McLaughlin, A. A., Keller, S. M., Feeny, N. C., Youngstrom, E. A., & Zoellner, L. A. (2014). Patterns of therapeutic alliance: Rupture–repair episodes in prolonged exposure for posttraumatic stress disorder. *Journal of Consulting and Clinical Psychology, 82*(1), 112–121. https://doi.org/10.1037/a0034696

McMahon, C. A., Gibson, F. L., Leslie, G. I., Saunders, D. M., Porter, K. A., & T ennant, C. C. (2003). Embryo donation for medical research: Attitudes and concerns of potential donors. *Human Reproduction, 18*(4), 871–877. https://doi.org/10.1093/humrep/deg167

Menning, B. E. (1976). RESOLVE; a support group for infertile couples. *The American Journal of Nursing, 76*(2), 258–259. https://doi.org/10.2307/3423816

Mihai, D., Bratila, E., Mehedintu, C., Berceanu, C., & Pituru, S. M. (2017). The ethical aspects regarding cryopreserved embryos. *Revista de Medicina Legala, 25*(3), 317–321. https://doi.org/10.4323/rjlm.2017.317

Miller, S., Wherry, L. R., & Foster, D. G. (2020). What happens after an abortion denial? A review of results from the Turnaway Study. *AEA Papers and Proceedings, 110*, 226–230. https://doi.org/10.1257/pandp.20201107

Mindes, E. J., & Covington, L. S. (2015). Counseling known participants in third party reproduction. In S. N. Covington (Ed.), *Fertility counseling: Clinical guide and case studies* (pp. 136–149). Cambridge University Press. https://doi.org/10.1017/CBO9781107449398.011

Mollen, D. (2006). Voluntarily childfree women: Experiences and counseling considerations. *Journal of Mental Health Counseling, 28*(3), 269–282. https://doi.org/10.17744/mehc.28.3.39w5h93mreb0mk4f

Moolhuijsen, L. M., & Visser, J. A. (2020). Anti-Müllerian hormone and ovarian reserve: Update on assessing ovarian function. *The Journal of Clinical Endocrinology & Metabolism, 105*(11), 3361–3373. https://doi.org/10.1210/clinem/dgaa513

Morey, L. C. (1991). *Personality Assessment Inventory professional manual.* Psychological Assessment Resources.

Murphy, D. A. (2013). The desire for parenthood: Gay men choosing to become parents through surrogacy. *Journal of Family Issues, 34*(8), 1104–1124. https://doi.org/10.1177/0192513X13484272

Myers, D., & Hayes, J. A. (2006). Effects of therapist general self-disclosure and countertransference disclosure on ratings of the therapist and session. *Psychotherapy: Theory, Research, Practice, Training, 43*(2), 173–185. https://doi.org/10.1037/0033-3204.43.2.173

Nachtigall, R. D., Becker, G., Friese, C., Butler, A., & MacDougall, K. (2005). Parents' conceptualization of their frozen embryos complicates the disposition decision. *Fertility and Sterility, 84*(2), 431–434. https://doi.org/10.1016/j.fertnstert.2005.01.134

Nakano, Y., Akechi, T., Furukawa, T. A., & Sugiura-Ogasawara, M. (2013). Cognitive behavior therapy for psychological distress in patients with recurrent miscarriage. *Psychology Research and Behavior Management, 6*, 37–43. https://doi.org/10.2147/PRBM.S44327

National Association of Social Workers. (2021). *Code of ethics for the National Association of Social Workers.* https://www.socialworkers.org/About/Ethics/Code-of-Ethics/Code-of-Ethics-English

National Institute of Mental Health. (2022). *I'm so stressed out!* https://www.nimh.nih.gov/sites/default/files/documents/health/publications/so-stressed-out-fact-sheet/im-so-stressed-out.pdf

Negris, O., Lawson, A., Brown, D., Warren, C., Galic, I., Bozen, A., Swanson, A., & Jain, T. (2021). Emotional stress and reproduction: What do fertility patients believe? *Journal of Assisted Reproduction and Genetics, 38*(4), 877–887. https://doi.org/10.1007/s10815-021-02079-3

Neimeyer, R. A. (2004). Fostering posttraumatic growth: A narrative elaboration. *Psychological Inquiry, 15*, 53–59.

Neimeyer, R. A., Klass, D., & Dennis, M. R. (2014). A social constructionist account of grief: Loss and the narration of meaning. *Death Studies, 38*(8), 485–498. https://doi.org/10.1080/07481187.2014.913454

Newton, C. R., Fisher, J., Feyles, V., Tekpetey, F., Hughes, L., & Isacsson, D. (2007). Changes in patient preferences in the disposal of cryopreserved embryos. *Human Reproduction, 22*(12), 3124–3128. https://doi.org/10.1093/humrep/dem287

Neyra, O. (2021). Reproductive ethics and family: An argument to cover access to ART for the LGBTQ community. *Voices in Bioethics, 7*, 1–8. https://doi.org/10.52214/vib.v7i.8559

Nikolettos, N., Asimakopoulos, B., & Hatzissabas, I. (2003). Intrafamilial sperm donation: Ethical questions and concerns. *Human Reproduction, 18*(5), 933–936. https://doi.org/10.1093/humrep/deg214

Norcross, J. C., & Phillips, C. M. (2020). Psychologist self-care during the pandemic: Now more than ever. *Journal of Health Service Psychology, 46*(2), 59–63. https://doi.org/10.1007/s42843-020-00010-5

Obergefell v. Hodges, 576 U.S.644 (2015). https://www.supremecourt.gov/opinions/14pdf/14-556_3204.pdf

O'Leary, J., & Thorwick, C. (2006). Fathers' perspectives during pregnancy, postperinatal loss. *Journal of Obstetric, Gynecologic, and Neonatal Nursing, 35*(1), 78–86. https://doi.org/10.1111/j.1552-6909.2006.00017.x

Olshansky, E., & Sereika, S. (2005). The transition from pregnancy to postpartum in previously infertile women: A focus on depression. *Archives of Psychiatric Nursing, 19*(6), 273–280. https://doi.org/10.1016/j.apnu.2005.08.003

Ombelet, W., & Van Robays, J. (2015). Artificial insemination history: Hurdles and milestones. *Facts, Views & Vision in ObGyn, 7*(2), 137–143.

Orenstein, P. (2007, July 15). Your gamete, myself. *The New York Times Magazine.* http://www.nytimes.com/2007/07/15/magazine/15egg-t.html?pagewanted=1

Ota, K., Takahashi, T., Katagiri, M., Miznuma, H., & Yoshida, H. (2021). Effects of Hatha Yoga on endocrine functions and assisted reproductive technology outcomes in women with infertility: A retrospective cohort study. *The Journal of Reproductive Medicine, 66*, 101–106.

Oxford University Press. (n.d.). Story. *Oxford Learner's Dictionaries.* Retrieved October 11, 2023, from https://www.oxfordlearnersdictionaries.com/us/definition/english/story

Öztürk, R., Herbell, K., Morton, J., & Bloom, T. (2021). "The worst time of my life": Treatment-related stress and unmet needs of women living with infertility. *Journal of Community Psychology, 49*(5), 1121–1133. https://doi.org/10.1002/jcop.22527

Paltrow, L. M., Harris, L. H., & Marshall, M. F. (2022). Beyond abortion: The consequences of overturning Roe. *The American Journal of Bioethics, 22*(8), 3–15. https://doi.org/10.1080/15265161.2022.2075965

Park, C. L. (2010). Making sense of the meaning literature: An integrative review of meaning making and its effects on adjustment to stressful life events. *Psychological Bulletin, 136*(2), 257–301. https://doi.org/10.1037/a0018301

Park, C. L. (2013). The meaning making model: A framework for understanding meaning, spirituality, and stress-related growth in health psychology. *The European Health Psychologist, 15*, 40–47.

Parker, G., Ker, A., Baddock, S., Kerekere, E., Veale, J., & Miller, S. (2022). "It's total erasure": Trans and nonbinary peoples' experiences of cisnormativity within perinatal care services in Aotearoa New Zealand. *Women's Reproductive Health, 10*(4), pp. 591–607. https://doi.org/10.1080/23293691.2022.2155496

Pašalić, M., & Hasanović, M. (2018). Treating childbirth trauma with EMDR—A case report. *Psychiatria Danubina, 30*(Suppl. 5), 265–270.

Pasch, L. A., Holley, S. R., Bleil, M. E., Shehab, D., Katz, P. P., & Adler, N. E. (2016). Addressing the needs of fertility treatment patients and their partners: Are they informed of and do they receive mental health services? *Fertility and Sterility, 106*(1), 209–215. https://doi.org/10.1016/j.fertnstert.2016.03.006

Patel, A., Sharma, P. S. V. N., & Kumar, P. (2020). Application of mindfulness-based psychological interventions in infertility. *Journal of Human Reproductive Sciences, 13*(1), 3–21. https://doi.org/10.4103/jhrs.JHRS_51_19

Patrizio, P., Mastroianni, A. C., & Mastroianni, L. (2001). Gamete donation and anonymity: Disclosure to children conceived with donor gametes should be optional. *Human Reproduction, 16*(10), 2036–2038. https://doi.org/10.1093/humrep/16.10.2036

Patterson, J. E. (2009). A birth gone awry. In S. H. McDonald, J. Hepworth, & W. J. Doherty (Eds.), *The shared experience of illness* (pp. 23–29). Basic Books.

Patton, J. (2009). Engendering a new paradigm: Self-disclosure with queer clients. In A. Bloomgarden & R. B. Mennuti (Eds.), *Psychotherapist revealed* (pp. 181–192). Routledge.

Paul, M. S., Berger, R., Berlow, N., Rovner-Ferguson, H., Figlerski, L., Gardner, S., & Malave, A. F. (2010). Posttraumatic growth and social support in individuals with infertility. *Human Reproduction, 25*(1), 133–141. https://doi.org/10.1093/humrep/dep367

Paulson, R. J. (2021). Reproduction reimagined. *F & S Reports, 2*(4), 361. https://doi.org/10.1016/j.xfre.2021.11.004

Pehlivan, T., & Guner, P. (2018). Compassion fatigue: The known and unknown. *Journal of Psychiatric Nursing, 9*(2), 129–134. https://doi.org/10.14744/phd.2017.25582

Pelka, S. (2009). Sharing motherhood: Maternal jealousy among lesbian co-mothers. *Journal of Homosexuality, 56*(2), 195–217. https://doi.org/10.1080/00918360802623164

Péloquin, K., Brassard, A., Arpin, V., Sabourin, S., & Wright, J. (2018). Whose fault is it? Blame predicting psychological adjustment and couple satisfaction in couples seeking fertility treatment. *Journal of Psychosomatic Obstetrics & Gynecology, 39*(1), 64–72. https://doi.org/10.1080/0167482X.2017.1289369

Peterson, C., Park, N., Pole, N., D'Andrea, W., & Seligman, M. E. P. (2008). Strengths of character and posttraumatic growth. *Journal of Traumatic Stress, 21*(2), 214–217. https://doi.org/10.1002/jts.20332

Peterson, Z. D. (2002). More than a mirror: The ethics of therapist self-disclosure. *Psychotherapy: Theory, Research, Practice, Training, 39*(1), 21–31. https://doi.org/10.1037/0033-3204.39.1.21

Pinto-Coelho, K. G., Hill, C. E., & Kivlighan, D. M., Jr. (2016). Therapist self-disclosure in psychodynamic psychotherapy: A mixed methods investigation. *Counselling Psychology Quarterly, 29*(1), 29–52. https://doi.org/10.1080/09515070.2015.1072496

Pirtea, P., Vulliemoz, N., de Ziegler, D., & Ayoubi, J. M. (2022). Infertility workup: Identifying endometriosis. *Fertility and Sterility, 118*(1), 29–33. https://doi.org/10.1016/j.fertnstert.2022.03.015

Popovic, M., Dhaenens, L., Boel, A., Menten, B., & Heindryckx, B. (2020). Chromosomal mosaicism in human blastocysts: The ultimate diagnostic dilemma. *Human Reproduction Update, 26*(3), 313–334. https://doi.org/10.1093/humupd/dmz050

Porcu, E., Cipriani, L., Dirodi, M., De Iaco, P., Perrone, A. M., Zinzani, P. L., Taffurelli, M., Zamagni, C., Ciotti, P. M., Notarangelo, L., Calza, N., & Damiano, G. (2022). Successful pregnancies, births, and children development following oocyte cryostorage in female cancer patients during 25 years of fertility preservation. *Cancers, 14*(6), 1429–1444. https://doi.org/10.3390/cancers14061429

Posluns, K., & Gall, T. L. (2020). Dear mental health practitioners, take care of yourselves: A literature review on self-care. *International Journal for the Advancement of Counselling, 42*(1), 1–20. https://doi.org/10.1007/s10447-019-09382-w

Practice Committee of the American Society for Reproductive Medicine. (2019). Fertility preservation in patients undergoing gonadotoxic therapy or gonadectomy: A committee opinion. *Fertility and Sterility, 112*(6), 1022–1033. https://doi.org/10.1016/j.fertnstert.2019.09.013

Practice Committee of the American Society for Reproductive Medicine and Practice Committee of the Society for Assisted Reproductive Technology. (2017). Recommendations for practices utilizing gestational carriers: A committee opinion. *Fertility and Sterility, 107*(2), e3–e10. https://doi.org/10.1016/j.fertnstert.2016.11.007

Practice Committee of the American Society for Reproductive Medicine and the Practice Committee for the Society for Assisted Reproductive Technology. (2021). Guidance regarding gamete and embryo donation. *Fertility and Sterility, 115*(6), 1395–1410. https://doi.org/10.1016/j.fertnstert.2021.01.045

Preimplantation Genetic Diagnosis International Society. (2016, July 10). *PGDIS position statement on chromosome mosaicism and preimplantation aneuploidy testing at the blastocyst stage.* https://www.pgdis.org/docs/newsletter_071816.html

Puddifoot, J. E., & Johnson, M. P. (1999). Active grief, despair and difficulty coping: Some measured characteristics of male response following their partner's miscarriage. *Journal of Reproductive and Infant Psychology, 17*(1), 89–93. https://doi.org/10.1080/02646839908404587

Purewal, S., & van den Akker, O. B. A. (2009). Systematic review of oocyte donation: Investigating attitudes, motivations and experiences. *Human Reproduction Update, 15*(5), 499–515. https://doi.org/10.1093/humupd/dmp018

Quinn, M., & Fujimoto, V. (2016). Racial and ethnic disparities in assisted reproductive technology access and outcomes. *Fertility and Sterility, 105*(5), 1119–1123. https://doi.org/10.1016/j.fertnstert.2016.03.007

Rabinor, J. R. (2009). Self-disclosure as a turning point in psychotherapy. In A. Bloomgarden & R. B. Mennuti (Eds.), *Psychotherapist revealed* (pp. 55–70). Routledge.

Raja, N. S., Russell, C. B., & Moravek, M. B. (2022). Assisted reproductive technology: Considerations for the nonheterosexual population and single parents. *Fertility and Sterility, 118*(1), 47–53. https://doi.org/10.1016/j.fertnstert.2022.04.012

Ramos, C., & Leal, I. (2013). Posttraumatic growth in the aftermath of trauma: A literature review about related factors and application contexts. *Psychology, Community & Health, 2*(1), 43–54. https://doi.org/10.5964/pch.v2i1.39

Rando, T. A. (1985). Bereaved parents: Particular difficulties, unique factors, and treatment issues. *Social Work, 30*(1), 19–23. https://doi.org/10.1093/sw/30.1.19

Rando, T. A. (1986). *Parental loss of a child.* Research Press.

Rayner, J. A., McLachlan, H. L., Forster, D. A., & Cramer, R. (2009). Australian women's use of complementary and alternative medicines to enhance fertility: Exploring the experiences of women and practitioners. *BMC Complementary and Alternative Medicine, 9*(1), 52. https://doi.org/10.1186/1472-6882-9-52

Redshaw, M., Hennegan, J. M., & Henderson, J. (2016). Impact of holding the baby following stillbirth on maternal mental health and well-being: Findings from a national survey. *BMJ Open, 6*(8), Article e010996. https://doi.org/10.1136/bmjopen-2015-010996

Richard-Davis, G., & Morris, J. R. (2023). No longer separate but not close to equal: Navigating inclusivity in a burgeoning field built on injustice. *Fertility and Sterility, 120*(3), 400–402. https://doi.org/10.1016/j.fertnstert.2022.11.013

Rienzi, L., Gracia, C., Maggiulli, R., LaBarbera, A. R., Kaser, D. J., Ubaldi, F. M., Vanderpoel, S., & Racowsky, C. (2017). Oocyte, embryo and blastocyst cryopreservation in ART: Systematic review and meta-analysis comparing slow-freezing versus vitrification to produce evidence for the development of global guidance. *Human Reproduction Update, 23*(2), 139–155. https://doi.org/10.1093/humupd/dmw038

Rinehart, M. S., & Kiselica, M. S. (2010). Helping men with the trauma of miscarriage. *Psychotherapy: Theory, Research, Practice, Training, 47*(3), 288–295. https://doi.org/10.1037/a0021160

Robinson, M., Baker, L., & Nackerud, L. (1999). The relationship of attachment theory and perinatal loss. *Death Studies, 23*(3), 257–270. https://doi.org/10.1080/074811899201073

Rocca, C. H., Samari, G., Foster, D. G., Gould, H., & Kimport, K. (2020). Emotions and decision rightness over five years following an abortion: An examination of decision difficulty and abortion stigma. *Social Science & Medicine, 248,* Article 112704. https://doi.org/10.1016/j.socscimed.2019.112704

Roe v. Wade, 410 U.S. 113 (1973). https://www.oyez.org/cases/1971/70-18

Rogers, C. (1951). *On becoming a person.* Houghton Mifflin.

Romney, J., Fife, S. T., Sanders, D., & Behrens, S. (2021). Treatment of couples experiencing pregnancy loss: Reauthoring loss from narrative perspective. *International Journal of Systemic Therapy, 32*(2), 134–152. https://doi.org/10.1080/2692398X.2020.1855621

Rooney, K. L., & Domar, A. D. (2018). The relationship between stress and infertility. *Dialogues in Clinical Neuroscience, 20*(1), 41–47. https://doi.org/10.31887/DCNS.2018.20.1/klrooney

Rosen, A. (2015). Fertility preservation counseling. In S. N. Covington (Ed.), *Fertility counseling: Clinical guide and case studies* (pp. 212–225). Cambridge University Press.

Rothaupt, J., & Becker, K. (2007). A literature review of Western bereavement theory: From decathecting to continuing bonds. *The Family Journal, 15*(1), 6–15. https://doi.org/10.1177/1066480706294031

Rubin, H. (2002). *The impact and meaning of childlessness: An interview study of childless women* (Publication No. 3023438) [Doctoral dissertation, California School of Professional Psychology—San Diego]. Proquest Dissertations and Theses Global.

Rumball, A., & Adair, V. (1999). Telling the story: Parents' scripts for donor offspring. *Human Reproduction, 14*(5), 1392–1399. https://doi.org/10.1093/humrep/14.5.1392

Ryninks, K., Wilkinson-Tough, M., Stacey, S., & Horsch, A. (2022). Comparing posttraumatic growth in mothers after stillbirth or early miscarriage. *PLOS ONE, 17*(8), Article e0271314. https://doi.org/10.1371/journal.pone.0271314

Saakvitne, K. W. (2002). Shared trauma: The therapist's increased vulnerability. *Psychoanalytic Dialogues, 12*(3), 443–449. https://doi.org/10.1080/10481881209348678

Sachdev, P. (1991). The birth father: A neglected element in the adoption equation. *Families in Society, 72*(3), 131–139. https://doi.org/10.1177/104438949107200301

Sachs, P. L., & Burns, L. H. (2006). Recipient counseling for oocyte donation. In S. N. Covington & L. H. Burns (Eds.), *Infertility counseling: A comprehensive handbook for clinicians* (2nd ed., pp. 319–338). Cambridge University Press.

Sachs, P. L., & Toll, C. B. (2015). Counseling recipients of anonymous donor gametes. In S. N. Covington (Ed.), *Fertility counseling: Clinical guide and case studies* (pp. 97–108). Cambridge University Press.

Safran, J. D., Muran, J. C., & Eubanks-Carter, C. (2011). Repairing alliance ruptures. *Psychotherapy, 48*(1), 80–87. https://doi.org/10.1037/a0022140

Safran, J. D., Muran, J. C., Samstag, L. W., & Stevens, C. (2001). Repairing alliance ruptures. *Psychotherapy, 38*(4), 406–412. https://doi.org/10.1037/0033-3204.38.4.406

Sallam, H. N., & Sallam, N. H. (2016). Religious aspects of assisted reproduction. *Facts, Views & Vision in ObGyn, 8*(1), 33–48.

Sandelowski, M., Harris, B. G., & Holditch-Davis, D. (1993). "Somewhere out there": Parental claiming in the preadoption waiting period. *Journal of Contemporary Ethnography, 21*(4), 464–486. https://doi.org/10.1177/089124193021004003

Santorelli, S. F., Kabat-Zinn, J., Blacker, M., Meleo-Meyer, F., & Koerbel, L. (2017). *Mindfulness-based stress reduction (MBSR) authorized curriculum guide.* Center for Mindfulness in Medicine, Health Care, and Society, University of Massachusetts Medical School. https://www.tarkustekool.ee/wp-content/uploads/2021/09/CFM-Teaching-UMass-MBSR-Curriculum-Teaching-Guide-2017.pdf

Saran, J., & Padubidri, J. R. (2020). New laws ban commercial surrogacy in India. *The Medico-Legal Journal, 88*(3), 148–150. https://doi.org/10.1177/0025817219891881

Schmidt, F. M. D., Fiorini, G. P., & Ramires, V. R. R. (2015). Psychoanalytic psychotherapy and the pregnant therapist: A literature review. *Research in Psychotherapy: Psychopathology, Process and Outcome, 18*(2), 50–61. https://doi.org/10.4081/ripppo.2015.185

Schmidt, L., Holstein, B., Christensen, U., & Boivin, J. (2005). Does infertility cause marital benefit? An epidemiological study of 2250 women and men in fertility treatment. *Patient Education and Counseling, 59*(3), 244–251. https://doi.org/10.1016/j.pec.2005.07.015

Schwartz, S. E. O., Benoit, L., Clayton, S., Parnes, M. F., Swenson, L., & Lowe, S. R. (2022). Climate change anxiety and mental health: Environmental activism as buffer. *Current Psychology, 42*, 16708–16721. Advance online publication. https://doi.org/10.1007/s12144-022-02735-6

Schwerdtfeger, K. L., & Shreffler, K. M. (2009). Trauma of pregnancy loss and infertility among mothers and involuntarily childless women in the United

States. *Journal of Loss and Trauma, 14*(3), 211–227. https://doi.org/10.1080/ 15325020802537468

Seligman, M. E. P., Steen, T. A., Park, N., & Peterson, C. (2005). Positive psychology progress: Empirical validation of interventions. *American Psychologist, 60*(5), 410–421. https://doi.org/10.1037/0003-066X.60.5.410

Seyhan, A., Ata, B., Chen, H. Y., Varghese, A. C., Mumcu, A., & Tan, S. L. (2012). Fertility preservation. *Current Obstetrics and Gynecology Reports, 1*(4), 182–189. https://doi.org/10.1007/s13669-012-0025-4

Shanley, M. L. (2002). Collaboration and commodification in assisted procreation: Reflections on an open market and anonymous donation in human sperm and eggs [Special issue]. *Law & Society Review, 36*(2), 257–284. https://doi.org/ 10.2307/1512177

Shapiro, C. H. (2009). Therapy with infertile heterosexual couples: It's not about gender—Or is it? *Clinical Social Work Journal, 37*(2), 140–149. https:// doi.org/10.1007/s10615-008-0149-1

Shapiro, F. (2002). EMDR 12 years after its introduction: Past and future research. *Journal of Clinical Psychology, 58*(1), 1–22. https://doi.org/10.1002/jclp.1126

Shapiro, S. L., Brown, K. W., & Biegel, G. M. (2007). Teaching self-care to caregivers: Effects of mindfulness-based stress reduction on the mental health of therapists in training. *Training and Education in Professional Psychology, 1*(2), 105–115. https://doi.org/10.1037/1931-3918.1.2.105

Sharma, P. (2020). Facing the 'baby bump': How a psychotherapist's pregnancy influences healing. *International Journal of Indian Psychology, 8*, 255–261. https://doi.org/10.25215/0801.030

Simopoulou, M., Sfakianoudis, K., Maziotis, E., Tsioulou, P., Grigoriadis, S., Rapani, A., Giannelou, P., Asimakopoulou, M., Kokkali, G., Pantou, A., Nikolettos, K., Vlahos, N., & Pantos, K. (2021). PGT-A: Who and when? A systematic review and network meta-analysis of RCTs. *Journal of Assisted Reproduction and Genetics, 38*, 1939–1957. https://doi.org/10.1007/s10815-021-02227-9

Simpson, T. H., & Hanafin, H. (2015). Counseling surrogate carrier participants. In S. N. Covington (Ed.), *Fertility counseling: Clinical guide and case studies* (pp. 122–135). Cambridge University Press.

Smith, J. F., Eisenberg, M. L., Millstein, S. G., Nachtigall, R. D., Shindel, A. W., Wing, H., Cedars, M., Pasch, L., Katz, P. P., & the Infertility Outcomes Program Project Group. (2010). The use of complementary and alternative fertility treatment in couples seeking fertility care: Data from a prospective cohort in the United States. *Fertility and Sterility, 93*(7), 2169–2174. https://doi.org/ 10.1016/j.fertnstert.2010.02.054

Smith, S. L. (2006). *Safeguarding the rights and well-being of birthparents in the adoption process*. Evan B. Donaldson Adoption Institute. http://www. adoptioninstitute.org/old/publications/2006_11_Birthparent_Study_All.pdf

Söderström-Anttila, V., Wennerholm, U.-B., Loft, A., Pinborg, A., Aittomäki, K., Romundstad, L. B., & Bergh, C. (2016). Surrogacy: Outcomes for surrogate mothers, children and the resulting families—A systematic review. *Human Reproduction Update, 22*(2), 260–276. https://doi.org/10.1093/humupd/dmv046

Soleimani, A. A., Najafi, M., Ahmadi, K., Javidi, N., Hoseini Kamkar, E., & Mahboubi, M. (2015). The effectiveness of emotionally focused couples therapy on sexual satisfaction and marital adjustment of infertile couples with marital conflicts. *International Journal of Fertility & Sterility, 9*(3), 393–402. https://doi.org/10.22074/ijfs.2015.4556

Stiel, M., McMahon, C. A., Elwyn, G., & Boivin, J. (2010). Pre-birth characteristics and 5-year follow-up of women with cryopreserved embryos after successful in vitro fertilisation treatment. *Journal of Psychosomatic Obstetrics & Gynecology, 31*(1), 32–39. https://doi.org/10.3109/01674820903537081

Stinson, K. M., Lasker, J. N., Lohmann, J., & Toedter, L. J. (1992). Parents' grief following pregnancy loss: A comparison of mothers and fathers. *Family Relations, 41*(2), 218–223. https://doi.org/10.2307/584836

Strasser, M. (2015). Traditional surrogacy contracts, partial enforcement, and the challenge for family law. *Journal of Health Care Law & Policy, 18*, 85–113.

Stricker, G. (2003). The many faces of self-disclosure. *Journal of Clinical Psychology, 59*(5), 623–630. https://doi.org/10.1002/jclp.10165

Stroebe, M., Finkenauer, C., Wijngaards-de Meij, L., Schut, H., van den Bout, J., & Stroebe, W. (2013). Partner-oriented self-regulation among bereaved parents: The costs of holding in grief for the partner's sake. *Psychological Science, 24*(4), 395–402. https://doi.org/10.1177/0956797612457383

Stroebe, M., & Schut, H. (1999). The dual process model of coping with bereavement: Rationale and description. *Death Studies, 23*(3), 197–224. https://doi.org/10.1080/074811899201046

Stroebe, M., Schut, H., & Boerner, K. (2017). Cautioning health-care professionals: Bereaved persons are misguided through the stages of grief. *Omega: Journal of Death and Dying, 74*(4), 455–473. https://doi.org/10.1177/0030222817691870

Svanberg, A. S., Lampic, C., Geijervall, A. L., Gudmundsson, J., Karlström, P. O., Solensten, N. G., & Sydsjö, G. (2012). Gamete donors' motivation in a Swedish national sample: Is there any ambivalence? A descriptive study. *Acta Obstetricia et Gynecologica Scandinavica, 91*(8), 944–951. https://doi.org/10.1111/j.1600-0412.2012.01430.x

Taylor, J. K. (2020). Structural racism and maternal health among Black women. *The Journal of Law, Medicine & Ethics, 48*(3), 506–517. https://doi.org/10.1177/1073110520958875

Taylor, L., McMinn, M. R., Bufford, R. K., & Chang, K. B. T. (2010). Psychologists' attitudes and ethical concerns regarding the use of social networking web sites. *Professional Psychology: Research and Practice, 41*(2), 153–159. https://doi.org/10.1037/a0017996

Tedeschi, R. G., & Calhoun, L. G. (1995). *Trauma and transformation: Growing in the aftermath of suffering.* Sage Publications. https://doi.org/10.4135/9781483326931

Tedeschi, R. G., & Calhoun, L. G. (1996). The Posttraumatic Growth Inventory: Measuring the positive legacy of trauma. *Journal of Traumatic Stress, 9*(3), 455–471. https://doi.org/10.1002/jts.2490090305

Tedeschi, R. G., & Calhoun, L. G. (2004). Posttraumatic growth: Conceptual foundations and empirical evidence. *Psychological Inquiry, 15*(1), 1–18. https://doi.org/10.1207/s15327965pli1501_01

Tedeschi, R. G., Calhoun, L. G., & Groleau, J. M. (2015). Clinical applications of posttraumatic growth. In S. Joseph (Ed.), *Positive psychology in practice: Promoting human flourishing in work, health, education, and everyday life* (pp. 503–518). Wiley. https://doi.org/10.1002/9781118996874.ch30

Thériault, A., Gazzola, N., Isenor, J., & Pascal, L. (2015). Imparting self-care practices to therapists: What the experts recommend. *Canadian Journal of Counselling and Psychotherapy, 49*, 379–400.

Thijssen, A., Provoost, V., Vandormael, E., Dhont, N., Pennings, G., & Ombelet, W. (2017). Motivations and attitudes of candidate sperm donors in Belgium. *Fertility and Sterility, 108*(3), 539–547. https://doi.org/10.1016/j.fertnstert.2017.06.014

Thorn, P. (2006). Recipient counseling for donor insemination. In S. N. Covington & L. H. Burns (Eds.), *Infertility counseling: A comprehensive handbook for clinicians* (2nd ed., pp. 305–318). Cambridge University Press.

Toedter, L. J., Lasker, J. N., & Alhadeff, J. M. (1988). The Perinatal Grief Scale: Development and initial validation. *American Journal of Orthopsychiatry, 58*(3), 435–449. https://doi.org/10.1111/j.1939-0025.1988.tb01604.x

Toedter, L. J., Lasker, J. N., & Janssen, H. J. (2001). International comparison of studies using the Perinatal Grief Scale: A decade of research on pregnancy loss. *Death Studies, 25*(3), 205–228. https://doi.org/10.1080/074811801750073251

Treff, N. R., Savulescu, J., de Melo-Martín, I., Shulman, L. P., & Feinberg, E. C. (2022). Should preimplantation genetic testing for polygenic disease be offered to all—Or none? *Fertility and Sterility, 117*(6), 1162–1167. https://doi.org/10.1016/j.fertnstert.2022.03.017

Triplett, K. N., Tedeschi, R. G., Cann, A., Calhoun, L. G., & Reeve, C. L. (2012). Posttraumatic growth, meaning in life, and life satisfaction in response to trauma. *Psychological Trauma: Theory, Research, Practice, and Policy, 4*(4), 400–410. https://doi.org/10.1037/a0024204

Trippany, R. L., Kress, V. E. W., & Wilcoxon, S. A. (2004). Preventing vicarious trauma: What counselors should know when working with trauma survivors. *Journal of Counseling & Development, 82*(1), 31–37. https://doi.org/10.1002/j.1556-6678.2004.tb00283.x

Tucker, M., Morton, P., & Liebermann, J. (2004). Human oocyte cryopreservation: A valid alternative to embryo cryopreservation? *European Journal of Obstetrics, Gynecology, and Reproductive Biology, 113*(Suppl. 1), S24–S27. https://doi.org/10.1016/j.ejogrb.2003.11.006

Uyehara, L. A., Austrian, S., Upton, L. G., Warner, R. H., & Williamson, R. A. (1995). Telling about the analyst's pregnancy. *Journal of the American Psychoanalytic Association, 43*(1), 113–135. https://doi.org/10.1177/000306519504300110

Valentine, C. (2019). Meaning-making in bereavement and grief. *Bereavement Care, 38*(1), 42–45. https://doi.org/10.1080/02682621.2019.1587850

Valerio, V. C., Downey, J., Sgaier, S. K., Callaghan, W. M., Hammer, B., & Smittenaar, P. (2023). Black–White disparities in maternal vulnerability and adverse pregnancy outcomes: An ecological population study in the United States, 2014–2018. *The Lancet Regional Health—Americas, 20*, Article 100456. https://doi.org/10.1016/j.lana.2023.100456

Valli-Pulaski, H., Peters, K. A., Gassei, K., Steimer, S. R., Sukhwani, M., Hermann, B. P., Dwomor, L., David, S., Fayomi, A. P., Munyoki, S. K., Chu, T., Chaudhry, R., Cannon, G. M., Fox, P. J., Jaffe, T. M., Sanfilippo, J. S., Menke, M. N., Lunenfeld, E., Abofoul-Azab, M., . . . Orwig, K. E. (2019). Testicular tissue cryopreservation: 8 years of experience from a coordinated network of academic centers. *Human Reproduction, 34*(6), 966–977. https://doi.org/10.1093/humrep/dez043

van Agteren, J., Iasiello, M., Lo, L., Bartholomaeus, J., Kopsaftis, Z., Carey, M., & Kyrios, M. (2021). A systematic review and meta-analysis of psychological interventions to improve mental wellbeing. *Nature Human Behaviour, 5*(5), 631–652. https://doi.org/10.1038/s41562-021-01093-w

Van den Broeck, U., Vandermeeren, M., Vanderschueren, D., Enzlin, P., Demyttenaere, K., & D'Hooghe, T. (2013). A systematic review of sperm donors: Demographic characteristics, attitudes, motives and experiences of the process of sperm donation. *Human Reproduction Update, 19*(1), 37–51. https://doi.org/10.1093/humupd/dms039

Van Gasse, D., & Mortelmans, D. (2020). With or without you—Starting single-parent families: A qualitative study on how single parents by choice reorganize their lives to facilitate single parenthood from a life course perspective. *Journal of Family Issues, 41*(11), 2223–2248. https://doi.org/10.1177/0192513X20911971

Vieira, T. (2002). When joy becomes grief. Screening tools for postpartum depression. *AWHONN Lifelines, 6*(6), 506–513. https://doi.org/10.1177/1091592302239621

Vignoles, V. L., Manzi, C., Regalia, C., Jemmolo, S., & Scabini, E. (2008). Identity motives underlying desired and feared possible future selves. *Journal of Personality, 76*(5), 1165–1200. https://doi.org/10.1111/j.1467-6494.2008.00518.x

Volgsten, H., & Schmidt, L. (2021). Motherhood through medically assisted reproduction—Characteristics and motivations of Swedish single mothers by choice. *Human Fertility, 24*(3), 219–225. https://doi.org/10.1080/14647273.2019.1606457

Vučina, T., & Oakley, S. (2018). Case study of EMDR therapy use in treating reproductive trauma—A case report. *Psychiatria Danubina, 30*(Suppl. 5), 262–264.

Wada, K., & Park, J. (2009). Integrating Buddhist psychology into grief counseling. *Death Studies, 33*(7), 657–683. https://doi.org/10.1080/07481180903012006

Waldman, J. (2003). New mother/old therapist: Transference and countertransference challenges in the return to work. *American Journal of Psychotherapy, 57*(1), 52–63. https://doi.org/10.1176/appi.psychotherapy.2003.57.1.52

Wang, G., Liu, X., & Lei, J. (2023). Effects of mindfulness-based intervention for women with infertility: A systematic review and meta-analysis. *Archives of Women's Mental Health, 26*(2), 245–258. https://doi.org/10.1007/s00737-023-01307-2

Wånggren, K., Alden, J., Bergh, T., & Skoog Svanberg, A. (2013). Attitudes towards embryo donation among infertile couples with frozen embryos. *Human Reproduction, 28*(9), 2432–2439. https://doi.org/10.1093/humrep/det252

Watson, R. I. (2005). When the patient has experienced severe trauma. In A. Rosen & J. Rosen (Eds.), *Frozen dreams: Psychodynamic dimensions of infertility and assisted reproduction* (pp. 219–235). Analytic Press.

Waugh, A., Kiemle, G., & Slade, P. (2018). What aspects of post-traumatic growth are experienced by bereaved parents? A systematic review. *European Journal of Psychotraumatology, 9*(1), Article 1506230. https://doi.org/10.1080/20008198.2018.1506230

Way, C., Lamers, C., & Rickard, R. (2019). An unavoidable bump: A metasynthesis of psychotherapists' experiences of navigating therapy while pregnant. *Research in Psychotherapy: Psychopathology, Process and Outcome, 22*(3), Article 386. https://doi.org/10.4081/ripppo.2019.386

Weiner, I. B. (1975). *Principles of psychotherapy*. Wiley.

Weingarten, K. (2010). Intersecting losses: Working with the inevitable vicissitudes in therapist and client lives. *Psychotherapy: Theory, Research, Practice, Training, 47*(3), 371–384. https://doi.org/10.1037/a0021170

Wenzel, A. (2017). Cognitive behavioral therapy for pregnancy loss. *Psychotherapy, 54*(4), 400–405. https://doi.org/10.1037/pst0000132

Westergaard, L. G., Mao, Q., Krogslund, M., Sandrini, S., Lenz, S., & Grinsted, J. (2006). Acupuncture on the day of embryo transfer significantly improves the reproductive outcome in infertile women: A prospective, randomized trial. *Fertility and Sterility, 85*(5), 1341–1346. https://doi.org/10.1016/j.fertnstert.2005.08.070

White, M., & Epston, D. (1990). *Narrative means to therapeutic ends*. Norton.

Wieland, L. S., Manheimer, E., & Berman, B. M. (2011). Development and classification of an operational definition of complementary and alternative medicine for the Cochrane collaboration. *Alternative Therapies in Health and Medicine, 17*(2), 50–59.

Wierckx, K., Van Caenegem, E., Pennings, G., Elaut, E., Dedecker, D., Van de Peer, F., Weyers, S., De Sutter, P., & T'Sjoen, G. (2012). Reproductive wish in transsexual men. *Human Reproduction, 27*(2), 483–487. https://doi.org/10.1093/humrep/der406

Wilson, J. F., & Kopitzke, E. J. (2002). Stress and infertility. *Current Women's Health Reports, 2*(3), 194–199.

Winograd, M. (2017). *Understanding the predictors of posttraumatic growth among those with a history of a reproductive trauma* (Publication No. 2319) [Doctoral dissertation, Seton Hall University]. Seton Hall University Dissertations and Theses.

Wise, E. H., Hersh, M. A., & Gibson, C. M. (2012). Ethics, self-care and well-being for psychologists: Reenvisioning the stress-distress continuum. *Professional Psychology: Research and Practice, 43*(5), 487–494. https://doi.org/10.1037/a0029446

Wojnar, D. (2007). Miscarriage experiences of lesbian couples. *Journal of Midwifery & Women's Health, 52*(5), 479–485. https://doi.org/10.1016/j.jmwh.2007.03.015

Wolfe, E. H. (2013). *The therapist's pregnancy and the client–therapist relationship: An exploratory study* [Unpublished doctoral Dissertation]. Smith College School for Social Work.

Wu, K. S., & Sonne, J. L. (2021). Therapist boundary crossings in the digital age: Psychologists' practice frequencies and perceptions of ethicality. *Professional Psychology: Research and Practice, 52*(5), 419–428. https://doi.org/10.1037/pro0000406

Yding Andersen, C., Mamsen, L. S., & Kristensen, S. G. (2019). Fertility preservation: Freezing of ovarian tissue and clinical opportunities. *Reproduction, 158*(5), F27–F34. https://doi.org/10.1530/REP-18-0635

Yee, S., Blyth, E., & Ka Tat Tsang, A. (2011). Oocyte donors' experiences of altruistic known donation: A qualitative study. *Journal of Reproductive and Infant Psychology, 29*(4), 404–415. https://doi.org/10.1080/02646838.2011.611938

Yee, S., Hitkari, J. A., & Greenblatt, E. M. (2007). A follow-up study of women who donated oocytes to known recipient couples for altruistic reasons. *Human Reproduction, 22*(7), 2040–2050. https://doi.org/10.1093/humrep/dem103

Yu, Y., Peng, L., Chen, L., Long, L., He, W., Li, M., & Wang, T. (2014). Resilience and social support promote posttraumatic growth of women with infertility: The mediating role of positive coping. *Psychiatry Research, 215*(2), 401–405. https://doi.org/10.1016/j.psychres.2013.10.032

Zeanah, C. H., Dailey, J. V., Rosenblatt, M. J., & Saller, D. N., Jr. (1993). Do women grieve after terminating pregnancies because of fetal anomalies? A controlled investigation. *Obstetrics and Gynecology, 82*(2), 270–275.

Zerubavel, N., & Wright, M. O. (2012). The dilemma of the wounded healer. *Psychotherapy, 49*(4), 482–491. https://doi.org/10.1037/a0027824

Zhang, X., Deng, X., Mo, Y., Li, Y., Song, X., & Li, H. (2021). Relationship between infertility-related stress and resilience with posttraumatic growth in infertile couples: Gender differences and dyadic interaction. *Human Reproduction,* *36*(7), 1862–1870. https://doi.org/10.1093/humrep/deab096

Ziv-Beiman, S. (2013). Therapist self-disclosure as an integrative intervention. *Journal of Psychotherapy Integration, 23*(1), 59–74. https://doi.org/10.1037/a0031783

Zlotogora, J. (2002). Parental decisions to abort or continue a pregnancy with an abnormal finding after an invasive prenatal test. *Prenatal Diagnosis, 22*(12), 1102–1106. https://doi.org/10.1002/pd.472

Zur, O. (2009). Therapist self-disclosure: Standard of care, ethical considerations, and therapeutic context. In A. Bloomgarden & R. B. Mennuti (Eds.), *Psychotherapist revealed: Therapists speak about self-disclosure in psychotherapy* (pp. 31–51). Routledge.

Zur, O. (2015). *The Google factor: Psychotherapists' intentional & unwitting self-disclosures on the net.* https://zur-institute.sfo3.digitaloceanspaces.com/migrated/media/google_factor1.pdf

Zur, O., & Donner, M. B. (2009, January/February). The Google factor: Therapists' transparency in the era of Google and MySpace. *The California Psychologist,* 23–24. https://zur-institute.sfo3.digitaloceanspaces.com/migrated/media/internet_transparency.pdf

Zweifel, J., Christianson, M., Jaeger, A. S., Olive, D., & Lindheim, S. R. (2007). Needs assessment for those donating to stem cell research. *Fertility and Sterility, 88*(3), 560–564. https://doi.org/10.1016/j.fertnstert.2006.12.042

Index

A

Abandonment, feelings of, 183
Abortion, 31, 50, 73–74
Abraham Center of Life, 102
Acceptance (stage of grief), 57
Access to care, 15, 46, 51
Acting out, 168, 171
Active grief, 70
Acupuncture, 127
Adair, V., 108
Adjunctive therapies, 172
Adjuncts to reproductive psychotherapy, 123–130
Adolescence, 88
Adolescents, 107
Adoptees, 117
Adoption, 12, 13, 156, 158, 172. *See also* Adoptive parents; Third-party reproduction and adoption
Adoptive parents, 74–75, 117–121
AFC (antral follicle count), 28
Agitation, 143
AI (artificial insemination), 25–26
Alienation, feelings of, 78
Alternative therapies, 172
Altruism, 112
American Counseling Association, 151
American Psychological Association (APA), 151
American Society for Reproductive Medicine (ASRM), 32, 46, 100, 105
　Ethics Committee, 30, 35, 99–100
　Practice Committee, 10, 13, 26–27
AMH (anti-Mullerian hormone), 28

Amniocentesis, 21
Anger, 71, 82, 173
Anger (stage of grief), 57
Anonymity, 147–148
Anonymous gamete donors, 97–100
Anti-Mullerian hormone (AMH), 28
Antral follicle count (AFC), 28
Anxiety, 16, 79, 89, 90, 141
Appreciation of life, 136, 140
ART. *See* assisted reproductive technology
Artificial insemination (AI), 25–26
ASRM. *See* American Society for Reproductive Medicine
Assessment of patients' needs, 79
Assisted reproductive technology (ART), 9, 12, 29
Assumptions, 43–52
Assumptive state, 134–135
Attachment, 60
Autonomy, 31, 50
Avoidant behavior, 42

B

Baby blues, 141
Backstories, 59
Baden, A., 120
Bakhbakhi, D., 62
Balance, 195
Bargaining (stage of grief), 57
Basal body temperature, 20
Bass, A., 170
Beauchamp, T. L., 31

About the Author

Janet Jaffe, PhD, is a clinical psychologist who has been working in the field of reproductive psychology for over 25 years. She is the cofounder and codirector of the Center for Reproductive Psychology in San Diego, CA, where she works in private practice with individuals and couples seeking psychological support on their journey to parenthood, using a combination of psychodynamic, cognitive, and narrative therapies. She has done extensive writing on infertility and pregnancy loss and is coauthor of *Unsung Lullabies: Understanding and Coping With Infertility* (2005), a book geared for the general public. She also coauthored the first edition of *Reproductive Trauma: Psychotherapy With Infertility and Pregnancy Loss Clients* (2011), a text written for professionals working in the field.

Sought out by major editors, Dr. Jaffe has contributed several chapters to books, as well as journal articles regarding fertility counseling and women's health. She is a member of the American Society for Reproductive Medicine (ASRM) Mental Health Professional Group and served as chair of the Connections Committee, overseeing educational forums for members. She has given talks on reproductive psychology for professional audiences, including several through ASRM, the American Psychological Association, and the California Psychological Association at their annual congresses; been interviewed by National Public Radio; and addressed patient audiences across the country.